Noble Brutes

ANIMALS, HISTORY, CULTURE

•

Harriet Ritvo, *Series Editor*

· *Noble Brutes* ·

How Eastern Horses Transformed English Culture

DONNA LANDRY

The Johns Hopkins University Press

Baltimore

© 2009 The Johns Hopkins University Press
All rights reserved. Published 2008
Printed in the United States of America on acid-free paper

2 4 6 8 9 7 5 3 1

The Johns Hopkins University Press
2715 North Charles Street
Baltimore, Maryland 21218-4363
www.press.jhu.edu

Library of Congress Cataloging-in-Publication Data
Landry, Donna.
Noble brutes : how eastern horses transformed English culture /
Donna Landry.
p. cm. — (Animals, history, culture)
Includes bibliographical references and index.
ISBN-13: 978-0-8018-9028-4 (hardcover : alk. paper)
ISBN-10: 0-8018-9028-4 (hardcover : alk. paper)
1. Arabian horse—History—Great Britain. 2. Arabian horse—
Social aspects—Great Britain. 3. Horsemanship—Great Britain—
History. 4. Great Britain—Social life and customs. I. Title.
SF293.A8L36 2008
636.1′120942—dc22   2008011842

A catalog record for this book is available from the British Library.

*Special discounts are available for bulk purchases of this book. For more
information, please contact Special Sales at 410-516-6936 or
specialsales@press.jhu.edu.*

The Johns Hopkins University Press uses environmentally friendly book
materials, including recycled text paper that is composed of at least 30 percent
post-consumer waste, whenever possible. All of our book papers are acid-free,
and our jackets and covers are printed on paper with recycled content.

CONTENTS

Noble Brutes

What the Horses Said

• • •

An Equine History

D eep within the echoing passageways of the Aleppo souk, in the Han al-Gümrük, where the English merchants lived, Nathaniel Harley schemed. He fervently hoped that his latest attempt to export horses from Syria to England would trump all previous endeavors. In the spring of 1715 he had shipped to his nephew a dun stallion. Known thereafter as Lord Harley's Dun (or Dun Arabian) after the English fashion, the horse had been so widely admired, Nathaniel's nephew reported proudly, that he was "thought by all that have seen him to be the finest Horse that ever came over."[1]

Such praise went a long way toward repaying Nathaniel for the vast "trouble, Expence and difficulty" he had faced "at first to procure, afterwards to keep, and now to send away" the horse.[2] He had spirited the stallion out of Aleppo to the port of Scanderoon (Iskenderun), evading the Ottoman authorities seeking to requisition for Sultan Ahmed III's imperial stables in Istanbul this remarkably fine specimen—"a Horse that has made more Noise and been more taken Notice of here then I desired."[3] Nathaniel bragged in a letter to his brother Edward that nobody else could have organized such a successful undercover operation: "[U]pon the first notice of it Three Expresses have been sent after him, and all the passes of the Mountains between this and Scanderone Ordered to be watched, and ye Marine Strictly guarded to prevent his being Ship'd off."[4] With such a provenance, Nathaniel thought the horse "above any price that can be offered," and declared himself "So little of a Merchant that I would not have him Sold Even thô a Thousand Pounds should be bid for him."[5]

Four years later, in January 1720, Nathaniel plotted to outdo himself:

By Capt. Oliver I Send a Grey Horse that I have had by me more than four Years, And have two or three times attempted to Send away but have been disappointed . . .

He is of the Gordeen breed of which there's few now Remaining, And is the Chief cause of My sending him, He is of great Spirit but no great Speed, Wou'd Soon learn anything in the Manage, He has got Colts thô but One of his Testicles is come down . . . And because you Will Observe A Redish Stain on One of his Shoulders, Which is now much wore Out but when I bought him was as red as Blood, I Will give you the Account the Owner of him gave me without afirming it to be true.[6]

The gray stallion belonging to a rare and valuable desert strain, who sported a distinctive mark on his right shoulder about which a romantic story would be told, was Nathaniel's last consignment. The Bloody Shouldered Arabian arrived safely in England and would bring the Harley family fame. Although he had made plans to sail home from Iskenderun to hear the horse praised in person, Nathaniel Harley was never to return to England; he died of a fever in July of that year.[7]

"His lordship's Arabian" was a phrase often heard in eighteenth-century England and Ireland. Although seemingly self-evident, the term represents something of a crux in the naming and classifying of members of the equine species. Between 1650 and 1750 alone, more than two hundred horses designated as Eastern or Oriental were imported into England. Wherever they came from, there developed a tendency to name these horses "Arabians" rather than "Turks" or "Barbs," the terms most commonly used to describe Oriental horses of superior bloodlines during the seventeenth century. Since many keen patrons of the English turf were Irish lords or gentlemen, some of these horses and their progeny made their way to Ireland, while others could be found in Wales and Scotland. However, Englishness dominated ethnic identity within the forging of a British nation just as Arabian-ness dominated equine identity.

During the eighteenth century, people in the British Isles came to identify themselves as Britons, as opposed to English, Irish, Scots, or Welsh, largely through a consciousness of their shared differences from the French and other Europeans, as Linda Colley has shown.[8] Amid this process, Englishness came to dominate over the other nationalities or "races" of the British Isles, while this internal colonialism, as such dominance is often called, became culturally muted.[9] What has not been sufficiently noticed, perhaps, is that there was a parallel movement in British horse culture at this time. Although a few imported horses could still be found being described as Turks or Barbs in Britain during the later eighteenth and nineteenth centuries, the designation Arabian became far more prevalent than these other terms for Eastern horses in the course of the eighteenth century. Within one generation their progeny were described as English Thoroughbreds. (The lower-cased term *thoroughbred* is commonly used to designate a pedigreed horse of pure blood. When capitalized, the term refers to the particular breed developed in England during the eighteenth century, genetically forged from crossing previously separate types of Eastern bloodstock.)

Thus it came to pass that, riding Eastern blood horses and their English Thoroughbred progeny, noblemen and gentlemen in the British Isles distinguished themselves from other Europeans by means of what came to be known as the English hunting seat. Both the new horses and the new disposition of the body on horseback came to signify the difference of the British Isles from the Continent, and a particular style of aristocratic and genteel self-display. This is another way of saying that equestrian culture and its offshoots, the sporting culture of hunting and racing, and the artistic culture of equine portraiture and sporting art, served imaginatively to express Britain's "gentlemanly capitalist" version of mercantilism during the nation's rise to global economic importance between the late sixteenth century and the mid-nineteenth century.[10] Financiers and great merchants became gentlemen, and some gentlemen became financiers. The English gentlemanly ideal retained symbolic power long after the gentry were no longer the important political force they had been at the Restoration. New mercantile wealth purchased traditionally genteel accoutrements—country houses, emparked estates, fine horses, sporting art. Whatever their social origins, merchants in the Levant trade and members of City livery companies avidly pursued what Gervase Markham in 1615 had called "Countrey Contentments."[11] As Britons transformed themselves into the "polite and commercial people"[12] suited to administering an empire, a new language of free forward movement and equine initiative developed as the new language of horsemanship, whether its practitioners were English or Irish, Scots, or Welsh. In Ireland particularly, the ideal of free forward movement of the horse and rider was and still is regarded as characteristically Irish. Yet the Anglo-Irish colonial relation assured that, at least in print, any significant innovations, wherever they originated, would be claimed to be English ones.

Indeed, the very question of an English seat on horseback may have been most hotly debated precisely during moments of national crisis and identity formation or reformation, though the evidence for this is not conclusive. What the evidence does support, I think, is that the style of riding developed to follow hounds in the British Isles, particularly when pursuing foxes over enclosed land, was developed with a sense of cultural superiority allied with imperial destiny. When eighteenth-

century Britons started jumping obstacles at flat-out racing pace on Thoroughbred, or part-Thoroughbred, horses while hunting, turning the tops of their boots
down and taking their stirrups up a notch or two in order to negotiate at a gallop
the new enclosures of the second or landlords' agricultural revolution,[13] they departed from Continental equestrian practice in the name of national superiority
and imperial sovereignty.

The legacy of imagined superiority in cross-country riding continues to this
day. That is why the British public who follow equestrian sports grow indignant
when British teams fail to win at international Combined Training or Three-
Day Event competitions, particularly if they have not at least distinguished themselves in the cross-country phase (the three phases consisting of dressage, cross-
country, and stadium or show jumping). As one longtime competitor observed,
"Britain used to dominate the world, and sadly we seem to have lost our edge."[14]
The rise and decline of the English hunting seat might stand as a metonym for
the fate of the British Empire.

Apologists for imperial Britain have often adopted the rhetoric of superior civility when dealing with other cultures, whether rival empires or colonized peoples. Beginning in the later seventeenth century, and gathering momentum during the course of the eighteenth, at the same time that the language of liberty and
property came to dominate politics, a new language of equine reasonableness and
a loosening and lightening of control became fashionable in equestrian circles.
Self-styled freeborn Britons, both men and women, sought to represent themselves as superior in civilization by riding lightly and exerting control by means
of a silken thread. What I am describing was certainly ideological. It was both an
ideal and an illusion, and it was often contradicted in practice. But it was a peculiarly powerful ideology because it could be physically experienced as if empiri-
cally true while riding a certain kind of horse in a particular way. The ideology of
free forward movement as an enactment of and analogy for political liberty and
imperial adventuring was thus fully embodied ideology, viscerally experienced by
riders in a largely horse-powered nation.

Early modern Britain and Ireland produced a rich verbal and visual record of
obsession with the equine species, revealing how crucial horses were to formu-
lating what emerged as English culture on the world stage. We might say that
horses functioned imaginatively as ideal selves for many people in the British
Isles. The Irishman Jonathan Swift, who lived in England as well as Ireland, satirized this confusion of horses with ideal selves in his expose of Houyhnhnmland
in Part 4 of *Gulliver's Travels*, published in 1726. In the land of the whinnying ones,
horses were the only rational creatures. Swift's contemporaries were so horse-

obsessed that many of them devoted their lives to dealing, breeding, stabling, shoeing, medicating, schooling, riding, driving, hunting, and racing horses, and to writing about them and painting them. If the rich were often obsessed with the status conveyed by ownership of famous bloodlines, the poor could be equally obsessed, often in a professional capacity, while deriving their very livelihood from horse coping.

And as the island nation rose to global eminence as a mercantile and imperial power, one sign of its new importance was the plethora of Eastern horses who had been acquired, by fair means or foul, from whom there issued forth a new equine breed, the English Thoroughbred—the epitome of equine nobility in the flesh. Such blood horses were objects of both utility and beauty. Indeed, *dulce et utile* so perfectly described them that it was as if that motto had been coined on their behalf. Eastern bloodstock in their fineness and surprising toughness, to say nothing of their remarkable intelligence, transformed the notion of what a horse was, or could be, in Britain. This coupling of the useful with the beautiful disrupted contemporary ideas about horses, horsemanship, and human-animal relations. Relations of economic necessity and traditional usage became overlaid with new kinds of pleasure and poetry.

This book investigates a particular cultural shift for which certain highly valued horses, representations of those horses, and stories about them were largely responsible. It is not the story of all horses in the British Isles between 1650 and 1750, for that would be a different book. Most horses, like most people, were not central to the story of "his lordship's Arabian," though a surprising number became caught up in this transformation of equine culture.

The blood horses of the East had long had a legendary status. Circa 1526, Leo Africanus, as adapted for English readers by Samuel Purchas in his collection of travel writings (over which Coleridge famously fell asleep in an opium daze), celebrated the Arabian and Barbary horses for their "swiftnesse and agilitie."[15] By the second half of the eighteenth century, zoologists had come to regard Eastern horses, epitomized by the Arabian, as the best and oldest or most "original" representative of the equine species. Thomas Pennant illustrated his 1770 entry on the horse, for instance, with an engraving of George Stubbs's portrait of Lord Grosvenor's Arabian.[16]

Although the Eastern imports were exotic and expensive, and their ownership was consequently restricted, nevertheless the diffusion of Eastern blood throughout the horse population of the British Isles was considerable. Not everyone had direct access to Thoroughbred horses up and down the social scale, but as early as the mid-eighteenth century, foreign observers remarked how like Eastern horses many common or ordinary English horses were. The Comte de Buffon, for example, claimed that the "finest *English* horses greatly resemble the *Arabians* and *Barbs* in shape; indeed they owe their origin to them," but that the English horses had larger heads and ears, and stood noticeably taller than their forebears, "even fifteen hands" not being "very extraordinary."[17] Buffon went on to comment on the English penchant for racing but described those "people in *England* who are extreamly expert in that part of the gymnastic art" by means of the common touch, giving as his example the story of Mr. Thornhill, the postmaster of Stilton, who wagered he could ride three times between Stilton and London, 250 miles, in under fifteen hours, and did it in eleven hours and 52 minutes, employing fourteen horses—clearly not racehorses in a Newmarket sense, but useful road horses.[18] By 1831, William Youatt could describe a general transformation of English horses indebted to the infusion of Eastern blood from the middle of the seventeenth century onward: "From that period to the middle of the last century, the system of improvement was zealously pursued: every variety of Eastern blood was occasionally engrafted on ours, and the superiority of the engrafted, above the very best of the original stock, began to be evident."[19] This revolutionary improvement was not restricted to racehorses or horses possessed by the gentry, Youatt continued: "[N]or is this true only of the thorough-bred or turf-horse; it is, to a very material degree, the case with every description of horse. By a judicious admixture and proportion of blood, we have rendered our hunters, our hackneys, our coach, nay even our cart horses, much stronger, more active, and more enduring, than they were before the introduction of the race-horse."[20]

This story of assimilation of the foreign within that icon of Englishness, the Thoroughbred, and then throughout the entire horse population, may be well known in some quarters, but it has been little analyzed. Two arguments will be here made regarding its importance.

First, although they might at first seem entirely incompatible, nobility and brutality were the defining characteristics of Eastern blood horses and their progeny in eighteenth-century England. No other animal, except the human laborer, suffered from such a contradictory identity. Fine horses and the people who looked after them often crossed otherwise less than porous boundaries. The social world of horse culture in the British Isles sometimes elevated members of the laboring and artisanal classes to close associations with aristocrats and wealthy gentlemen. Whether we want to see this as an instance of a rough democratizing influence or not, it provided a countercurrent to the spread of urbanized, if not yet urbane, metropolitan polite culture, from which laborers were definitely excluded. If after 1750, country gentlemen were less likely to permit unqualified sportsmen to hunt and shoot game than they had been in earlier decades, closing ranks and consolidating gentry privilege in the right to chase a hare or bag a pheasant, they did not close ranks on the racecourse quite so early or in the same way.[21]

Even wagering and betting, despite great disparities in the fortunes of prospective punters, were endemic to sporting culture and crossed class boundaries. As the radical writer Thomas Holcroft remembered from boyhood, a King's Plate fought out at Nottingham races in 1757 between two renowned horses, Careless and the Duke of Devonshire's Atlas, galvanized the whole district, and betting was universal:

> Careless, who had been bred by a worthy and popular Baronet of the county (I forget his name) was the decided favourite of every man in Nottingham, gentle or simple . . . As for my own little one [referring to his heart], it was all in rapture for Careless. He was so finely made, his coat was so bright, his eye so beaming, his limbs so animated, and every motion seemed so evidently to declare, "I can fly, if I please," that I could not endure the thought of his being conquered. Alas for the men of Nottingham, conquered he was! I forget whether it was at two or three heats, but there was many an empty purse on that night, and many a sorrowful heart.[22]

Long before the nineteenth-century development of mass betting, then, at local race meetings the countryside turned out, regardless of rank, and backed their favorite. The laying of odds would come later, as an inner turfite betting group emerged by the end of the century, including a few working-class bookmakers, described as "legs."[23] When Birmingham won the St. Leger in 1830, the "Warwickshire gentlemen" were "almost the only winners," so few had backed him.[24] Protests against laboring-class involvement in racing belonged to a later era than the eighteenth century, when racing and betting were local, racecourses were open rather than enclosed, no attendance fees were charged, and women and children as well as men of all classes made up the audience.[25] Mike Huggins concludes his recent social and economic history of English racing with what he considers "perhaps the most important finding": that "racing had cross-class support." Huggins elaborates: "Working people possessed a spectrum of identities which were not just those of class but included those of the workplace and the community in a non-class sense, the county or the region, and this allowed participation in racing."[26] When racing became more commercialized in the nineteenth century than it had been in the eighteenth, Ross McKibbin has argued, mass betting could in fact be seen as "the most successful example of working-class self-help in the modern era."[27]

Second, from the late sixteenth through the eighteenth century, within discussions of horsemanship, a discourse of comparative imperialisms developed, in which the ways in which Christian Europeans related to their equine charges were contrasted with the ways in which Ottoman and Arab horsemen related to theirs. Christian European policy entailed the paradox of noble brutality. Eastern Islamic policy entailed the paradox of cruel leniency or cruel kindness. Christian European cudgeling and shouting at the noble brute produced cowed submission. Ottoman kindness, even in the context of a government whose practices could appear arbitrary or cruel, produced willing obedience, which never ceased to amaze Westerners. One consequence of this lenient intimacy, it was argued, was that Eastern horses were perceived to be more sensitively attuned to human wishes than other horses, and to live within and according to human domestic arrangements. This idea may well have inspired Swift's Houyhnhnmland.

In perhaps the earliest testimony by an Englishman on the superiority of Eastern horses, John Sanderson, deputy to the English ambassador at Constantinople, reported in 1597 traveling overland to Aleppo with a dark gray "Babilonian" horse, who never wearied, unlike all the other horses in his entourage, and was also remarkable in other ways. Although he was of "a meane stature; rather to[o] little for me," Sanderson observed, nevertheless the horse was "the best," in his opinion, "that ever I shalbe master of. He would walke by me, licking my hand; stand still when I backed [mounted] him; and kneele at my pleasure."[28] Gallantry, toughness, and apparent friendship or affection: this combination of qualities impressed early modern European horsemen who traveled East.

Western observers were often perplexed by what they observed of Eastern horsemanship. Cruel kindness came in many forms, as Dr. John Covel's 1675 eyewitness account of horse racing at Adrianople (modern Edirne), during the reign of Sultan Mehmed IV, testifies. Covel is struck by the length of the races, twenty-five or thirty miles, which draw fields of thirty or thirty-five horses. He reports that only four horses did the distance in two and a half hours. According to Covel, these races were "more to prove the utmost yt a horse can doe, rather then for any pleasure ye spectators can take," and he laments that although "there were very excellent horse indeed amongst them," some were run off their legs and "were bastinadoe'd in by footmen." By the end of the race, "some few had so much mettle and strength left as to offer at something which you might call a gallop," and Covel adds,"it would have greived your soul to have seen them so miserably hackney'd of of their legs." However, the treatment of the horses after the race surprises him more than the extreme arduousness of the race itself:

One peice of horsemanship I learned there when ye horse come in gasping and pant-
ing for life, so soon as if ye rider is dismounted there are men on purpose to pull ye
horses eares, his tayle, chafe his gullet, and rub him all over, but above all they take
up whole handfulls of dust and throw it in their mouths; I expected it should quite
choke them, but it happen'd quite otherwise; for it makes them drivel at chops extreamly, and cause them to work their toung and jawes, and without doubt refresh
them extreamly.[29]

Cruelty or kindness? There is certainly a hands-on intimacy in the ear- and tail-
pulling, gullet-chafing, and all-over body massage that strikes the Englishman as
curious but effective. But what at first seems to him a horrible thing to do to ex-
hausted horses—throw dust into their mouths—he then admits appears to work
"extreamly" well to refresh them. The detail is described as "one peice of horsemanship I learned." Covel is prepared to take instruction from Ottoman horsemen. The severe testing of horses' endurance and speed must be understood in
a context in which every care is taken of them afterward, if in curious Eastern
ways.

By the later eighteenth century, the mystique surrounding Eastern horsemanship, like the desire for importing the horses themselves, had ceased to be
fashionable. Between the sixteenth and nineteenth centuries, Britain, like other
European nations, gradually ceased being humbled and intimidated by the luxurious splendor of the Eastern empires and began to assert imperial dominance.
Acquiring such symbols of rank and power as so-called thoroughbreds (or blood
horses) from the East was a matter of cultural exchange but also of appropriation.
These goods could be assimilated by the West—consumed and digested, as it
were—as if rightfully native produce.

The arrival of Turkish, Barb, and Arabian horses revolutionized not only English racing and equestrian culture but early modern culture more broadly, in-
spiring new forms of painting and writing as well as riding. Along with the horses
came Eastern ideas about horsemanship, about the relation between horses and
humans, and about forms of representation of this relationship. The story of the
arrival on the English scene of horses like Lord Harley's Dun and the Bloody
Shouldered Arabian is a mercantile story. It is also a story about agricultural improvement, about the growth of leisure industries like racing and hunting, and
about the horse breeding that accompanied these activities. The story of "his lordship's Arabian" as a noble brute is also a story about art. Connoisseurship and
cross-cultural difference both play a part in its unfolding. As precious cargo and

as sentient beings with a striking appearance of intelligence, the Dun and the Bloody Shouldered Arabian disturbed certain distinctions between the animate and the objectified, the human and the animal. The many horses known from racing calendars as "his lordship's Arabian" usually did. Equestrian culture would never be quite the same again after the Eastern invasion.

The new work on animals that has arisen within cultural, historical, and literary studies (rather than zoology or animal science) has been preoccupied with a presumed human/animal divide, with how "the animal" has been employed to constitute and define "the human," and how things might be arranged otherwise. Scholars have been quick to document the exploitation and abuse of horses and other animals in early modern Europe. Indeed, animal studies as a field has emphasized cruelty to animals as a way of unpacking the history of human-animal relations. Many animal studies scholars see themselves as animal advocates, striving for a less exploitative, more just set of relations between humans and other animals. Animals, after all, cannot author their own historical accounts. Just as Marx found French peasants incapable of representing themselves politically during the revolution, so also animal studies scholars have found in animals a group that cannot represent themselves but must be represented.[30] Erica Fudge has recently called for scholars in animal studies to "work toward a more equitable relation with animals":[31]

> If it is to impact upon questions about the way in which we treat animals today, if it is to have something to add to debates about factory farming, cruel sports, fur farms, vivisection, and the numerous other abuses of animals in our cultures, then the history of animals cannot just tell us what has been, what humans thought in the past; it must intervene, make us think again about our past and, most importantly, about ourselves. The history of animals can only work at the expense of the human.[32]

Fudge's essay has been enthusiastically cited as marking a way forward for animal studies.[33] But what exactly might "working at the expense of the human" mean?

The Green or environmentalist movement, ecological theory, and animal rights and animal welfare activism have obviously shaped the emergence of animal studies within the academy. Working toward justice for animals, our fellow creatures, requires decentering human interests by engaging in a critique of anthropocentrism, or human sovereignty.[34] Like its predecessors feminism, anti-racism, anti-imperialism, and gay rights, the pro-animal movement entails a process of unlearning.[35] Animal rights and animal welfare activists have to date largely equated this anti-anthropocentric commitment with an exposure of human cruelty, and historians have found no shortage of cruelty in the archives.[36] A rigorous animal rights position condemns and rejects any form of domestication as enslavement.[37] Some scholars have questioned the animal rights emphasis on freeing animals from bondage to humans as a fantasy that reveals more about human desires than about animal needs.[38] Others have objected that seeking to liberate animals from domestication or other close relationships with humans is reductive, and perhaps even unethical, given how many species' evolutionary trajectories are closely intertwined with ours.[39]

Must physical proximity and communication between humans and other species always result in exploitation? Must close, hands-on, skin-to-skin relations between humans and animals always constitute oppression? Might there not be more in the historical record to understand than simply humans' cruelty and abuse of animals? The training situation is one site in which the possibility of mutual trust, of a certain reciprocity, between humans and animals arises, at least as an ideal. As Vicki Hearne observes of domesticated dogs, "The better trained a dog is—which is to say, the greater his 'vocabulary'—the more dog and human can rely on each other to behave responsibly."[40] Training takes place by means of working through narratives about the capabilities of various kinds of dogs. "The moral transformation of the dog comes about through stories," Hearne insists, "stories that provide a form of life within which responding to what is said is a significant possibility."[41] The same holds true for horses, according to Hearne, with the sense of touch, rather than the sense of smell, being the part of our sensory apparatus most crucial for human communication.[42] "Some people can learn to remain articulate in the ordinary human way while honoring the horse's intricate kinesthetic language," Hearne argues, "but some can't, and this is a large part of why riding is terrifying, as it is a large part of what is scary about initial immersion in any alien tongue."[43] How might such communicative practices disturb the emerging narrative of one-way cruelty and exploitation?

A pro-animal training position like Hearne's, or more recently, Donna Haraway's, questions the necessity of condemning domestication as equivalent to chattel slavery. "I believe that all ethical relating, within or between species," Haraway argues, "is knit from the silk-strong thread of ongoing alertness to otherness-in-relation."[44] The silken thread between human hand and equine mouth is an important idealization of communication in equestrian discourse, as we shall see. Following Hearne, Haraway proposes that "something new and elegant" comes into being through "the *relational* work of training," something "much more exacting" than "the relief of suffering as the core human obligation to animals."[45]

"[A]ll the participants are remodeled," according to Haraway, by "the relational practice of training," which nurtures an "ethic of flourishing" in which "animal happiness" is at stake.[46] The training relationship, then, would seem to elicit human stewardship of and care for animals. Not merely utilitarian considerations, or expectations of animal servitude and obedience, have a bearing on this relationship, but also ethics and aesthetics. The animal's welfare, and even pleasure— animal happiness—are the governing criteria in this connection between human and animal. If presuming to know what is good for another suggests paternalism—human benevolence toward nonhuman animals—we should remember that benevolence, as a guide to action, means the benign, the good, use of power: *bene-volens.*

Although inspired, as is Haraway, by Hearne's advocacy of training, Paul Patton questions Hearne's conclusion that obtaining absolute obedience from the trained horse or dog might constitute something other than a relation of coercion, of human dominance in a situation of inequality. If, as Patton puts it, we "understand coercion to mean causing the animal to act in ways that it would not otherwise have acted," then even the most sympathetic training techniques are "coercive in the broader sense"; the difference between good (noncoercive) and bad training merely lies "between more and less sophisticated techniques of exercising power over other beings."[47] However, far from arguing that because such relations are contaminated by inequality, no ethical human-animal relations are possible, Patton insists that we need to question our assumption that ethical relations are possible only between equals. What training demonstrates is that "hierarchical forms of society between unequals are by no means incompatible with ethical relations and obligations toward other beings," that "certain kinds of emphasis on equality in all contexts are not only misleading but dangerous," and that we would "do well to attend to the requirements of the hierarchical and communicative relations in which we live."[48] This is a call for humans to take responsibility for their species' disproportionate share of power in the world. With that power come obligations. Animal training entails the obligations of engagement, not a spurious freedom from engagement.

To reject the possibility of communication, of a mutual responding to what is said and of responsible behavior on both sides, would be to condemn humans and other animals to a kind of apartheid. Even as, globally speaking, animals have disappeared from most urban people's economic lives, all animals have become increasingly involved in interactions with humans. No wild species is entirely immune to human influence. And even urban people often keep pets, living in close companionate-species relations. Given that animal freedom from human intervention has become ever more a fantasy, it appears more ethically responsible to attend to human-animal relations, to attempt to understand them in their full complexity, than to ban them or dismiss them by means of what Haraway calls "puritanical critique" of the kind that "indulge[s] in historical structural analysis in a way that denies both emotional bonds and material complexity and so avoids the always messy participation in action that might improve lives across many kinds of difference."[49] Improving lives, both human and animal, across many kinds of difference, might take us some way toward putting into practice Fudge's call for working "at the expence of the human." Once animal happiness becomes as compelling an ethical ideal as human happiness, cruelty, but also indifference to animals' needs and pleasures, might become a thing of the past. That ethical ideal will also challenge human sovereignty in favor of human responsibility, which after all means, literally, a call to respond.

The emergence of animal studies within the humanities means that it is now possible to ask certain new questions about the past. Can animals be understood as agents of history, or as agents in history? I agree with Garry Marvin that cultural specificity is more compelling than Fudge's philosophical concern with "the animal," and that we need to interrogate the significance of the various "social, cultural, economic, political and environmental contexts" that gave shape to particular relationships between humans and animals, and to particular representations of animals, in specific times and places.[50] Horses are a specific species, not just or any "animals," let alone "the animal." Marvin attempts to "puzzle through the complex feedback systems" looping between "representations and constructions that create the conditions or contexts for relationships with embodied animals in the world" and "the relationships themselves that create or generate representations which then create . . . Relationships out of representations, representations out of relationships."[51] He concludes that such "feedback systems are not, however, timeless, fixed or mechanical, and it is necessary to consider carefully how and why both social, economic, political and cultural changes within human societies, and the continuities and changes of how animals behave in their world, give rise to new representations and relations."[52] Here the attribution of agency to animals refers specifically to animals' making changes within their own world. My question for Marvin is this: Is the animal world the only domain within which to register the agency of animals? Might it not be possible to pursue another line of enquiry regarding animal agency: have animals caused changes within human culture?

The historical record suggests that in early modern Britain something far more uneven and complex was going on than unmitigated domination and exploitation of the equine species. The horse as servant to man was ideologically crucial to equestrian culture, but not a universal description of it.

Equestrianism and horse-keeping were far more central to an understanding of early modern European and Asian culture than has generally been acknowledged within scholarship of the recent past. As Karen Raber and Treva J. Tucker observe in their introduction to *The Culture of the Horse* (2005), a collection of essays that seeks to restore horses to history, only people who combine academic training with some experience of horse culture today are likely to be able to make sense of early modern equestrian matters or make plausible connections and distinctions between past and present practices. As Raber and Tucker put it, "To write anything intelligent on the subject of the horse, it is often necessary to combine training in the academic professions with training in, or at least substantial exposure to, the arts and nuances of horsemanship."[53] In her essay in the collection, Elisabeth LeGuin echoes this claim, countering the impossibility of entering into the past, of being there "when 'there' was 1556," with the belief that "being here, now, astride, can provide a meaningful window on the past—especially, perhaps, in a discipline as consistent and self-conscious as Western European horse training."[54] This book seeks to contribute to a collective project of rectifying the imbalance between the equestrian saturation of early modern culture and today's marginalization of matters equine. As Raber and Tucker comment, it may be instantly understandable to most of us why

> artworks, or architecture, or textiles, or educational practices, or violent crime, or cartography, or race . . . are important to our achieving a comprehensive picture of the early modern world, because we still in some part of our lives interact with versions of these. It is, however, much, much more difficult for us to instantly see why *horses* are so central to various domains of early modern culture and, more importantly, what they meant to that culture.[55]

If animal studies has so far emphasized how humans have not only domesticated but dominated and exploited animals, it is time to look at the other side of the story. Might not horses have had some effects on human culture as well as the other way around?

CHAPTER ONE

Horsemanship in the British Isles
before the Eastern Invasion

• • •

As if an angel dropp'd down from the clouds
To turn and wind a fiery Pegasus,
And witch the world with noble horsemanship.
— *Henry IV, Part 1*, IV.i.108–10

Horse ownership in England increased dramatically during the seventeenth century. In the 1590s only a fifth of the householders of a modest parish such as Yetminster in Dorset had owned horses, but by the 1660s three-fifths owned them.[1] By 1767, Arthur Young had cause to protest that even farmers with the smallest acreages often indulged in horse-keeping, to their cost. Prudent and profitable husbandry on a small scale, Young insisted, meant the employment of oxen, which were much cheaper to keep than horses, for plowing and pulling wagons and carts. Young appeared quite bemused by the prejudice against oxen, strongest in the "horse counties" but clearly widespread elsewhere. By the second half of the eighteenth century, horses had become sufficiently fashionable to appear indispensable to the farming classes.[2] By the nineteenth century, even in a metropolitan center like London, horses were "ubiquitous."[3] Burgeoning traffic and greater mileages increased the demand for draft animals of all kinds, and the first thing visitors to London noticed "was that it smelt like a stable yard."[4]

Intrinsic to the economy in an era of horsepower, then, early modern horses were social actors. And as social actors, they could act up. They might rebel against the constraints of work and sharp discipline, and be severely punished for it. Like domestic servants, horses could be well or badly treated. But because horses served as engines and vehicles, they could be employed as if they were machines rather than sentient beings. In Victorian London, as Diana Donald has shown, "the most shaming instance of the mercenary callousness of the age was its treatment of horses."[5] Servitude could all too easily become chattel slavery. Horses performed a powerful metonymic function, as Donald claims, both as "living evidence of the tragic effects of metropolitan commercialism, and hence a symbol of the ills of capitalism," and as embodiments of what Carlyle called the "'half-frantic velocity of impetus' of the 'brute-world' of British national ascendancy and capitalist competition."[6]

In short, horses were property. Yet horses were also powerfully symbolic. To ride a horse well was to possess the virtues necessary for social authority and even political rule. Commanding a horse required both technical skills and an ability to reason with a creature that embodied the passions but showed signs of being capable of a degree of reason. Indeed, in the later seventeenth and early eighteenth centuries the horse began to figure as an idealized version of the human self. The arrival in the British Isles of Eastern horses—whether called Turks, Barbs, or Arabians—was crucial to this transformation.

Cultural historians have recently begun to investigate the evidence of animals' contributions to human culture. Explanations of domestication and the relationships that have evolved between companion species such as humans and canines, and humans and equines, are currently shifting. As Donna Haraway has observed, the old domestication story was that "Man took the (free) wolf and made the (servant) dog and so made civilization possible." This is the story told by both deep ecologists, who hated it "in the name of Wilderness before the Fall into Culture," and by humanists, who have used it "in order to fend off biological encroachments on culture."[7] Haraway argues that the new "distributed" versions of domestication stories, in which dogs and other nonhuman species get to make the first moves, although they may sound faddish and tailored to fit an animal-loving audience, in fact have a "better chance of being true" than the older stories.[8] Might what happened in prehistoric times have also happened subsequently, in very different circumstances, in early modern Europe? What is the likelihood of horses having effected change within English culture during the age of empire?

Horses were economically central in early modern Britain, but the richness of the verbal and visual record of equestrian culture suggests a preoccupation that exceeded the requirements of mere economic necessity. If examined with an eye toward the newer, "distributed" stories of domestication and human-animal relations proposed by Haraway, this verbal and visual record reveals how crucial horses were to what came to be classified as distinctively "English" culture in early modern Britain. And when a superior kind of horse, the Eastern blood horse, became widely known, Britons altered their attitudes toward horses in keeping with the aptitudes of this particularly sensitive and peculiarly rational animal.

Both the Eastern incursion among the equine population and the formulation of a potentially imperial identity within the human one were products of mercantilism. That is to say, Britain's participation in global maritime trade as a newcomer on the world stage enabled both developments. *Asia before Europe*, K. N. Chauduri's study of Indian Ocean trade from the rise of Islam to 1750, boldly reminds us that all European nations were latecomers on the scene of world economic power.[9] This is an argument also made by Andre Gunder Frank in *Re-Orient: Global Economy in the Asian Age* (1998), which shows how before 1800, "Europe used its American money to muscle in on and benefit from Asian production, markets, trade," and how the "Chinese Ming/Qing, Indian Mughal, and even Persian Safavid and Turkish Ottoman empires carried much greater political and even military weight than any or all of Europe."[10] So-called blood or thoroughbred horses, the wellspring of equine quality, were much coveted by Eastern rulers for both military and ceremonial purposes. Arabians, North African Barbs, and the Turanian, Turkmen, or Turcoman from further north and east (Persia and Central Asia, originating near the shores of the Caspian Sea) had been a staple of trade among Eastern nations long before the sixteenth century. "The medieval trade of Asia was really founded on the economic and social acceptance of the four great products of eastern civilisation—silk, porcelain, sandalwood, and black pepper—which were exchanged for incense (Arabian gum resins), thoroughbred horses, ivory, cotton textiles, and metal goods," notes Chauduri.[11] The earliest evidence of domestication of the horse has been found in the geographical arc spanning "the Ukraine to the region of Turkestan," in which horses were first employed as food animals, than as draft animals, and finally as vehicles ridden under saddle.[12] Much of the traffic consisted of Central Asian horses being sold to India.[13] Within the Bukharan trade, as many as one hundred thousand horses were exported annually during the seventeenth century.[14] Gifts sent by the Ottoman sultans to Mughal India, as Naimur Rahman Farooqi observes, "always consisted of Turkish horses of purest breed," which included horses from Greater Syria and Arabia as well as Anatolia.[15] When the Mughals wished secretly to form an alliance with the Ottomans and Uzbeks against the Persians, it made sense to use the cover story of an embassy to Istanbul expressly to bring back horses of the highest quality from Anatolia and Arabia.[16]

The British importation of Eastern equine bloodstock on a grand scale between 1650 and 1750, then, was an important material and economic as well as symbolic and cultural phenomenon. Like so much of British trade in this period, the horse trade depended on imports, rather than British manufactures. By forcibly appropriating and rapidly assimilating this Eastern resource, the remote island nation promoted its shores as a breeding ground of equine purity and nobility. The heterogeneity of horse genetics in the British Isles was miraculously transformed into a myth of exotic prepotency derived from the breeding practices of the Ottoman and Persian empires, Bedouin tribesmen, and North African "Barbary" states. The blood horse, a creature with mythic resonance in Islamic culture, became the totem of an aggressive accumulationist policy, however "gentlemanly" the dominant social identity of Britain's *arriviste* capitalists was to remain during the long eighteenth century.

An Equestrian Nation

One reason that the assimilation of Eastern bloodstock appeared so seamless and aroused so little curiosity was that Britons believed that they had a right to the finest horseflesh, dating from time immemorial. From prehistory onward, inhabitants of the British Isles have imagined themselves as belonging to an equestrian nation. The least disputed early record for the domestic horse in Western Europe comes from Ireland, where, at New Grange in County Meath, Late Neolithic (Beaker) level horse remains provide evidence of their importation and domestication from about 2000 B.C.E.[17] The Celtic vocabulary is peculiarly rich in words for horses and vehicles, which entered the Romanic and Teutonic languages.[18] The name of the Celtic goddess Epona means simply the Great Mare, but there were other versions: in Welsh, Rhiannon, the Great Queen, and in Ireland, Macha, the Holy Queen.[19] *Marca* means "war-horse" in various Celtic tongues.[20] A Venetian ambassador "remarked with some surprise and disapproval as early as 1558 that English peasants (by which we should understand yeomen) usually rode on horseback: 'miserable must that man be who follows his cart on foot. Thus the rustic on horseback drives the oxen or horses of his team, and hence comes it that England is also called the land of comforts.'"[21]

Thus when addressing his countrymen between 1579 and 1580, Sir Philip Sidney could think of no more persuasive analogy for recommending his chosen art of poetry than equitation. In his *Apologie for Poetrie*, which is also a theory of governance, the subtle control of intellect and rhetoric that Sidney endorsed took as its model *haute école* riding, what we would today call dressage. Remembering a visit he and his friend Edward Wotton had paid to the court of the Habsburg emperor Maximillian II at Vienna in 1573, during which the emperor's Italian equerry John Pietro Pugliano had lectured to them about the art of horsemanship, Sidney recalled Pugliano's describing how "no earthly thing bred such wonder to a Prince as to be a good horseman," and that "Skill of gouernment was but a Pedenteria in comparison":

> Then would hee adde certaine prayses, by telling what a peerlesse beast a horse was, the onely seruiceable Courtier without flattery, the beast of most beutie, faithfulness, courage, and such more, that, if I had not beene a peece of a Logician before I came to him, I think he would haue perswaded mee to haue wished my selfe a horse.[22]

Sidney adopted Pugliano's strategy of expressing "strong affection" for his art.[23] To value horses more highly than people was not quite logical, but it was compelling. Sidney hoped that this vindication of horsemanship would work for poetry, since poetry, like horsemanship, was a kind of learning that served ethical and political ends beyond itself:

> Euen as the Sadlers next end is to make a good saddle, but his farther end to serue a nobler facultie, which is horsemanship; so the horseman to souldiery, and the Souldier not onely to haue the skill, but to performe the practise of a Souldier: so that, the ending end of all earthly learning being vertuous action, those skilles, that most serue to bring forth that, haue a most iust title to bee Princes ouer all the rest.[24]

The proper governance of horse and rider *is* virtuous action, but it also *promotes* virtuous action, just like poetry. As a man governs his horse, so will he govern his text—or a ruler his people.[25]

Culturally Hybrid Horsemanship

The equestrian culture of Sidney's England was by no means parochial. Horsemanship in the British Isles was indebted from its earliest beginnings to immigrants. The earliest recorded horse races in England may have been those held by the Romans in the reign of the Emperor Severus Alexander (A.D. 210) at Netherby in Yorkshire, where the horses were reported to be "delicate Arabs of famous speed and stamina, but so unsuitable to this climate that their owners were obliged to construct an enclosed training ground in order to prepare them for their engagements."[26] What came to seem most intrinsically British or English or Irish thus often had its origins considerably further east. But these alien practices, goods, and species were eagerly incorporated into the nation and became very quickly a naturalized part of its identity.[27]

Importations of exotically bred horses and of foreign equestrian techniques were mutually reinforcing phenomena. Since the horsemasters of Naples, Ferrara, and Mantua were the leading theorists of equitation in Europe in the six-teenth century, ambitious young gentlemen like Sir Philip Sidney studied horse-manship abroad. Sidney advised his brother Robert that Italian theory should be studied alongside actual foreign practice in order to gain the greatest benefit from Continental riding instruction:

> At horsemanship when you exercise it, read Crison Claudio and a book called "la gloria del Cavallo" withal, that you may join the thorough contemplation of it with the exercise; and so shall you profit more in a month than others in a year; and mark the bitting, saddling, and curing of horses.[28]

Sidney recommends not only the trusty "Crison"—Federico Grisone of Naples, known in England as "Grison," whose 1550 treatise, *Gli Ordini di Cavalcare*, had been translated into English in 1560 by Thomas Blundeville[29]—but also Claudio Corte, who wrote *Il Cavallenzzo* (1573), and the Neapolitan Pasquale Caracciolo, author of *La Gloria del Cavallo* (1567).[30] During the years in which he was receiv-ing gifts of Barbary horses from the Gonzaga family of Mantua, Henry VIII had benefited from the expertise of Alexander de Bologna, an expounder of Grisone's rules, who worked at the king's stables from 1526 until his death, and perhaps con-tinued to serve Elizabeth;[31] he is referred to in *The Duchess of Malfi*, act 1, scene 1.

If Sir Philip Sidney typifies Renaissance man, we might understand his learn-ing from Italian riding masters as a typically Renaissance gesture. European horsemanship has long been thought to have undergone a rebirth in the sixteenth century, partly through the rediscovery of Xenophon's work *Hippike* or *On Horse-manship*, circa 365 B.C.E., which was disseminated through the publications of Grisone and others. Manuscripts of this work existed in Italy (two of the thirteenth century and five of the fourteenth are known); an edition of it was printed at Florence in 1516, and a Latin translation, *De re equestri*, was published in 1539.[32] R. H. C. Davis observes that Xenophon's short treatise "conveys very clearly, at-tractively and persuasively the idea that horses are best trained with kindness."[33] The first printed work on horsemanship in Europe had been Spanish, published in 1495.[34] Italian works were printed in 1499, 1517, and 1518, and a flurry of pub-lications appeared across Europe during the 1550s and 1560s.[35] As John Astley commented in his "breefe treatise," with its "due interpretation of certeine places alledged out of Xenophon, and Gryson," in 1584, Xenophon "setteth downe that shape and forme that Art should imitate."[36] Grisone's treatise appeared in new editions almost every year during the 1550s, and by 1568 had been translated and published in France, Germany, and Spain, as well as England.[37] Thomas Blunde-ville's *A newe booke containing the arte of ryding, and breakinge great Horses* brought

England into the picture in 1560.[38] Other English translations of Italian works subsequently appeared.[39]

Imagining the Renaissance as a parochially European phenomenon is something of a distortion, however. Looking to the East for some of the cultural origins and forms we associate with this rebirth—whether in the arts, architecture, or horsemanship—has begun to transform the field of Renaissance studies. Scholars influenced by the work of Ottoman historians as well as Eastern European and Asian scholars have given us a new conception of the Renaissance as emerging in rich exchanges between East and West.[40] There are grounds for speculation that a visit to Constantinople may have been as important for European horsemanship as was the rediscovery of Xenophon. Grisone was one of several riding masters working in Naples during this earliest period in the history of European riding schools. Another was the nobleman Giovanni Battista Pignatelli, who may have been persuaded to open a riding school after a visit to Constantinople.[41]

Naples led the other Italian cities in theories of horsemanship and the discipline of the manège, or *haute école,* because of "its court and its links with Spain," and Spain in turn was saturated by Islamic North African and Asian influences.[42]

What might have been the effect of seeing up close the forward style of riding common, by this time, to the Turkic horsemen of the Central Asian steppe and Ottoman, Mameluke, Arab, and Berber horsemen? How influential might this example of a fundamentally different seat—with very short stirrup leathers, riding forward—have proved to be? Blundeville, translating Grisone for publication in 1560, "more than once refers to 'riding short after the Turkey fashion.'"[43] In *The arte of ryding,* Blundeville describes *corvetti* and the *capriole,* two of the *haute école* "airs above the ground," and recommends that *corvetti,* "a certaine continuall prauncynge and dauncynge uppe and downe stil in one place, and sometimes sydelynge to and fro," be undertaken only if the rider and horse have sufficient aptitude and have accustomed themselves to this new seat:

> If your horse be very light, and you have accustomed to ryde shorte upon hym, after the Turkey fashion: you may teache him also the *Coruetti,* but if he be great of stature and that you ride longe upon him, after oure fashion, then the Capriole is most meete for him.[44]

Blundeville also observes how the Spaniards practice the *corvetti* "moste uppon their Jennettes, and specyallye when they ryde shorte after the Turkey fashion."[45] A hundred years later, William Cavendish, Duke of Newcastle, would chastise Blundeville for his use of "Turkey fashion" here:

To Ride short, he calls after the *Turkish* Fashion, wherein he is Deceived; for it is *A La Genette*, which is the *Spanish* Fashion too; and to Ride Short in *Corvets* is his Mistake, for I would Ride Longer in *Corvets* than any other Ayre.[46]

Cavendish insists that the Spaniards, whom some thought closer kin to the English in belonging to Christian Europe, are as good exponents of riding short as the Turks. He evades the question of a different tradition—"A La Genette," *à la gineta*—which came to Spain from the Barbary states of North Africa, where Arab-Islamic horsemanship was practised, displaying Mameluke and Ottoman influences. Elsewhere in his book the duke confesses that he had never traveled to Constantinople, but had "Spoken with many Gentlemen that have been There, as Likewise with diverse Merchants that came from Thence," and that all who had seen the horses of the Ottoman capital agreed, "That there are *There*, the most *Beautifull-Horses* in the World . . . And certainly they are Brave *Horses!*"[47] Might this acknowledgement of the horses' bravery be a covert hint of appreciation for the virtues of the ferociously effective Ottoman cavalry? Cavendish also praised what he had heard of Turkish grooms and described the clothing in which Ottoman horses were dressed.[48] There is every reason to think that English training regimens for horseracing, including the wearing of clothing to sweat a horse to a lean, hard state of fitness, were influenced by Ottoman, and more broadly, Turkic, practice. Asian equestrian culture was disseminated alongside European ideas. Ottoman practices may have been absorbed and become as influential as European ones.

The Italian riding masters, and hence Blundeville, may have been influenced by the brilliance of both Ottoman horses and horsemen. Walter Liedtke speculates that, like the Crusaders before him, Pignatelli "must have been impressed by the small but fast and agile Arabian horses" he would have seen in the Ottoman capital, which, "imported to the West, were used to develop new breeds, especially in Italy and Spain."[49] The influence of Arabian blood on European breeds was well known in the early modern period. As the Aleppine English merchant Nathaniel Harley commented in 1705, the Arabian was "probably the Root of the best Breeds in the World, The Barbary & Spanish Horses are descended from 'em, and the Naples from the last."[50] The relation between the importation of Eastern bloodstock to Europe and changes in equitation should not be underestimated. The appeal of horses from the Near East in contrast with the weight-carrying European war horses and other native stock was profound. The Eastern bloodstock was small but fast, agile, and highly sensitive to human demands through centuries of intimate domestication. Different modes of dealing with these new physical and mental capabilities were required.

Ottoman influence, however, might well have extended beyond the favorable impression made by Turkish horses of Arabian and Turanian or Turcoman breeding.[51] Liedtke does not speculate about the possible impression made by Ottoman horsemen on Western European visitors. And yet it seems likely that if a visitor such as Pignatelli was inspired to open a riding school, that inspiration might have owed something to what he saw of horsemanship and cavalry training as practiced at Constantinople, over and above the superior qualities of the horses themselves.

Between Xenophon and the Renaissance revival of Greek equestrian ideas, there existed from the eighth century onward in the Islamic world an elaborate discourse on horsemanship or *furusiyya*—the theory and practice of hippology, veterinary care, farriery, and equitation. This discourse combined Islamic with pre-Islamic, especially Sasanian, ideas,[52] and was transmitted orally as well as by means of treatises in Arabic, Persian, and Ottoman Turkish, displaying a mixture of Arab, Iranian, Turkish, and Greek influences.[53] As Rhoads Murphey has observed, the horse and horse culture were "formative" as a "central element in state institutions in the steppe," as in the desert, so that horses were both materially and symbolically important for the Ottomans and Mongols; however, the question "as to whether the horse played a more significant role in the mythology or the reality of rule" remains, according to him, "still open."[54] Robert Irwin finds Qipchak Turkish and Mongol Mamelukes, long after their conversion to Islam, continuing to consume horse meat and mares' milk ceremonially in Egypt, a practice that he concludes was not so much a challenge to Islam as a reflection of "an innocuous nostalgia for the ways and tastes of nomadic life that they had known as children on the steppes."[55] As Michael Rogers concludes in the best study of Ottoman *furusiyya* to date, despite Ottoman historians' "pride in their nomadic past," the traditions they recorded "do not go back earlier than the origins of the Ottoman state in the early fourteenth century," and thus display strong Mameluke influences.[56] Mameluke treatises have traditionally been beset by problems of sources, dating, authorship, translation, and other bibliographical difficulties, so the scholarly treatment of *furusiyya* remains underdeveloped.[57] What does seem clear is that *furusiyya,* as the complete training of horse and rider in both courtly and military modes, was often publicly exhibited in the hippodrome or *maydan,* the outdoor enclosure where schooling was conducted, of which there were particularly famous examples at Cairo and Baghdad.[58] In Constantinople it would have been displays of horsemanship in open squares, including the *at meydanı,* or horse maydan, built on the site of the classical hippodrome, that impressed European visitors such as Pignatelli.

Figure 1. This portrait medal of Mehmed II, "the Conqueror," made by the Italian artist Costanzo de Moysis or Costanzo da Ferrara, probably in 1478, depicts the Ottoman sultan riding very short in the "Turkish fashion," as described by Thomas Blundeville and others. The Samuel H. Kress Collection, National Gallery, Washington, DC.

On the reverse side of a portrait medal depicting Sultan Mehmed II—"Fatih," the Conquerer—who took Constantinople in 1453 (fig. 1), the Italian artist Costanzo de Moysis registers similar details of his Ottoman patron's seat while, as Jerry Brotton observes, broadcasting the sultan's"imperial power" across the realm.[59] Note the short-stirruped seat, the loose reins, the horse's balanced forward movement, and Mehmed's use of the snaffle rather than the Mameluke curb. Mehmed noticeably bends his knees over his short stirrups, keeping his weight forward like a jockey and encouraging the horse's free forward movement, while remaining regally upright.

With the exception of Blundeville's mention of riding "after the Turkey fashion" and the Duke of Newcastle's criticism of it, the early modern sources are not very forthcoming regarding European opinion of the Eastern seat. This is rather surprising, given the military might of the Ottoman empire for several centuries before its first significant defeat at the hands of Hetman Jan Sobieski, the Polish king, in uneasy alliance with the Habsburg empire at the siege of Belgrade in 1683.[60] Jeremy James dramatizes this first of a number of defeats suffered by the Ottomans between 1683 and 1699 as particularly demoralizing because of the way Sobieski's forces had acquired Turkish horses and tactics. The Ottoman cavalry were now facing a European mirror-image of themselves.[61] And although cavalry was becoming increasingly less important in actual warfare from the sixteenth century onward as more accurate, quicker-reloading firearms and field artillery were developed, the symbolic significance of equestrian mastery remained undiminished both on and off the battlefield, in Europe as well as the East, at least until the First World War.[62]

As the light-horse cavalry enthusiast Captain Lewis Edward Nolan observed in 1853, "For ages, the finest cavalry seen in Europe was indisputably that of the Turks."[63] By the late eighteenth century, the influence of Ottoman and Hungarian cavalry methods on British military thinking had become transformative. Captain Nolan himself, a pupil of Colonel Haas, instructor of the Austrian cavalry, had also served for some time in the Hungarian Hussars.[64] Impressed by their performance during the Seven Years War, British commanders attempted to imitate the mobility and fire-power of Hungarian light dragoons, using Hungarian-type saddles and a better class of troop-horse.[65] The Napoleonic campaigns resulted in a near-reversion to "the original Danubian type," as Anthony Dent puts it, even to the adoption of the name Hussar, so that by the time "the Light Brigade of Balaclava fame" charged the Russian guns they "had the clothing, the saddlery, and the accoutrements partly of Polish Ulani (in the Lancer regiments) and partly of Hungarian light horsemen."[66]

These borrowings have become so completely normalized that today at a state reception at Windsor Castle, for instance, the Household Cavalry will most likely be led by a drum-horse "accoutred in the Turkish manner and bearing brass kettledrums ultimately of Turkish or Tartar origin," while the King's Troop of the Royal Horse Artillery will parade "in their full-dress uniform of Hussar (that is, Hungarian) pattern."[67]

Why should this rich and varied legacy of Eastern influence on British horsemanship, and on European horsemanship in general, have gone so relatively unacknowledged? In Edward Said's terms, the ideological mechanism at work would appear to be the West's tendency in modern times to imagine itself superior to, and thus entitled to appropriate, the substance of the so-called Orient. By the late eighteenth century, Orientalist scholarship had become indispensable as an imperial administrative tool, saturating popular culture and manifesting itself as "a battery of desires, repressions, investments, and projections."[68] Orientalist assumptions so commonplace in Western culture that they go unremarked include the failure to recognize Oriental knowledges as knowledge, possessed of any scientific or systematic value. A related function of Orientalist thinking has been to regard the Orient as a source of raw materials but never of cultural practices or end-products. Eastern techniques and technologies, like exotic luxury goods, were highly prized, but they were also seized upon and more or less unconsciously absorbed into European culture. Thus whatever was imported into Britain became British by dint of use and habitual consumption.

From the sixteenth century onward, then, and thus nearly a hundred years before the major importation of Eastern bloodstock occurred, equestrian culture in the British Isles was already profoundly hybrid. The Italian influence was explicitly acknowledged, the Ottoman and Arab-Islamic one scarcely so. And so it would continue after the celebrated Arabians and other foreign horses had been fully naturalized and assimilated as English on English or Irish soil.

The Arts of Equitation and Political Rule

Rival empires emulated one another in both arms and arts. The renaissance of European horsemanship, likely to have been inspired by Ottoman and Arab-Islamic example as much as by Greek ideas, represented a period of both re-theorization as well as changes in equestrian practice. In early modern Britain, the art of horsemanship, at a rudimentary level a very necessary form of knowledge in a horse-powered nation, always simultaneously embodied authority and power. As a twentieth-century historian once quipped, "It is impossible to be chivalrous without a horse."[69] Sir Thomas Elyot thought there was no more suitable knowledge for the governing classes to possess if they hoped to impress "inferior persones" by appearing "aboue the common course of other men, dauntyng a fierce and cruell beaste."[70] Lord Herbert of Cherbury proclaimed that "a good rider on a good horse is as much above himself and others as this world can make him."[71] It was certainly difficult to elevate oneself above the masses without one. A horse performing obediently for a rider while giving off an aura of contained wildness, of massive physical power and independent spirit, was indeed a daunting spectacle. Early modern writing about horsemanship sought to make the most of the paradox of enormous physical power contained and directed by art rather than violence, although there were exceptions.

In the *Arcadia*, probably composed during the same period as the *Apologie*, Sidney again wrote about equitation, demonstrating that the rider's governance of the horse ought to be achieved by subtle and graceful means rather than force. In the second book of the *Arcadia*, although the Centaur-like rider sports both spurs and a "wand" or rod, these aids to correction

seemed rather marks of sovereignty than instruments of punishment, his hand and leg, with most pleasing grace, commanding without threatening, and rather remembering than chastising; at least, if sometimes he did, it was so stolen as neither our eyes could discern it, nor the horse with any change did complain of it: he ever going so just with the horse, either forthright or turning, that it seemed, as he borrowed the horse's body, so he lent the horse his mind. In the turning one might perceive the bridle-hand something gently stir: but indeed so gently, as it did rather distil virtue than use violence.[72]

"Marks of sovereignty" in the right hands are not to be confused with "instruments of punishment," Sidney insists. Human authority goes unquestioned, but the horse's compliance, even willing cooperation, is to be solicited rather than the rider's will imposed. The narrator looks for signs of ongoing chastisement of the horse but fails to discern any. The horse thus constitutes the best witness to the lack of any objectionable domination—for the horse does not complain of any. So either there is no coerced obedience being exacted, and the horse participates willingly in the exercise, or the horse has been so totally infused with the rider's will that complaint is impossible. Sidney neither explores nor answers this question, which remains implicit in his analysis.

However, the handling of the bridle, the one observable aid, is less ambiguously treated. This most obvious means of control, with all its attendant metaphors—the bit in the mouth, the hand upon the rein, the whole package of governance as curbing the other's will, or reining it in—can be seen in action, but only just. The bridle hand can be seen to "stir"—but "so gently" that there is a "distillation" of "virtue" rather than any violent exacting of obedience.

The art of horsemanship as an exercise in negotiation rather than coercion could hardly be more persuasively described. In "riding the great horse" in the manège or indoor school, such a sympathetic form of communication was meant to develop between horse and rider that it would be as if some peculiar osmosis had occurred. The horse would have allowed his body to be "borrowed" by the rider, and the rider in turn would have "lent" his mind to the horse. The rider commands, expresses "sovereignty," but by commuting the horse's will into the virtue of a beautiful performance. This exhibition of the horse's intrinsic beauty and nobility can only be achieved through sympathetic or empathetic rather than violent means.[73]

Early modern writers returned repeatedly to a passage in Xenophon for representing what the art of equitation sought to achieve. Xenophon had described a stallion showing off for mares as the height of equine beauty and called upon his readers to seek to imitate this ideal when they rode. Teaching the horse "to go with a slack bridle, to hold his neck up and to arch it towards the head," Xenophon opined, "you will cause the horse to do the very things in which he himself delights and takes the greatest pleasure."[74] The proof of this delight lay in how a horse exhibited himself before an audience of admiring females, raising "his neck highest" and arching "his head most, looking fierce," lifting his legs "freely off the ground," and tossing his tail up. "Whenever, therefore, you induce him to carry himself in the attitudes he naturally assumes when he is most anxious to display his beauty," Xenophon concluded, "you make him look as though he took pleasure in being ridden, and give him a noble, fierce, and attractive appearance."[75] In recreating a horse's original delight in showing himself to best advantage, the rider invites his mount to comply with being ridden, in a state of enjoyment, not cowed obedience.

Xenophon's ideal of equitation as the recreation of a horse's natural beauty inspired sixteenth-century riding masters such as John Astley, who adapted Xenophon as follows:

> When you see a Horse . . . make haste to meet with other horses, that be in his view, or mares rather, then shall you see how nature mooueth him to shew himself in his best forme and lustiness of courage, yea, both terrible and beautiful to behold: for then he will set vp his crest, bow in his head, pricke vp his eares, gather vp his legs high and nimble, swell in his nostrils, and start out his taile, &c. This is now the patterne that the curious painter with all his skill dooth diligentlie indeuor to imitate, but how much more should the skilfull Rider doo the same?[76]

Carrying himself in a mode of high collection and animation, from pricked ears to flaglike tail, the horse displays the arched neck and elevated paces of which he is capable but not always inclined to show. This aesthetic ideal was to be reproduced in the manège, preparing horses for service in the formal pageantry of state, as well as war, hunting, and other public displays. Once again the principle at issue was an ethic of just governance—the rider controlled the horse and directed the creature to perform according to human will, yet the object of the exercise was to display the inherent beauty and physical prowess of the horse, its cooperation and partnership with human designs, rather than its brutalization or forced submission.

Cruelty or Kindness? The Question of Training

Reading between the lines, we may be tempted to wonder how such idealization mapped onto actual practice. One of the ironies of reading early modern horsemanship treatises is that their writers perpetually set out to correct the work of

predecessors, advocating a more reasonable, gentler, less cruel system of training, while simultaneously recommending at least one or two methods likely to
strike modern readers as peculiarly outlandish or brutal. This combination of
reason and compassion with traces of residual violence threatens to disturb read-
erly confidence in the humaneness of such training methods. It also invites the
suspicion that the elevated discourse of the manuals existed in sharp contrast
with the routine use of violence in everyday interactions between horses and humans.

This contrast is nowhere more apparent than in the writing of William Cavendish, Duke of Newcastle. Cavendish manages to sound both sophisticated and coercive at the same time. While his advice is couched in terms that imply that force
absolutely rules other people's ideas of horsemanship, he also claims to bend the
horse more firmly to his will than do other horsemen, who take their cues from
the horse's individual character:

> I follow not the Horses *Disposition*, as most do; but I *Make* the Horse follow my
> *Wayes*, and *Obey* me: I seldom Beat them, or Punish them with either *Rod*, or *Spur*,
> but when I meet with a great *Resistance*, and that *Rarely*: And yet I must tell you, that
> I use *Force*, which they *Obey* willingly, for the most part; and, however, all Yeeld, and
> Render themselves at last, with much Satisfaction to me; which I wish others may
> find in following their Wayes.[77]

Cavendish describes himself as being more systematic with the equine kind than
are "most" people, who tailor their training techniques to an individual horse's
"Disposition" or temperament. His system, which brooks no resistance or he applies "Force," will, he claims, apply equally well to all horses, regardless of their
idiosyncrasies. He professes thus to be able to impose his will equally on all
equine subjects. And yet he also announces himself to be less violent in his corrections than other people, "seldom" beating horses or punishing them with the
rod or spurs. His comments here suggest that such punishments were common.
By being both systematic and implacable, Cavendish insists, he can assert his authority over a horse without resort to such devices. The art of horsemanship con-
sists in gaining the horse's confidence to submit "willingly" to the will of the
rider, and countering all resistance with appropriate "Force"—a calculated correction.

A century earlier, violent punishments seem to have been even more routine.
Translating Grisone, Blundeville recommends correcting a "restive" horse—a
horse who "naps" or "sticks" and refuses to go forward—by outlandish means,
entailing what most modern readers would probably consider abuse of cats and

hedgehogs as well as horses. "Get a footma[n] stand behind you with a shrewed catte teyed at the one ende of a long pole with her belye upwarde, so as shee maye haue her mouth & clawes at liberty," suggests Blundeville:

> And when your horse doth stay or go backward, let him thrust the Catte betwixt his thyes so as she may scratche and bite him, somtime by the thighes, somtime by the rompe, and often times by the stones. But let the footman and al the standers by threaten the horse with a terrible noyse, and you shall see it will make him to goe as you woulde haue him. And in so doing be ready to make much of him.[78]

This scenario appears to contradict in every way the sympathetic partnership described by Sidney and advocated by Cavendish. Blundeville continues:

> Also the shirle crye of a hedgehog beinge strayt teyed by the foote under the Horses tayle, is a remedye of like force, which was proued by Maister *Vincentio Respine a Napolytan* who coirected by this meanes an old restiue horse of ye kinges in such sort as he had much a do afterwarde to kepe him from the contrarye vice of running away.[79]

The repertoire of the Italian riding masters would appear to have included such cruel tricks as well as sophisticated communication techniques. Modern readers are likely to wish to applaud the king's horse for running away.

We should consider, however, that Blundeville's advice here, in the form of these extreme measures, is directed towards those whose "art" is lacking: this chapter is entitled "Other corrections to be used agaynste restivenes when the rider lacketh art, and knoweth not by order of ridinge howe to gette the mastrye of his horse and make him to know his faulte."[80] Where proper "order" or technique in riding had been acquired, such violence would prove unnecessary, according to the logic of the text. We should also note that, following the thrusting of the cat between the horse's hind legs, and sundry loud noises, as soon as the horse responded correctly, by going "as you woulde haue him," Blundeville recommends "making much" of the animal, a practice also known as "cherishing."

The treatises' reiteration of the desirability of securing a horse's cooperation rather than beating a horse into submission suggests that the latter was a common enough practice to require chastisement. Yet ideals too need to be taken into account alongside abuses. The early modern language is often oddly affecting to the modern ear used to more scientific-sounding terminology for schooling. "But aboue the rest," wrote Thomas Bedingfield in his 1584 translation of Claudio Corte's *Il Cavallenzzo,* "make him to loue your person, and (as it were) be in loue with you."[81] Cherishing was an effective means of securing a horse's loyalty, which could never be acquired by coercion. "You shall likewise please him much, to cherish him with your hands, when you weare sweete gloues, wiping his face, and chieflie his nostrills with perfumes & sweet handkerchiefs: for neatnesse & sweetnes be two things wherein a horsse dooth singularie take pleasure," wrote Bedingfield.[82] This courtly language suggests an erotic and mimetic relation between horse and rider, a far cry from brutalization. Horses undoubtedly occupied a special place in the imagination of horsemen and women in the British Isles, as elsewhere. The catalogue of abuses, therefore, must be understood in relation to these other practices that bespeak affection and mimetic complicity of human with equine.

Throughout this period, from the mid-sixteenth century to the early eighteenth, equestrian manuals repeatedly addressed the question of the horse's capacity for reason and understanding. As is argued by many of the contributors to Karen Raber and Treva Tucker's *The Culture of the Horse,* equine rationality is increasingly stressed in riding manuals during this period. By the mid-seventeenth century, William Cavendish was directly comparing a horse's ability to reason, and thus to learn, with a human schoolboy's. Just as "a boy is a long time before he knows his alphabet, longer before he has learn'd to spell, and perhaps several years before he can read distinctly," wrote Cavendish, so also a horse should be educated gradually: "The horse is taught first to know, and then by frequent repetition to convert that knowledge into habit."[83] The duke waxed even more explicit on equine reason when challenging Descartes and other "scholasticks," especially Oxford and Cambridge dons, who condemned horses' mental abilities without having any proper knowledge of them:

> What makes scholasticks degrade horses so much, proceeds (I believe) from nothing else, but the small knowledge they have of them, and from a persuasion that they themselves know every thing. They fancy they talk pertinently about them, whereas they know no more than they learn by riding a hackney-horse from the University to LONDON, and back again. If they studied them as horsemen do, they would talk otherwise.[84]

Empirical experience was thus the basis for both horses' knowledge of schooling by humans and human knowledge of horses' potential to learn. Cavendish in the following passage describes his system of training in terms consonant with John Locke's on human understanding. He explicitly refutes Descartes's assertion that animals are mere machines, without any capacity for reasoning:

> A horse must be wrought upon more by proper and frequent lessons, than by the heels, that he may know, and even think upon what he ought to do. If he does not

think (as the famous philosopher DES CARTES affirms of all beasts) it would be impossible to teach him what he should do. But by the hope of reward, and fear of punishment; and when he has been rewarded or punished, he thinks of it, and retains it in his memory (for memory is thought) and forms a judgment by what is past of what is to come (which again is thought;) insomuch that he obeys his rider not only for fear of correction, but also in hopes of being cherish'd.[85]

According to Cavendish, not only could horses think, but they ought to be encouraged to think in the course of training. More specifically, they ought to be encouraged to look forward to the reward of "being cherish'd," a form of pleasure that could only be derived from human contact, rather than simply fearing corrections or punishments.

This emphasis on a horse's capacity for thought, in the sense of having memory and thus an ability to anticipate the future based on the past, grants the horse a form of agency in relation to human action and designs. We might consider Paul Patton's fine distinction between the imposing of human will on a horse as plain coercion—"an exercise of power that blindly seeks to capture some of the powers of the animal for human purposes"—and good, ethical training, which is based on mutual understanding and a sense of human obligation and responsibility toward the animal: "an exercise of power that seeks to capture the powers of the animal in ways that enhance both those powers and the animal's enjoyment of them."[86]

Certainly Cavendish, like Corte and Bedingfield before him, appreciates the horse's potential for enjoyment in the training situation. "Cherishing" is described as a positive good, a form of mutual pleasure and even moral value. Thus, even in the manège, which could and would be contrasted with the relative freedom of the racecourse and hunting field, a sense of give and take between horse and rider was an accepted fact of equestrian partnership. Kindness was expected to reap greater rewards than cruelty, outbreaks of violence indicated a failure of human knowledge and technique, and the use of force in training or schooling horses was a last resort rather than the first, theoretically the exception rather than the rule, and a sign of the horseman's lack of "art," not a failing on the horse's part.

That the duke's affection for his horses was reciprocated, his wife Margaret Cavendish, Duchess of Newcastle, was pleased to point out. "So great a Love" had William Cavendish for his horses, she wrote in her *Life* of her husband, that he refused to part with them even for high prices, and as a consequence, the horses had also a particular Love to my Lord; for they seemed to rejoice whensoever he came into the Stables, by their trampling action, and the noise they made; nay, they would go much better in the Mannage, when my Lord was by, then when he was absent; and when he rid them himself, they seemed to take much pleasure and pride in it.[87]

Herself no horsewoman, the duchess nevertheless registered vividly this equine testimony to the duke's loving horsemastership. There was no surer sign of nobility than the capacity to manage and evoke affection from horses.

Native Tastes and Preferences

Defending his system of equitation as well as the Restoration of Charles Stuart to the throne, Cavendish celebrated a human authority in the manège, and a royal one at the head of the body politic, that were both less than absolute.[88] Although he spent many years in exile on the Continent, following his defeat during the Civil Wars at the battle of Marston Moor, Cavendish was not untouched by the political, social, and intellectual upheaval of the Interregnum that forever altered the balance of class power. The very Restoration of 1660 that he defends represented a compromise between the sovereignty of the crown and the constitutional authority of Parliament, between aristocratic power and something approaching popular mandate.[89] Like his philosophy of riding, in which horses must be won over to obeying him willingly, Cavendish's political philosophy is less absolutist, less concerned with violently repressing, and more with reforming, the "ungovernable people" of the British Isles than it might at first appear.[90]

Cavendish's writing remained popular well into the eighteenth century. He had staked an English claim to the art of equitation as Enlightenment system or science that could be compared favorably with the treatises of the Italians and Antoine de Pluvinel's *Maneige Royal* (1623).[91] A Dublin edition of his English treatise appeared in 1740, and the English translation of his French one in 1743.[92] Particularly in his English treatise, Cavendish sought to persuade, and in some cases satirically goad, his countrymen into a more elegant, gentlemanly school of riding, one more amenable to Continental practice than had been their recent wont. Although manège riding had been fashionable during the peaceful years between 1550 and 1580, after 1580 a new vogue for racing arose among the nobility and gentry, as Joan Thirsk has observed; she quotes Thomas de Grey, in *The Compleat Horseman and Expert Ferrier* (1639), referring to "the neglect of the horse of manège" in his dedication to James, Marquess of Hamilton, Master of the Horse.[93] Racing had already achieved fashionable status by 1585, when a horse race at Salisbury was attended by the Earls of Cumberland, Warwick, Pembroke, and Essex, along with many gentlemen, and prizes of a golden bell and a golden snaffle were awarded.[94] James I was a keen racing man, who established the racecourse at Newmarket that would prove an irresistible draw for his grandsons Charles II and James II.

Confident of the superiority of his system, Cavendish contrasts it with what he takes to be the unenlightened horsemanship of his fellow Englishmen. Advocating the superiority of manège riding, especially the *haute école* or "high shool" maneuvers, the "airs above the ground" of *levade* (rearing on the hind legs with the front legs tightly tucked), *courbette* (a balanced leap on the hind legs), and *capriole* (a leap with a backward kick of the hind legs), Cavendish implies a great deal about his audience's expectations. Given his loyalties, we should take his judgments on the state of early modern English equestrianism with several grains of salt. But from the very defensive strategy of his argument, we can detect something of what English horsemen were likely to say about manège riding and the *haute école*.

Cavendish's chief anxiety is that such maneuvers as the *levade, courbette,* or *capriole* will be dismissed as useless, a series of tricks more akin to dancing than to pleasurable or purposeful getting across country. "Many say, that all things in the *Mannage* is nothing but Tricks, and Dancing, and Gamballs, and of no Use,"[95] Cavendish lamented, but he retorted:

> I wonder how men are so Presumptious, to think they can Ride as *Horse-men,* because they can Ride forward from *Barnet* to *London,* which every body can do; and I have seen Women to *Ride* Astride as well as they.[96]

Merely getting around on horseback was not the point. The proving ground of the art of horsemanship was the manège, and it should be the proper study of all who called themselves gentlemen horsemen:

> Another, because he hath *Ridd a Hundred Miles* in a *Day,* (which a *Post-Boy* can do) thinks Himself a *Horse-man;* or, Because he can Run a *Match* with his *Groom,* or Leap a Ditch, or a Hedg, in *Hunting,* and Hold by the *Main,* he thinks he is a *Horse-man;* but his *Hunts-Boy* doth as much . . . And I have seen many Wenches Ride *Astride,* and Gallop, and Run their *Horses,* that could, I think, hardly Ride a *Horse* Well in the *Mannage.*[97]

The untutored Englishman, outridden by a mere groom, or worse, a woman, is no gentleman. And women of the bolder sort were apparently to be seen riding astride and even racing in Cavendish's day. Jumping a ditch or hedge on the hunting field, gripping the horse's mane for security, was clearly a common practice and what came to mind when "leaping" was mentioned. Fast forward movement across country was the desideratum, whether for business or sport, not the elegant discipline of the manège.

Bits

All this forward movement suggests the unrestrained use of the snaffle bit. Archaeological evidence shows the snaffle to have been the earliest European bit as well as the earliest Asian bit. The snaffle was probably invented on the Eurasian steppe, but it underwent major improvements in the Near East.[98] Juliet Clutton-Brock reports that snaffle bits were used in harnessing chariot horses in Mesopotamia from 1600 B.C.E. onward, and that the fifth-century B.C.E. Scythian bronze and iron bits from the frozen Iron Age tombs of Pazyryk in the Altai Mountains of Siberia are jointed snaffles.[99] The Archaeological Museum in Istanbul contains Iron Age snaffle bits thought to be Cimmerian (from ninth to eighth century B.C.E.) and Urartian (eighth to seventh century B.C.E.). During this time (ninth to seventh centuries B.C.E.), the Celtic peoples, with antecedents in "the bronze and horse using" cultures of South Russia, began moving into Europe, and it has been argued that "a significant chapter of the European history of the horse began with the Celts' keeping horses: equestrian traditions of western Europe originated with the Celts."[100] The Celts used snaffle bits, and in Britain and Ireland, Celtic snaffles with three links have been found. These bits may imply "the emergence of a finer breed, more sensitive to skilled control," since such a bit is a less severe device than the more common two linked snaffles.[101]

As Michael Baret argued in 1618, the snaffle could stimulate a pleasing sensation in the horse's mouth; "his mouth" would be "truely relished with the snaffle," is how Baret put it.[102] This pleasant contact would maximize communication, the horse's mouth being "neither too much dulled, so that hee would disquiet the man to hold him in, nor yet so tender that vpon the feeling thereof he should either moue a stay or checke his head" (21). The object of the exercise was a Xenophonian picture in which the horse:

> must haue a perfect placing of his eye head and reyne with his nose inward, resting his iawes vpon the thropell, shewing his crest in his greatest grace, his mouth truely relished with the snaffle. (21)

This description could apply either to a snaffle bit employed on its own or to one used in combination with a curb, as we shall see. Being ridden properly in either case ensured that the horse could no longer hold his head any way he liked but had to carry himself and his rider in a balanced fashion, not altering the natural position of the horse's head "from his true place, but onely to giue him the meane betwixt them both" (21). The rider's part of the bargain was to cultivate a sensitive feel of the horse's mouth, not a heavy-handed contact:

> Now therefore the true vse of the hand is onely to guide the Horse by sweet and gentle motions, neither carrying it so hard that it shall make his mouth more dull, nor so slack, that he shall loose the true and stayed carriage thereof: . . . that whensoeuer his Horse shall assay to thrust his head or nose forth, the stay of his hands will not giue him liberty. (51)

"The true and stayed carriage" of the head and "the stay" of the rider's hands are most at issue. Achieving a horse's going well with "snaffle relish" demanded considerable artistry of the hands and seat.

The horsemen of Continental Europe, however, had during the Middle Ages embraced the curb bit, which was as crucial for knights to control their war horses as for the later discipline of the manège. In Egypt, and elsewhere in North Africa and parts of Arabia, the Mamelukes employed a curb bit with an additional jaw-encircling ring. Ottoman *furusiyya* was indebted to Mameluke treatises as well as Central Asian steppe example, so depictions of Ottoman riders display both Mameluke and snaffle bits. Both the curb and the curb-plus-ring-bit could be severe if harshly used, since they employed leverage by means of the curb's long side pieces to lower the horse's head, as well as acting upon the bars of the mouth as did the snaffle.

The curb invites collection of the horse, a rebalancing that shifts the weight back onto the hind legs, generating a containment of energy, not free forward movement. Although collection may be achieved with a snaffle, the leverage provided by the curb bit promises greater powers of collection, and hence greater submission of the horse to the will of the rider. Lowering and fixing the position of the horse's head and neck not only give the appearance of submission, limiting the animal's freedom of movement theoretically, but actually restrict the horse's capacity for independently judging and negotiating the obstacles that go with any terrain other than the confines of the indoor school.

The famous engravings in Blundeville's Grisone translation are of curb bits of various punishing-looking sorts.[103] William Cavendish had nothing but scorn for "Mr. *Blundevils* Bitts," but these engravings circulated widely. Cavendish found these devices so "very Ridiculous" that he ranted:

The Eyes are Naught, the Cheeks as ill, and the Mouths Worst of all; . . . and his Compleat Bitts, are completely Abominable, with their Water-Chain and Trench, the Mouth of the Bitt too being as Bigg as my Wrist; and the Branches as Long as my Arm; and the Curb as Bigg as a Chain for a Horse Nose, with two Stories flying Trench, with is a Snaffle tyed to the Bitt, and such other Tormenting ignorant Follies: The Leggs of it are to be so Loose, as if they were Broken, in the Knees, and are to Help up and down, as if they were Wind-Mill-Sayls.[104]

Cavendish evidently preferred bits that were not "complet" in Blundeville's terms, lacking the second chain across the mouthpiece that Blundeville called a "complet" "Cattes foot." Cavendish's own pictured bits are not so different from Blundeville's "halfe Cattes foote" bits, numbered 24 and 25, though the ports are somewhat lower and thus not quite so severe in their action on the mouth. Despite Cavendish's ridicule, Blundeville's bits were still being discussed in 1829 when John Lawrence quipped that such "instruments of torture" bespoke an inventiveness that had never been more "uselessly employed," and recommended that "the inventors of them ought to be compelled to wear them experimentally themselves, for a season."[105]

Three years into his reign, Charles I decreed that curb bits replace snaffles in the army, and in riding generally, and that snaffles be used only in *"Disport"*—hunting and racing.[106] Yet snaffle bridles never disappeared from common use in Britain, as the visual evidence of paintings and engravings amply shows. During the 1760s and 1770s, the Earl of Pembroke, whose system was adopted by the British cavalry, argued strongly on behalf of the snaffle in cavalry training, that the horse's mouth might be "kept fresh by its own play" in order to produce "the proper, gentle, and easy degree of *appui* or bearing." As his use of *appui* suggests, Pembroke saw the advantages of Continental high school training for the making of a good mouth.[107] In 1772, the London riding master Charles Hughes praised the snaffle and cautioned against too free a use of the curb:

There is no kind of bit equal to the snaffle, nor any that should be more sparingly used than the curb . . . I do not propose to lay down exact rules for the management of the curb; suffice it only to observe, that the greatest caution is required in the use of it. It is the gentle turn of the wrist you must apply to it, not the strength of the arm. If a horse cannot perform any thing readily, never put on a curb to compel him to it. A snaffle will give you power enough over his head to turn it any way . . . Such is the right treatment of a horse of spirit and a good mouth.[108]

As late as 1829, John Lawrence eulogized the "old attachment to 'a good snaffle-bridle horse'" as "a very rational one."[109] "Racers are always, hunters generally, ridden in a snaffle bridle, a check cord and rein being appended to it, in the case of a hard pulling horse, that cannot otherwise be held," Lawrence reported (41). A defender of the rights of animals, Lawrence encouraged fellow riders to consider a horse's pleasure in being ridden:

> Enthusiastically fond of the horse from infancy, one of my greatest pleasures has been derived from riding a horse with a good mouth. Such a one as champs and takes pleasure in his bit, and with jaws of such a temper and feeling as readily to obey every motion of the hand, and yet sufficiently hard to bear a good pull, and even delight in it . . . I have experienced great pleasure in riding true snaffle-bridle horses, which being in high spirits and good humour, would on a brisk trot now and then stretch out the neck and immediately curve it, returning the head and playing with the bit; and I remember a famous racer that had the same habit in his exercise, to the great pleasure of the lad who rode him. (168–70)

Light-mouthed horses would cherish themselves, as it were, and invite being cherished by their riders, by playing with their bits, especially if those bits were snaffles.

John Adams emphasized how this exquisite mouth-to-hand contact was, at its foundation, nothing other than the *appui* celebrated by manège devotees, and manège riding was "the science whereby you become acquainted with, and learn, the superiority you have over the horse, by a proper correspondence of the hand."[110] Adams assured his audience that there was utility as well as beauty to be derived from manège training, with its full repertoire of bits and bitting techniques. The educated rider above all had educated hands and thus could achieve the desired *appui* with either a snaffle or a curb:

> By this method of riding, you ride with perfect security; for though you ride with the highest animation, and occasional rapidity, you never suffer the ascendency of the hand to be transferred to the horse: thus by the continual restraint the horse is under, he is prevented from making the speed his capacity would admit; and the more he exerts himself to that purpose, the sooner he is exhausted.[111]

Thus collection—forward-going energy contained—leads to impulsion, animation, and brilliance rather than ground-covering movement. Adams acknowledged that many "who want to trot at the rate of from 12 to 16 miles an hour; or gallop at the rate of 20" would not find this attractive (1:xix). However, if safety were to be considered, mere jockeyish repudiation of the manège simply would not do. Even if not engaged in manège riding, but going fast across country, it was important to know how to regain the upper hand after allowing a horse the freedom of extension, so that

> whenever you adopt the proper style for these extended paces, and suffer the horse
> to take a support and ascendency of the hand, you can, when you find it necessary,
> more readily recover the superiority of the hand than those who are totally ignorant
> of the science. Many of these you see pulling and labouring with all their might, to
> no effect; and frequently exposed to imminent danger, from not being able to man-
> age their horses: and this they never attribute to their want of skill, but to the hard-
> ness of the horse's mouth. (1:xix–xx)

Only a poor artisan blames his tools. A horseman should never blame a horse for disobedience, but only his own lack of proper "management." After all, how did the horse acquire this so-called hard mouth in the first place, if not through ignorant usage? Adams's description of the unskilled rider being run away with, or physically laboring to the limit of his strength not to be, gives us a glimpse of the long-term effects of that native tendency to give the horse a free head in the interests of efficient ground covering.

Cavendish had warned his countrymen 150 years before to learn manège discipline. By the early nineteenth century, the horse's relative autonomy, if not agency, was so fully embedded in English riding that a return to Cavendishian basics appeared advisable.

The snaffle versus curb bit debate was effectively resolved when a hybrid piece of equipment became the gentlemanly tackle of choice—the double bridle or "bit and bradoon," consisting of a combination of a curb bit and a small snaffle. As Lawrence summarized its appeal, "On the whole, mild bits, comfortable to the horse, and it is a pleasure to find him playing with his bit, are more profitable and more conducive to good management."[112] "The double reined bridle, with curb and snaffle," he concluded,

> may well come under this description, the curb not being inordinately severe. It has
> been long the fashionable bridle for the road, and the curb may be enforced or slack-
> ened, according to the direction of the hand. The single curb [one lacking a snaffle
> rein] may be classed with severe and unfavourable bits. (41)

By the nineteenth century, the double bridle had become the mark of the educated gentleman rider, and the conventional bridle for all forms of riding except racing. Even George Morland's downmarket country sportsman in *The Benevolent Sportsman* (1792)—who is sympathetic to gypsies, rides a hairy-heeled horse (though one with a fine head bespeaking quality), and dresses in a shabby, rough-hewn fashion—rides in a double bridle.[113] However, he holds his mount's snaffle rein only, leaving the curb rein slack on the horse's neck. His benevolence extends to his horse as well as to the gypsies.

Free Forward Movement

Until 1800, the entry "To Ride" in the *The Sportsman's Dictionary* still designated "riding the Great Horse" or "learning the manage" (1735, 1778, 1785, 1792)—a gentlemanly nicety of which Cavendish would have approved.[114] However, by the end of the eighteenth century, native predisposition and the spirit of expedition had won the day. The duke's efforts had failed to convert the equestrian public to systematic management.

As Lawrence remarked in 1798, "The decline of Riding-house forms in this country, and the universal preference given to expedition, fully confirm the superior use and propriety of a jockey-seat."[115] Adams confirmed that the manège was out of fashion in 1805, while defending it:

> For, certain it is, masters of old taught only one style of riding, which was the *manege;* and this being the truth and foundation of all good riding (which I must acknowledge it is, and shall make it so appear) they neither practise nor taught any other. The obvious consequence is, that gentlemen are as emulous of riding fast, as of riding well; and finding persons who had learned to ride in a style so ill calculated to travel far, or fast, or endure its fatigue; they ridiculed the idea of learning to ride at a school, but preferred, or sought to copy, a hunting-groom, or racing-jockey.[116]

The result of that venerable British preference for riding from Barnet to London as expeditiously as possible was, as Adams commented in 1805, that "reciprocal contempt has subsisted between the *manege* riding and *jockey* riding ever since" (1:xvii).

Himself a figure of worldly compromise, Adams made it his business to "reconcile both, and make them friends with each other," which he hoped to do by playing to both sides, "making each party appear to be in the right; which is certainly the case here, since both styles of riding will be found proper for their respective purposes" (1:xvii–xviii). That Adams succeeded in this admirably modern appeal to reason and utility is borne out by his emergence in the twentieth century as an early hero of the modern forward seat so important in Three-Day Eventing or Combined Training competitions.[117] An Olympic sport, eventing bridges the gap between Cavendish's "mannaged riding" and the legacy of hunting and military reconnaissance by including the three disciplines of dressage, cross-country jumping at speed, and the more precise art of show or stadium jumping.

By the end of the seventeenth century, riding on horseback was no longer restricted to an elite few. As the Frenchman Guy Miège admiringly stated in 1699, "I may say the English nation is the best provided of any for land travel as to horses and coaches . . . Travelling on horseback is so common a thing in England that the meanest sort of people use it as well as the rest."[118] Cavendish's countrymen liked nothing more than expediting matters, the efficient use of time in a commercial sense, and making expeditions, the positive seeking out of adventure and even danger. The sports of the aristocracy and gentry no less than business and commerce partook of this spirit of enterprise.

The spirit of expedition may have contributed most crucially to what appears to have been a truly British invention: rising to the trot (in American usage, "posting"). Jankovich suggests that a horse's natural gaits are the walk and the gallop, and the trot only occurs when passing from one to the other, usually when "changing down" from the gallop to the walk.[119] Hence Eastern horsemen rode at the walk and gallop, not rising to the trot but leaning forward from the waist to sit out the occasional trotting stride. Arabian and some steppe horses may travel easily at a canter for long distances, but other breeds, including the long-striding English Thoroughbred, last longer at the trot.

How could commerce have been conducted, we are invited to wonder by the early modern sources, if the mass of Englishmen and women had not been able to travel freely on horseback, covering the miles as expeditiously as possible without excessively tiring themselves or their horses? For this, fast trotting was essential, and only rising to the trot enabled fast trotting on a big-going horse without severe discomfort. "Since the rider's ease and convenience is the principal consideration in riding on the road, it is admissible when the trot is extended to an unpleasant roughness, to ease the jolting by rising in the stirrups," Adams politely conceded in 1805.[120]

Rising or posting to the trot has been popularly attributed to eighteenth-century postillions or post-boys who had to bestride coach horses going full-tilt at a "spanking trot." However, in the late eighteenth century it was recognized that this easing of human and horse had been going on for much longer in Britain than just the previous few decades. John Lawrence commented in 1798, "It is somewhat remarkable, that the seat on horseback, recommended by Baret in the reign of James I, is precisely the same as that practised by our jockies and sporting men of the present day."[121] In the entry on "Horsemanship" in the *Sports-*

man's Dictionary of 1800, Lawrence again remarks, "We cannot speak to the antiquity of the English fashion of rising in the stirrups during a trot, and of preserving time with the motions of the body, in unison with those of the horse; but the knowledge of it is discoverable in BARET, and in no author before him."[122]

Michael Baret had recommended rising to the trot as early as 1618, and neither Lawrence, who knew of Baret in the 1790s, nor anybody else seems to have found any earlier mention in print:

> If he would help his horse in his trot, pace or any other assault, for delight, then let him clap both his knees close to the points of the saddle, and onely keepe time with his seate, to moue the better spirit to the horse: and not to sit as some doe, (which are not esteemed the worst horsemen) without any motion, (like logges) on their horse backes, with their legges stretched out in their stirrops, (as if they were on the racke) but as their horse causeth them, (they forcing him by extremities,) hauing no agility to helpe him.[123]

Encouraging ground-covering action at all costs, including at the price of what could be an awkward or uncomfortable gait for the inexperienced, came to seem peculiarly English. The spirit of expedition inspired rising to the trot.

Thus we can see that before the Eastern importations of 1650–1750, there was already in place in the British Isles a predisposition toward a forward-going style of riding that might have owed something to Eastern, especially Ottoman, example, although it had Celtic and antique British roots as well. The arrival of the Eastern blood horse encouraged this predisposition. These horses not only raced unbelievably well across difficult terrain but could be ridden thus with a minimum amount of fuss. The radical writer Thomas Holcroft, once a stableboy at Newmarket, wrote of being "borne" by racehorses "over hill and dale, far outstripping the wings of the wind."[124] The boldness of blood horses encouraged intrepidity in their riders. Whether racing, crossing rivers, or leaping fences or precipices, the new "through-bred" horses of Eastern extraction combined "force and ardour" in the field with "mild and gentle manners" and a "social" temper.[125] Riders in the British Isles experienced for the first time the thrill of being borne away by athletic, finely tuned racing machines who also possessed a particular sensitivity to human demands and requirements that suggested a nearly human rational intelligence. It is no coincidence that the horses listed in Erica Fudge's recent book *Animal* who were the subjects of experiments in animal intelligence, whether in turn-of-the-twentieth century Germany or turn-of-the-seventeenth century England—Zarif and Muhammed, Clever Hans, Marocco—were either of Arabian blood (the first three) or have a name suggesting an Eastern origin (Bankes's Marocco).[126] Rational intelligence and Eastern equine blood were equated from the start.

The arrival of Eastern blood horses gave a new infusion of energy to British self-stylings as different from and superior to their European neighbors across the channel. English merchants' and diplomats' special trading relationship with the Ottoman empire encouraged an absorption of matters and manners Eastern that rendered culture in the British Isles surprisingly hybrid. As the equine population changed, so too did the new horses' riders evolve new seats and saddles, giving the impression that these horses demanded to be ridden differently. One consequence of this new equestrian partnership was a hybrid style of riding, neither entirely Eastern nor entirely native or European, that emerged from a literal jockeying for position on horseback: we shall call this phenomenon the making of the English hunting seat.

CHAPTER TWO

The Making of the English Hunting Seat

• • •

> This riding and tumbling, this being blown upon and rained
> upon and splashed from head to heels with mud, have worked
> themselves into the very texture of English prose and given it that
> leap and dash, that stripping of images from flying hedge and
> tossing tree which distinguish it not indeed above the French but
> so emphatically from it.
>
> —Virginia Woolf, "Jack Mytton," *The Common Reader*

George Stubbs's painting *William Henry Cavendish-Bentinck, 3rd Duke of Portland, and His Brother Lord Edward Bentinck, with a Groom and Horses* (1766–67; fig. 2), portrays the gentlemanly ideal of horsemanship as it had come into being by the middle of the eighteenth century. Stubbs's nineteenth-century biographer Sir Walter Gilbey observed, "The portraits of the Duke and his brother were pronounced by contemporaries to be 'the very spit of the subjects portraid.' The artistic merit of the work is patent to the most casual observer."[1] More recently, Martin Myrone has used this picture to exemplify how "Stubbs's images of horses and the men and women who rode, owned and cared for them are widely prized not just as great works in their genre, but as among the greatest works in the whole history of art."[2] This particularly fine example of Stubbs's art, then, might well repay close scrutiny. Might we not profitably read it for its cultural and social content as well as its aesthetic mastery, especially since Stubbs's aesthetic was above all a scrupulously realist one?

Stubbs's bid to be not only a painter of horses but a great painter, an innovative and scientific painter, is visible even in this casual grouping of young sporting aristocrats, a groom, a dog, and two horses—a black hunter and a bay cob, as Gilbey notes. It would appear that a schooling session is in progress, involving a "leaping bar." The schooling is not taking place in a manège, we notice, but in a

Figure 2. Here in George Stubbs's painting of *William Henry Cavendish Bentinck, 3rd Duke of Portland, and His Brother Lord Edward Bentinck, with a Groom and Horses* (1766–67), an interest in hunting and racing does not preclude manège traditions of schooling and the "leaping bar," which continue within sporting culture. Private collection.

paddock in the open air. Everything about the young gentlemen and their equipment broadcasts that they are sportsmen. The black dog with a white chest looks like a spaniel, likely to accompany them when they go shooting. The hunter wears a minimal, lightweight-looking saddle—a hunting saddle nearly worthy of the racecourse—and the cob's saddle on the ground appears to be of the same type. The extremely short docked tails of the horses are similarly sporting, designed to be mud-free out hunting, but also erroneously thought to increase a horse's speed. Dressed identically as if for hunting, in green frock coats and boots with brown tops (the fashionable outcome of turning the tops of traditional riding boots down in order to bend the knees), the brothers look as though they wish to be seen above all as keen horsemen and sporting gentlemen.[3]

For, ironically, it is the Welbeck estate where their hunting-oriented schooling is taking place. The brothers William Henry (1738–1809) and Edward (1744–1819) are the direct descendants of William Cavendish, the Duke of Newcastle, who had returned to a wrecked and deforested Welbeck after the Restoration, shortly before publishing his English treatise. They were descended from the Duke through their mother, Margaret Harley, who had married William Bentinck, the second Duke of Portland. She was a great-great-granddaughter of the Duke of Newcastle through the maternal line, the only daughter and heiress of Henrietta Cavendish Holles and Edward, Lord Harley, the second Earl of Oxford. Henrietta was the only daughter and heiress of John, fourth Earl of Clare, created Duke of Newcastle, and Lady Margaret Cavendish, third daughter and co-heiress of Henry, second Duke of Newcastle, William Cavendish's younger son by his first wife (his second wife, Margaret Cavendish, the author, had no children).[4] Although he did not own Welbeck until the death of his mother in 1785, William Henry, the third Duke of Portland, lived there and managed the estate after his marriage to the daughter of the fourth Duke of Devonshire in November 1766, the year he commissioned this picture from Stubbs.[5]

On the walls of the hall of the house, Welbeck Abbey, presumably nearby but out of the frame, would still have hung the original oil paintings from which were engraved the famous illustrations of the Duke of Newcastle's French treatise, showing various breeds of horses. The Turkish horse Mackomilia for example, is exotically presented, complete with black groom, a status symbol in early modern England, as Kim Hall observes.[6] The horse displays natural impulsion and proud self-carriage. There were also illustrations of manège maneuvers, including how to sit properly on horseback, and scenes of hunting and riding at Welbeck and elsewhere. Illustrating *"la plus parfaitte posture du Cavallier,"* the duke sits upon his horse in an upright, long stirrup-leathered seat (fig. 3). He appears to be naturally master of his horse and of all he surveys, a properly cosmopolitan man of the world as well as an English nobleman. And he is very much in control of his powerful, heavily muscled but well-disciplined and submissive mount. The historian of the turf Theodore Cook pointed out how distinctly not Arabian or otherwise Eastern the duke's horse is, observing that "if His Grace's ideas of 'shape' are to be judged from the illustrations of his famous book, the only sort of horse he cared about was of the massive Flemish build of Van Dyck's chargers."[7] The duke, in fact, claimed to prefer Spanish and Barbary horses to all others,[8] but it is true that the horses represented in the plates of his treatise (by artists themselves from the Low Countries, we should remember) appear heavily built and even rather hairy-heeled.

Despite the presence of the duke's original illustrations hanging in the house, his heirs do not seem particularly inclined toward manège riding. If he had been

Figure 3. The Duke of Newcastle illustrates the "perfect posture" of the manège seat in an engraving by Lucas Vorsterman the Younger after Abraham van Diepenbeke, from the duke's *Methode Et Invention Nouvelle de dresser Les Chevaux* (1658). The British Library.

alive in Stubbs's time, the duke might well have been disappointed to observe the presence of a leaping bar, which suggested that hunting and jumping were the focus of the young men's horsy interests, not the *haute école* leaps of the airs above the ground, such as the capriole. And yet William Cavendish might not have despaired utterly of the tastes of his heirs and descendants. The leaping bar may not have signified the *haute école* as plainly as would the twin pillars of the manège, but it nevertheless indicated that schooling—the literal meaning of the French *dressage*—was still part of the young gentlemen's preparation for equestrian pursuits. That is to say, the Cavendish-Bentinck brothers have learned to ride according to the old school, Continental-style, and could no doubt perform "riding the Great Horse," if necessary. They may often have chosen the hunting field and fast forward riding over the discipline of the manège, but they almost certainly understood the value of the latter in making a horse supple and responsive to the rider. After all, they did not simply "make" or train their horses to jump by taking them hunting, using the heat of the moment and the adrenaline rush of the equine herd instinct to get them over obstacles. Rather, they schooled them at home over a bar, calmly and in cold blood, as it were.

The brothers had been pupils of the celebrated riding master Dominico Angelo, and his riding school in Carlisle Street would have been the venue where they were introduced to George Stubbs. As Walter Shaw Sparrow reported in 1929, Angelo's riding school was instrumental in helping Stubbs, "when a newcomer from the country," gain "a footing as a painter on the Turf and in London," because Angelo's "great reputation as a horseman" assured that

> his riding-school in Soho was frequented by animal painters and by all who were sportsmen. A friendship sprang up between him and young Stubbs, and to this friendship Stubbs owed most of the early patronage that he obtained after he came to London.[9]

As Dominico's son Henry reminisced,

> All the celebrated horse painters of the last, and some of the veterans of the present age, were constant visitors at our table, or at the *manège* which my father erected on the space between Carlisle House and Wardour Street.
>
> It was reserved for the late Mr. Stubbs, however, to raise the reputation of this department of painting to that high state of excellence which it had formerly atttained in the old Flemish and Dutch schools; and I shall never cease to remember that it was to the friendship of the elder Angelo that this most distinguished early member of the British school principally owed the patronage which he obtained. Some of his earliest and best studies were made by his faithful pencil from my father's stud, who had, indeed, some magnificent horses. Certain of these he painted for my father, and, through his recommendations, he was employed by many of the noblemen and others, gentlemen of rank, who frequented this fashionable place of resort.[10]

The elder Angelo, from a rich commercial family of Leghorn, had studied in France under the celebrated Monsieur François Robichon de la Guérinière,[11] a riding master schooled in the tradition of *Maneige Royal* (1623),[12] the treatise by Louis XIII's riding master, Antoine de Pluvinel (1555–1620), who had himself learned from the Italian masters. Guérinière's teaching has continued to govern the training of horse and rider at the Spanish Riding School of Vienna into modern times.[13]

Gentlemanly horsemanship of the 1760s, therefore, appears to have combined the techniques of equestrian sports—hunting and racing—with those of manège riding. It was not precisely a racing jockey's seat that they adopted, nor was it the manège seat advocated by Newcastle. It was an eclectic hybrid that owed something not only to those hedge- and ditch-leaping, hunting-mad ancestors who held on by the mane but also to the "Turkey fashion" of riding short which Blundeville had mentioned two hundred years before.

A National Seat?

No book codes nationality more blatantly in equestrian terms than John Buchan's First World War thriller, *Greenmantle* (1916). The narrator, Richard Hannay—English-identified, of Scottish extraction, brought up in South Africa: a perfect colonial cocktail—delights in distinguishing the nationalities of his fellow secret agents by their seats. Approaching the novel's denouement, as the British and their allies strive to outwit the Germans and Ottoman Turks in order to join forces with the Russians, our heroes are forced to gallop "furiously" in the dark on small Turkish horses.[14] John S. Blenkiron, the fat American, whose "thighs were too round to fit a saddle leather," and who preferred "a gentle amble and a short gallop" to this "mad helter-skelter," loses both his stirrups and finds himself sitting on his horse's neck.[15] Americans had better have brains and guts, in other words, because economic prosperity has physically softened them. The Scotsman Sandy Arbuthnot, on the other hand, who possesses a remarkable ability to get "inside the skin of remote peoples,"[16] is a "wonderful fine horseman, with his firm English hunting seat."[17] Even the Scots ride like the English when they ride well, and to ride well is to have been formed in the cut and thrust of the hunting field.

By the First World War, then, the English hunting seat would appear to have become an achieved and recognizable thing. It is spoken of by Buchan's narrator Hannay as an embodiment of nationality, of belonging or not belonging to the us-ness of Englishness. Being a Scot, Sandy Arbuthnot provides evidence that it is in fact Britishness, signified by an identification with things English, that is at issue in the construction of the nation. The particular disposition of the body on horseback works most powerfully, most evocatively, to summon nationality as a visible sign, a rallying cry, a point of identification on the testing grounds of rival national and imperial powers—the battlefield in *Greenmantle*.

Olympic Rivalry

It should come as no surprise, therefore, that where the Great Game of political and diplomatic intrigue was played, and where it has gone on being played in a displaced fashion, these equestrian rivalries continue. The recent history of the Olympic Games is a case in point. From the 1990s to the twenty-first century,

British fears of a postimperial decline have been mirrored in anxiety not only about rival European and former colonial economic prowess but about rival European and former colonial athletic prowess, and horsemanship in particular.

After the British Eventing team went so cautiously on the cross-country phase at the Olympics in Barcelona in 1992 that they were seriously outclassed by the Australians, the New Zealanders, and, most heart-burningly, the Germans, the British equestrian press engaged in patriotic soul-searching. Where had British training gone wrong? The famous British event rider Lucinda Green (née Prior-Palmer) contributed a piece to *Horse and Hound* examining the history and meaning of eventing:

> Eventing was primarily devised to produce a multi-dextrous horse and rider, obedient, athletic and reliable enough to perform vital message-carrying in war. Communications—the delivery of messages—was and is crucial to success in battle. The dressage test (judged coincidentally by "the enemy"—try as they might to be on our side), has come a long way from this concept. Imagine spending time going sideways or backwards when speeding a communication from one place to another.[18]

Being judged by "the enemy" here must carry a distinct whiff of anti-German prejudice; the Second World War, if not the First, is still being fought on the undulating fields of Three-Day Event courses and the oblong boxes of dressage rings. What Green just stops herself from saying is that too much "Germanic" Continental influence on riding in the form of dressage, like too much German economic and political dominance in the European Union, is edging out that traditional British sense of sovereignty and superiority.

The indignity of not winning a medal at Barcelona was compounded by the fact that the team had begun by scoring well in the dressage, traditionally the phase in which Continental riders, particularly the Germans and the Dutch, excel, and which has never been the British forte, as William Cavendish lamented in 1667. So British resistance to the nonjumping ("flatwork") phase of Combined Training competitions dates at least to the seventeenth century. Thus for the British team, having mastered internationally commendable dressage, to look cautious, lackluster, and rather slow on the cross country while the Australians, New Zealanders, and Germans were galloping and jumping the course with dash and style, was a national image and public-relations disaster. It represented a mini-crisis in postimperial British identity.

Britain's struggle for supremacy in eventing competitions continues. The sport itself has evolved during the last twenty-five years along increasingly technical and dressage-based "Euro" rather than "Anglo" lines. As recently as the summer of 2005, the Junior European Eventing Championships, held at Saumur in France, saw the German team retaining their gold medals while Britain's team came away without any medals at all. Once again dressage had proved the downfall of the young Brits, whose cross-country rounds were their best effort. But the team's horses came in for scrutiny as well, as it seems that now the once supreme English or Irish Thoroughbred is being displaced as the ideal eventing horse by Continental "warmbloods" who, though less athletic and bold, are calmer and easier to ride in a highly controlled fashion in the dressage and show jumping phases. Robin Balfour, chairman of the British selectors for the national team, remarked, "Dressage has been our weak point for many years. It is improving but we don't have the warmblood horses the Germans have. Also the Germans have focused on the flatwork and it shows."[19]

With the ostensible banning of fox hunting in England and Wales from February 2005 onward, the future of the hunting field as a typically British route to equestrian superiority remains uncertain. Drag hunting—sending hounds and a mounted field after a humanly laid trail of scent—is permitted, as is flushing a fox with hounds either to be shot or pursued by a bird of prey. As of early 2007 there has been one successful prosecution of a huntsman for violating the Hunting Bill. The legislation appears to contain a number of loopholes that at least in some parts of the country have allowed hunting to carry on much as usual. Far from having diminished, therefore, support for hunting appears to be growing. There were record turnouts of both mounted and foot followers at meets throughout the country during the Christmas–Boxing Day–New Year's period of 2006–7 and a BBC Radio 4 "Repeal the Ban" telephone campaign. Fox hunting remains a hotly contested and highly political issue. Whatever the outcome of movements to repeal the ban, the future of hunting is far from assured.

Would the end of hunting, should it happen, mean that people would then learn to ride differently? What *was* the English hunting seat, that it served so well both fictional characters like Sandy Arbuthnot and Olympic competitors like Lucinda Green?

A Nationalist History?

British popular historians of horsemanship present a progress narrative that culminates, unsurprisingly, in the superiority of English riding. The story goes something like this. Beginning in the late seventeenth or early eighteenth century, people in the British Isles departed from European example by shortening their stirrup leathers so that they could ride ever faster horses ever faster over fences. They simultaneously created the English Thoroughbred to go faster on, and bred faster hounds to chase foxes, who were faster and more straight running than hares, and ran longer and straighter across country than deer. Shortening the stirrup leathers to a length that made standing in them easy encouraged free forward movement of the horse (an instance of enacted liberty) while increasing the security and comfort of the rider over rough terrain (preserving the precious body of the enlightened Englishman).

This shorter-is-better difference from Continental Europe appears to have held from sometime in the eighteenth century until very late in the nineteenth, when from 1897 onward the Italian cavalry officer Captain Federico Caprilli (1868–1907) and the American jockey Tod Sloan put theirs up even higher, thus causing the English to look askance at the practice.[20] Caprilli's was a scientific, logically consistent *sistema* for covering all types of terrain, based upon close observation of equine and human anatomy in action. Sloan's seat was designed solely for flat racing and was perhaps not invented by him so much as copied "from diminutive Negro stable-boys," as the historian of horsemanship Charles Chenevix Trench speculates.[21]

Recent research has confirmed Chenevix Trench's hunch about the influence on Thoroughbred racing of African American jockeys such as Isaac Murphy, Abe Hawkins, Tony Hamilton, and Willie Simms.[22] African American jockeys led their profession throughout the years of slavery and for several decades after emancipation, until, after post–Civil War Reconstruction, increasingly violent racial prejudice caused their exclusion from prestigious flat racing, which became a lucrative whites-only sport. The departure of black jockeys left a vacancy that the white Sloan could fill, becoming a celebrity on two continents.[23] According to Chenevix Trench, whether or not Caprilli was influenced by what he had read or heard of Sloan, who after 1897 was "engaged in making himself painfully conspicuous in the most expensive London restaurants," remains "extremely doubtful."[24]

Once Sloan's and Caprilli's seats had become fashionable, the traditional English hunting seat looked like riding long and sitting down and back, comparatively speaking—almost like dressage, except that the lower legs and feet were carried more forward than was desirable in the dressage seat. It appeared as a sort of middle way, a splendid British compromise.

There are important differences between Caprilli's extremely practical forward seat for riding across country and the relatively insecure, though aerodynamic, "monkey up the neck" flat-racing jockey's seat adopted by Sloan.[25] One might

even see Caprilli's *sistema* as the logical extension, influenced by Eastern precedents, of taking those stirrups up a notch or two in order to jump fences at speed,
while the Sloan jockey's seat is only good for flat racing on racecourses, where
balance will be comparatively undisturbed, with most of the strain of the perilous
crouching position being taken by the thighs, and the knees clearing the saddle,
limiting grip to the barest essentials.

The consensus among British historians of horsemanship as to the state of
riding styles before Caprilli could be summarized as follows. By the end of the
eighteenth century there remained "the two ancient styles of horsemanship," the
Eastern and the Western, but a third was emerging:

> The natural style developed by the horsemen of Eurasia who rode short, on a snaffle-
> bridle, with no thought of collection but allowing their horse free forward movement:
> and the style of western Europe, where educated, scientific horsemen rode long and
> concentrated above all on collection induced by spurs and a curb-bit. But there was
> also a third school of horsemanship, if anything so thoughtless and unscientific can
> be so pretentiously termed; that of the English (and American) hunting-man, who
> rode fairly long like his ancestors, but whose riding was based, like the Cossack's,
> on extension rather than collection.[26]

During the next 170 years, according to Chenevix Trench, the history of horsemanship is one "of the interaction, and, in certain cases, coalescence of these
three rival schools."[27]

Setting the stage for Caprilli's revolutionary *sistema,* another British historian,
Elwyn Hartley Edwards, not only falls back on the Anglo-German opposition we
have encountered before in Lucinda Green's comments on cross country riding
versus dressage but waxes lyrical on the subject of free forward movement so that
those in the know about dressage cannot fail to miss the implicit criticism therein.
The European cavalry seat, he argues, had by the end of the nineteenth century
become largely dominated by the German schools, not by the innovative French
or the Habsburg Spanish Riding School of Vienna. Following classical principles
of high collection, but hardly ever putting them into practice outside a manège,
the German school of military jumping as revealed in early photographs looks
"not far short of horrific," as the riders "leant well back, ungiving hands held at
chest height, while the horses jumped with hollow backs and mouths wide open
in an agonised attempt to avoid the punishing action of the bit."[28]

The British, on the other hand, although "their approach may not have been
exactly scientific," produced a grand compromise anticipating Caprilli. Because

"no tradition of indoor riding existed," and because enclosures were established much earlier than on the Continent, British cavalry officers and country gentlemen "rode across country in pursuit of the fox, jumping what obstacles were met . . . [T]hough they leant back over their fences they did not interfere with their horses' mouths and the very nature of the sport encouraged a degree of self-balance and initiative in the horse."[29] Indoor schools and dressage are Germanic and impractical because they lead to having bad, unyielding hands and giving a horse a brutish ride across country.

When this attitude is combined with the notion that horses show initiative in fox hunting because they enjoy it, we have a potent recipe for free forward movement of horse and rider as the quintessential experience of Englishness. Lieutenant Colonel S. G. Goldschmidt put this idea particularly forcefully in 1927: "One often hears it said that a polo pony has a fondness for the game. This is not true. The only work that a horse is put to in this country from which it derives any enjoyment is hunting."[30] Knowing how to ride across country without hindering an English hunter who enjoys his work is the essence of the English hunting seat, and thus the essence of being British.

Here is Edwards's paean to Caprilli's system of cross-country riding in what might be called the prose of the modern English hunting, but now international forward, seat:

> In brief, he discarded the system of school riding with its accent on the slow, collected paces and evolved a "forward system," training horses to acquire a natural balance by schooling them over the sort of country in which they would have to operate. The curb bit was replaced by the snaffle and the horse was allowed free extension of the head and neck, especially over fences.
>
> Instead of the completely dominated, collected school horse he asked for unfettered extension. Instead of the rider insisting upon the horse conforming to his hand and to a form which was in itself unnatural, he asked his riders to conform to the horse's natural movement and outline. They rode with a much shortened stirrup, perching forward so that their weight was carried as nearly as possible over the horse's centre of balance, where it would be the least possible encumbrance to a free and even movement. They sat forward over every type of fence and even when riding up or down the most fearsome inclines. It was, in essence, the very same sort of seat that generations of steppe nomads and eastern horsemen had used for centuries.[31]

That "much shortened stirrup" must be in relation to the length of the cavalry or classical seat, not the English hunting seat, which was already several holes shorter anyway. And "perching forward" sounds ever so slightly insecure, not only over fences but in the general run of things. Captain F. C. Hitchcock, writing in 1938, comments that "the Italian seat has indeed been tried out by officers belonging to the Weedon Equitation School over the Pytchley and Grafton countries, but it did not prove practical for hunting,"[32] presumably because the stirrups were too short to allow for old-fashioned "leaning back" security over rough terrain and awkward fences and ditches (backsliding from free forward movement). Jokes about the Italian influence on riding style included contempt for the snaffle bridle, which Caprilli also advocated.[33] British officers and gentlemen had grown so attached to the double bridle as a mark of both status and control that they were reluctant to relinquish it. Nevertheless the "Weedon seat" characteristic of Britain's most successful Three-Day Event riders (such as Lucinda Green) owed its origins to Caprilli's system.[34]

Edwards's argumentative pay-off lies surely with his last idea: that Caprilli had not so much invented something as scientifically theorized the practice of steppe nomads and other Eastern horsemen. Sandy Arbuthnot's "firm English hunting seat" thus owed its origins as much to the romance of the East as did his undercover mission in *Greenmantle*.

Chenevix Trench, Elwyn Hartley Edwards, and Dorian Williams all tell stories about English horsemanship that are patriotically satisfying. Their books appeal to horse-owning audiences because they are grounded in a knowledge of actual riding practice.[35] None of these popular-history books, however, quite observes the cautious protocols of scholarly history. Where the authors glimpse a resemblance between riding styles, they declare an influence. Where there appears to be a difference, it signifies nationality in an unproblematical way. Unfortunately, a close reading of the early modern sources does not offer plentiful evidence of the sort we might wish for either to substantiate or to disprove their claims. Rather, it becomes necessary to read against the grain of the early modern English sources, both visual and verbal, as well as against the grain of the popular histories. We must remember that the early modern English sources have a tendency to naturalize and assimilate, often silently and unconsciously, whatever luxury goods or technical knowledges their authors wished to appropriate from the East.

Sitting Like an Englishman

Descriptions of how to sit on horseback occur throughout the centuries in English manuals of horsemanship. In 1618, Michael Baret recommended sitting down in the saddle and putting weight in the stirrups in order to stop a horse, but otherwise he advised sitting lightly:

If he would serue his horse for any other motion, as to helpe his horse in his trot, pace or any other assault, for delight, then let him clap both his knees close to the points of the saddle, and onely keepe time with his seate, to moue the better spirit to the horse: and not to sit as some doe, (which are not esteemed the worst horse-men) without any motion, (like logges) on their horse backes, with their legges stretched out in their stirrops, (as if they were on the racke).[36]

Hence a light, active seat was to be encouraged. Two centuries later, John Lawrence still found this advice apt: "It is somewhat remarkable, that the seat on horseback, recommended by Baret in the reign of James I, is precisely the same as that practised by our jockies and sporting men of the present day," wrote Lawrence, noting that Baret also "describes and recommends (under the de-nomination of a help) the wriggling motion of the bridle in a race, as we see it practised at present, by jockies."[37] "Rising in the trot, and lifting and working the horse along with the reins in the gallop by the jockey, are, no doubt, practices purely English," opined Lawrence in 1829.[38]

William Cavendish went so far as to describe "How a Man should SIT PER-FECTLY on Horse-Back":

Being Plac'd upon his *Twist*, in the middle of the Saddle, advancing towards the Pommel of the Saddle, as much as he can; leaving a handful of Space between his Hinder-parts and the *Cantle*, or *l'Arson* of the Saddle, his *Leggs* being straight Down, as if he were on *Foot*, his *Knees* and *Thighes* turned inwards to the Saddle; holding both of them Fast, as if they were Glewed to the Saddle, (for a *Horse-man* hath noth-ing but those two with the *Counterpoize* of his *Body* to keep him on *Horse-Back*) his *Feet* planted firmly upon the Stirrups; his *Heels* a little Lower than his *Toes*, that the end of his *Toes* may pass the Stirrups half an Inch, or a little more, and Stiff in the *Hamms*, or *Jarrets*, his *Leggs* not too far from the Horse's *Sides*, nor too near, that is, not to Touch them; which is of great Use for *Helps*, that I will Shew you here-after . . .

You must Look a little *Gay*, and *Pleasantly*, but not *Laughing*; and Look directly between the Horses *Ears*, when he goes Forwards: I do not mean, you should be Stiff, like a Stake, or like a Statue on *Horse-Back*, but much otherwise; that is, Free, and with all the Liberty in the world, as the *French-Man* sayes, in Dancing, *A la neg-ligence* . . .

The Seat is so much, (as you shall see hereafter) as it is the only thing that makes a Horse go Perfectly; and the very Manner of Sitting is beyond all other *Helps*: There-fore Despise it not, for I dare Boldly say, He that is not *Bel homme de Cheval*, shall never be *Bon homme de Cheval*.[39]

Once again the dictum that distinguished Oriental bloodstock from common horses, the uniting of the aesthetically pleasing with the practical, has a bearing on equestrian matters, in this case the horseman's seat rather than the horse. This description of the seat will continue relatively unchanged for decades and even centuries, despite the gradual shortening of the stirrup leathers. Such basic information appeared to bear repeating because the state of equestrian knowledge in Britain was perpetually thought to be in jeopardy.

In 1798 Lawrence marveled at how ignorance prevailed despite that fact that "for the moderate sum of one shilling" the "judicious and humane rules" of the "truly excellent pamphlet of my old acquaintance, Professor Charles Hughes" (1772), had "long since" been "attainable."[40] Lawrence then offered his own description of the proper seat:

> The modern seat on horse-back, and it seems to have owed its establishment to reason, confirmed by experience, is, to set naturally and easily upright upon your saddle, as you would in your chair; your knees about as much bent, and turned inward, your toes somewhat out, and upward, your leg falling nearly straight, and your foot home in the stirrup; your backbone prepared to bend in the middle, upon occasion, your elbows held close to your sides, your hands rather above the horse's withers, or the pommel of the saddle, and your view directed between his ears.[41]

So far, so much like Cavendish's seat. But Lawrence's conclusion suggests a radical shift:

> This is the true turf or Newmarket seat, and the best exemplification of it, that I am able to give, is the portrait of Samuel Chifney, the jockey, upon a horse named Baronet, once the property of his Royal Highness the Prince of Wales.[42]

With such a pedigree, combining royal and turf-professional associations, the modern English seat could mask its mixed origins—in hunting as well as manège riding, to say nothing of Eastern example. If, as Lawrence insisted, modern Englishmen all rode in a "Newmarket" racing seat, racing's triumph within the English imagination could appear to be an unassailable truth. Thus could patriotic Britons exaggerate their difference from their European neighbors, particularly when they were at war with France.

English Saddles, a Breed Apart

During the last decade of the seventeenth century the French noticed that the English were doing some things differently. A predilection for a shorter-stirruped jockey seat, coupled with rising or posting to the trot, was evident down to the kind of saddle the English preferred. According to Sir William Hope's translation of Monsieur Solleysell's *The Parfait Mareschal, Or Compleat Farrier* in 1696, even the equerry to the king of France had to concede the superiority of English tack in this respect. The passage is so unusually detailed in its description of national differences that it deserves quoting in full:

> When English Saddles are put upon a Horse's Back, they immediately appear as if they rested close upon the withers, but when a Man is set upon them, the weight being placed in the middle, makes them rise before, so that it is hardly possible for them to rest upon the Withers or hurt the Horse, by reason of the exact turn given to the Bands: Our French Sadlers have attempted to make theirs after the same fashion, but few as yet have come that length . . .
>
> Those however who are accustomed to Ride upon English Saddles, find difficulty to make use of Ours, although very well made, and people may indeed say in behalf of the good English Sadlers, that they make their Hunting Saddles lie closer to the horse, Lighter, and more commodious and easy, than any whatsoever; so that a Man who hath made use of them for some time, cannot accommodate himself with others, without a great deal of inconveniency; because although the most part of them be hard and little, yet a man sits firmer upon them than any other, because he is nearer to the Horse, either when he is Hunting, or even Riding Post; those who are accustomed to such Saddles, never gall or loose their Leather, as they will do if they posted upon French Saddles, because the Seats of them being large, and stuffed with wool, Feathers, or hair, do become warm, and afterwards heat a Mans breech and Thighs, and the skin being thus heated, doth immediately gall; however, there are few people of this opinion, although a very true one, unless they have been long accustomed with English Saddles . . .
>
> People at first using of them, find some of these English Saddles very hard, especially those with skirts, and untill a man be a little accustomed to them, he findeth them uneasy, and his Breech suffers by it; but, the habit once acquired, and buttocks hardened, people never quit them, unless they be very lean, or have their skin near to the bones; or that they are not much accustomed with Riding.
>
> Observe all the *Horse-Coursers* which are most firm and vigorous on Horse-back, and you will find, that they never make use of any other but English Saddles.[43]

Solleysell himself appears convinced that the English saddlers have outdone the competition, but he leads his French audience gently toward this conclusion, since they may find fault with these foreign appurtenances while getting used to them. National prejudices are not easily overcome. The indisputable proof of superiority, according to this professional horseman, lies in what professional "Horse-Coursers"—nagsmen or jockeys—routinely adopt, and that is the light-weight, minimal, short-skirted, flat, hard English saddle that fits most horses without discomfort.

The all-purpose close-lying or, in modern tack parlance, "close contact" English saddle, which at a pinch could be used for racing, hunting, or just plain riding, remained a feature on the British scene well into the twentieth century. It may even have been the model for the first seats in British aircraft, on the grounds that what a chap could sit in for a long day's hunting, he could sit in for a long day's or night's flying. It is symptomatic of a shift in the international equestrian balance of power that in recent years, beginning in the 1980s and 1990s, heavier saddles, more cushioned in the seat and padded at the knees, and with higher pommels and cantles—owing their inspiration to French and German dressage saddles rather than to racing or hunting saddles—have become increasingly popular even in England.

Boots and Saddles

A jockey seat required that Englishmen turn the tops of their boots down in order to be able to bend their knees sufficiently to get into a shorter-stirruped position on horseback. This caused them to look different from their European colleagues, who continued to be portrayed in top boots that extended over their knees, as was the Duke of Newcastle. The difference of the English was henceforth legible in their very bodies as well as their boots.

This new seat, the turning down of top boots, and the new saddles were all inspired by racing and hunting ever faster across country. And this faster pace was a direct consequence of the arrival of Oriental blood horses in significant numbers.

The Eastern Invasion

From the evidence of paintings of this period it is clear that these horses were a breed apart, strikingly different from native British or European horses. Even granting a considerable degree of painterly license, a tendency to stylization, and the likelihood of pressure to idealize in order to please horse-owning patrons, the arrival of large numbers of Eastern horses in England and the appearance of recognizably Oriental types in painting coincided. Sporting painting itself changed as these delicate creatures flew or capered over the landscape. Horse portraiture and sporting painting generally obey the dictates of realism. Such pictures may be idealized, to be sure, but they would have been found utterly lacking in appeal for their essentially practically minded audience if they had proved wrong in important details. Eighteenth-century horse pictures therefore provide important evidence of equestrian culture, especially in its idealized aspect—of how owners and riders wished themselves and their charges to appear.

James Seymour's *Mr. Peter Delmé's Hounds on the Hampshire Downs* (1738; fig. 4) exemplifies the new style of riding to hounds on the new Eastern horses—jolly, capering, delicate, and not at all hairy-heeled, unlike native breeds. Looking back in 1897 at pictures painted around 1720, Thomas Lister, Lord Ribblesdale, might just as well have been describing Seymour's horses:

> The horses are exceedingly well bred and full of character, but narrowish and not up to more than twelve stone. They *all* show much more Eastern blood in their heads— the bump on the forehead, the full eye, which we only find here and there in an individual now. They were, of course, much nearer the blends of Arab and Arabian blood to which we are indebted for everything we prize most in horseflesh.[44]

Ribbesdale took for granted the importance of Eastern, especially Arabian, genetic contributions to English bloodstock. This is a controversial position, as we shall see, and confidence in the importance of native hobbies, Galloways, and Yorkshire running-horses in Thoroughbred pedigrees continues. In any case, the evidence shows that eighteenth-century English breeders were greatly indebted to nonindigenous bloodstock for all they prized most, and that they transmuted this debt imaginatively into images of Englishness on the hoof. Regarded as sporting long before being censored as cruel, docked tails were common at this time and remained so for decades. The more "common" or less breedy-looking horses in this field—the cream, the dun, and the gray—have had their ears cropped as well, to make them conform more closely to the small-eared ideal set by the Eastern bloodstock.

If the wintry Hampshire downs in Seymour's painting look strangely desertified, might there not be a fanciful Eastern resonance to the openness of the landscape that mimicked the clearly Arabian quality of the horses? The short-coupled bay horse in the lower right hand of the foreground is particularly Arabian-looking, with a dished face and characteristic upright head and tail carriage. He appears to be leaping exuberantly forward, making light of his rider, who sits tight while keeping a light hand on the snaffle rein, the curb rein hanging loose. Notice the preponderance of single-rein snaffle bridles. Where the two reins of the double bridle appear, the riders leave the lower, curb rein slack and ride on the

Figure 4. In *Mr. Peter Delmé's Hounds on the Hampshire Downs* (1738), James Seymour represents the look of quality and feel of sporting power typical of Eastern-bred horses in the hunting field. Virginia Museum of Fine Arts, Richmond, Paul Mellon Collection.

bradoon or snaffle rein. The huntsman, around whom the hounds cluster, sits forward (compare Mehmed II, fig. 1) on a rangy bay who looks more Turcoman or Thoroughbred than Arabian—a real racing sort—and does not even hold his curb rein but leaves it loose on his horse's neck. If the hounds "find" or put up their quarry, the field will be in for a challenging day's riding.

Poised over their horses' centers of gravity, the withers—rather than sitting back, driving with their seats, and engaging in collection to alter their horses' corporeal outline, as the Duke of Newcastle would have them do—the riders appear to sit easily and the horses to be moving freely. Peter Delmé himself (1710–70), the young man mounted on the chestnut horse, third in the foreground lineup, has turned the tops of his boots down in a rakishly innovative fashion, accentuated by the flash of scarlet waistcoat showing under the skirts of his hunting coat. He leans forward attentively to listen to the older rider on the gray preceding him, as Judy Egerton notes.[45]

There could be no clearer instance of the English model of gentlemanly capitalism on the hoof. Peter Delmé, self-styled country gentleman and M.P., was the eldest son of Sir Peter Delmé (1667–1728), who had been knighted on the accession of George I in 1714; Delmé père was a London banker of Huguenot descent, Governor of the Bank of England 1715–17 and Lord Mayor of London in 1723. Seymour, the painter, whose father was in banking (and went bankrupt in 1737), obtained much of his patronage from sporting bankers.[46] Traditional country sports, Gervase Markham's "Country Contentments," were underwritten by City finance.

And country contentments were increasingly enlivened by the infusion of Eastern horses supplied by members of the Levant Company. Nathaniel Harley, anticipating his imminent return from Aleppo to England by sending ahead a weight-carrying hunter he hoped to keep for his own use, described the horse as follows:

> He is plain and Strong, Able I hope to carry my Weight, and to pull his Leggs out of your Brittish Dirt, I designe him for my own Rideing, and hope God willing Soon to follow him, he is of a high Spirit and may be in danger of being Spoyl'd if a bad Rider should mount him; this being a Country where theres neither Hedge nor Ditch the horses are not Used to leaping, you may therefore please to Order your Groom to use him to the Leaping Post and I hope his Stroke may be altered, which is now Short haveing been train'd up to the Midan and Short turnings.[47]

A high-spirited and handy horse from Syria, probably of Turcoman blood, who had been trained to turn on a sixpence in the *meydan,* would, Harley believed, readily take to leaping obstacles in the hunting field and to galloping "long" across country.

Sitting Like an Englishman, Sitting Like a Turk

It therefore seems highly likely that the English departure from Continental manège riding during the seventeenth and eighteenth centuries occurred with some regard to Ottoman example. Blundeville provides a touchstone by describing riding short as "after the Turkey fashion." The chief difference of the Eastern seat, especially as derived from Eurasian steppe horsemen through Ottoman and Mameluke examples, was riding short.

Stirrups were themselves an Asian invention. Miklós Jankovich has argued that the first people in the Arab world to use the stirrup "were persons of Turkish origin."[48] Lynn White Jr. suggests that the iron foot stirrup was most likely a Chinese invention, inspired by the Indic cultures to the south where a toe stirrup for the unshod foot had been developed, a simple loop attached to the saddle girth.[49] Impractical for colder climates, the toe stirrup gave rise to the foot stirrup no later than the early fifth century c.e. in China—very likely in the Altai mountains, among the Turkic-speaking nomads who lived by horse-keeping.[50] The stirrup was beginning to be adopted by Muslim horsemen—first the Persians, then the Arabs—by c.e. 694, and was widely diffused in the Islamic world by the ninth century c.e.[51] Although the precise timing of the arrival of the stirrup in the West is still a source of debate, most scholars agree that its adoption by European horsemen had begun to have a profound effect on military tactics by the tenth century.[52]

If Turkic-Chinese stirrups were an Eastern piece of technology that revolutionized military culture in the West, the short stirrup leathers of Eastern horsemen took rather longer to catch on. Apart from Blundeville's mentioning of riding short "after the Turkey fashion" and Cavendish's objection to it, there appears to be silence regarding an Eastern seat until the eighteenth century, when Richard Berenger, George III's Gentleman of the Horse, wrote dismissively in 1771, "The Turks ride with their stirrups so short, that their knees are almost as much bent, as when they sit upon their hams upon a sopha."[53] Berenger implies, without explicitly stating, that the Turks, like the Arab horsemen he has previously criticized for using harsh bits and "working upon false rules, or perhaps without any," consequently "never attain that grace, exactness, and certainty, which the principles of the *Art,* if known, would insure to them."[54] For Berenger, equitation is an art as well as an enlightened system of rules, and hence aesthetics and practical utility are inextricable. The Arabs receive the full brunt of what, after Edward Said's exposé, we cannot fail to recognize as ripening Orientalist prejudice, while the Turks are represented more ambivalently. Berenger adds, "The Turks seldom use *Spurs,* or carry a whip or switch, nevertheless they have an absolute command over their horses, and make them do whatever they please."[55] Such grudging acknowledgment of equestrian effectiveness is hardly evidence of influence, especially since Berenger's evidence regarding the Turks and the Arabs is entirely citational—based not upon his own observations but upon accounts provided by Dumont and Hasselquist, respectively.[56]

Not until its glory days had passed, in the mid-nineteenth century, did enthusiastic admiration for the Ottoman cavalry appear in print in English. A proponent of a more forward seat than was practiced in any European army, and an advocate of free forward movement of the horse, the Irishman Captain Nolan went so far as to opine that Pignatelli and Grisone's "Neapolitan school" was "of Eastern origin" and therefore "doubtlessly good," but that "whatever ease" the school may have possessed had been "stiffened out of it in France and Germany, as also in every part of Italy."[57]

A split between the East (origin of the stirrup and its proper use in riding short) and Continental Europe (where excessively long stirrup leathers defeated the stirrup's purpose) dominated Nolan's thinking. He wished to put his fellow Irish and English cavalrymen on the better side, the Eastern side, of this divide.

Had views like Nolan's been adopted by the British cavalry sixty years before, perhaps Samuel Taylor Coleridge, alias Silas Tomkyn Comberbache, would have had an easier time in military service. Having run away from Cambridge, the young poet enlisted in the cavalry, describing himself as "a very indocile Equestrian."[58] Finding sitting to a fast trot cavalry-style excruciating, he soon discovered his backside covered in saddle sores and boils, and was temporarily declared unfit to ride. Upon returning to training, he was mounted on "an horse, young and as undisciplined as myself," which ran away with him during each parade, so that he had three falls in one week.[59] Like many a trooper before him, Coleridge failed to gain a firm and independent seat, let alone cut a dashing figure on horseback, in the long-stirruped cavalry fashion.

Sitting Like an Englishman, Not Sitting Like a Turk

As Nolan himself admitted, Ottoman equitation was itself undergoing change in the first half of the nineteenth century. Ottoman saddles of the old-fashioned kind were nothing like the hunting and racing saddles or even the military saddles in which Nolan hoped his fellow cavalrymen would reproduce his idea of the forward seat.

By the nineteenth century, the Ottoman empire had begun attending ever more keenly to Western example, even in military matters. According to a source well known to Ottoman historians, Charles MacFarlane's *Constantinople in 1828* (1829), Sultan Mahmud II, a consummate horseman, had been so impressed by the ability to master an "unruly horse" shown by an Italian cavalry officer, Signor Calosso, a Piedmontese exile, that he employed him as his personal riding master and as cavalry instructor to his favorite troops, the lancers.[60] MacFarlane observed that Mahmud "appears to the best advantage on horseback," whether riding "in our style," "on a Frank military saddle," or while "going to the mosque on Fridays, or in any other grand ceremonies prescribed by religion, when every thing is strictly oriental."[61] In J. Clarke's frontispiece to MacFarlane's first volume, the exaggeratedly high pointed pommel of the sultan's saddle looks likely to impale anyone bending forward from the waist. Mahmud II rides with very short stirrups and very bent knees, like Mehmed II before him.

Although he continued to perform his ceremonial functions in Oriental kit,

Mahmud insisted on learning a European cavalry seat in the traditional fashion, beginning by riding bareback, and, as a result, impressed MacFarlane as "the best horseman, *a l'Europeene,* in his regular army," who sat "firm and erect, and might really pass muster among a regiment of our fine horse-guards, and that with credit."[62]

The troops, however, were having difficulty adjusting to the European saddle, which they found easier to fall out of than their Turkish "cradles" had been, quipped MacFarlane, and they were constantly taking up their stirrups "'a point or so' to make themselves comfortable."[63] Not until the Turks ceased to sit cross-legged "like tailors" and grew accustomed to chairs and stools of "Christian-like elevation," MacFarlane opined, would they take naturally to the flatter European saddle and long-legged seat.[64] MacFarlane himself had felt "in purgatory" when riding extremely short on a bulky Turkish saddle, and he thought it natural that the Turks should feel the same about the European seat.[65] Western travelers had so often commented on the uncomfortable experience of Eastern difference they endured in the saddle that by 1842 Viscount Castlereagh "was agreeably surprised" to find himself "more at home than I expected in a high Turkish saddle."[66]

By the time Nolan's book appeared in 1853, one consequence of the Tanzimat reforms of Mahmud II and his son and successor, Sultan Abdulmejid I, was that, as Nolan himself reported, the Ottoman cavalry was now so contemptible in its inept imitation of the French manner of riding long and wearing tight pantaloons that "it may now safely be said that the Turkish cavalry is the very worst in the world."[67]

> We have seen, quite in our own day, this effective and really brilliant cavalry reduced, by the spirit of imitation and ill-understood reform, to a condition beneath contempt . . . The men, always accustomed to sit cross-legged, and to keep their knees near the abdomen, cannot be taught to ride with the long stirrup, *à la Française.* They are always rolling off, and are frequently ruptured; they . . . have seldom any other weapon except an ill-made, blunt, awkward sabre. Their horses are now wretched *rosses.* The good breeds have died out.[68]

"Mounted as they are, armed as they are, and riding as they do," Nolan concluded, they could be dispatched by "any English hussar" "armed only with a stout walking-stick."[69] The term *hussar* is a clue to what had already been suppressed from British military history—that by the late eighteenth century, the influence of Ottoman and Ottoman-influenced Hungarian cavalry methods on British military thinking had been profound.

Nolan's mission as a light-horse cavalry enthusiast was to make good on these

Eastern borrowings by infusing them throughout the British army by advocating "The Military Seat As It Ought To Be," portrayed in his frontispiece.[70] By the mid-twentieth century, Nolan's idea of a proper forward-going cavalry seat had become the standard for all-purpose riding in Britain. The young woman pictured in the frontispiece to Major-General Geoffrey Brooke's contribution to the Beaufort Library is sitting much as Nolan would have wished. This seat (captioned: "Top: The natural seat. If the beginner adopts this seat from the start, it can easily be modified for any official purpose by shortening the stirrups. Bottom: Riding too long") is presented by Brooke as an entirely "natural" one. The only conceivable modifications to it would now consist of *shortening* the stirrups—for racing and jumping. The classical manège seat is here summarily dismissed as "Riding too long."[71]

A further historical irony in these equestrian East-West cultural exchanges is that in the early twentieth century, Turkish cavalry officers attended the Italian Cavalry Schools of Pinerolo (Turin) and Tor di Quinto (Rome): Lieut. Anni Effendi (1925–26), Capt. Vehli Bey (1928–29) (Pinerolo); Lieut. Anni Effendi (1927), Capt. Wekki Omar (1929) (Tor di Quinto).[72] After the—singularly unsuccessful, according to Nolan—reeducation of the Ottoman cavalry to something like a European seat during the empire's moment of modernizing by Europeanizing itself, the new Turkish republic sent its officers to Italy to relearn riding forward, with shorter stirrups: a reinvention of the Turkish seat, now packaged as the modern Italian—but also international—forward seat.

The Language of Liberty

What was at stake in English self-representations on horseback, beginning in the later seventeenth century when the importation of Eastern bloodstock burgeoned, was an image of liberty, of free forward movement of horse and rider with a minimum of restraint. This was an image with undoubted political significance. Liberty became a political watchword. Racing fast across country became its embodiment, its most euphoric, adrenaline-fueled bodily reenactment. Taking a ride on the wild side became synonymous with being English, with enjoying the liberties of the free-born Englishman or Briton. This ideology-in-action, however, also had a sinister side. English riding, conceived as a superior technology of horsemanship, and imperialism, conceived as a civilizing mission, have much in common as ideological projects. Clothing the often brutal realities of colonialism in the language of moral uplift could come to sound remarkably like transmogrifying the often brutal realities of equestrian culture into riding with a silken thread.

Karen Raber and Treva Tucker agree that "democracy and fast riding have something in common: both resist strict adherence to traditional forms; both involve liberty, setting free 'natural' impulses.'"[73] It was no accident, they claim, that "the freedom and liberty represented by fast riding" soon spread beyond "the confines of England," coinciding with political upheavals against traditional monarchical government.[74] Although Raber and Tucker are quick to point out that such a convergence of democracy and free forward movement is no guarantor of political liberties, they do not pursue this argument with regard to the American and French revolutions or repressive British imperial and domestic policies. Instead they note that the Cossacks "rode 'freely' while coexisting with fairly repressive forms of government."[75] According to the logic of their argument, Raber and Tucker ought rather to include the Russian revolution in the very convergence they posit between riding freely and democratic impulses—for what else is socialism in its ideal form but democracy by another name?[76]

The same self-congratulatory language of English liberties experienced in the saddle can be found in descriptions of the English style of landscape gardening, as opposed to more rigid Continental styles. Horace Walpole described William Kent's ostensibly wilder, more natural gardening aesthetic in terms remarkably similar to those used by the riding masters, rhapsodizing that "Freedom was given to the forms of trees; they extended their branches unrestricted," and positing that the English had "discovered the point of perfection" and "given the true model of gardening to the world; let other countries mimic or corrupt our taste; but let it reign here on its verdant throne, original by its elegant simplicity, and proud of no other art than that of softening nature's harshness and copying her graceful touch."[77] Freedom, nature (or at least the appearance of naturalness), and Englishness were one and the same.

Like the English landscape garden, the English hunting and jockey seats were described by their advocates in language that was patriotically charged, as an enactment of English freedoms. As John Lawrence remarked in 1798, "The decline of Riding-house forms in this country, and the universal preference given to expedition, fully confirm the superior use and propriety of a jockey-seat."[78] In 1805 the riding master John Adams put it the other way round, giving precedence to the hunting seat: "The system of riding adapted for racing, is exactly the same as the hunting seat, when rode in the stirrups."[79] Free forward movement of the horse with a minimum of interference from the rider embodies the liberties of the freeborn subject in action. As Adams enthused, "The rider participates the like ease or unrestrained liberty . . . laying aside all unnecessary restraint when we can perform to our satisfaction without it."[80] This is the politically potent rhetoric of liberty, which would be appropriated by both Whigs and Tories, and which was often employed to distinguish Britain from the Continent, especially France, both before and after the Revolution. It is also an ideology of the superiority of English native values, one that would be used to counter protests of inequality and injustice from within the body politic.

Transcending partisan divisions, the language of liberty when applied to the English seat exuded a theory of governance as well as an equestrian ideal. What this ideology promised, in however mystified a fashion, was less oppressive relations with horses as well as fellow subjects—less oppressive because more "natural." On the same grounds, Thomas Paine argued for the rights of man and Mary Wollstonecraft the rights of woman, to which Hannah More replied sarcastically that the rights of children would be next on the list.[81]

Throughout the eighteenth century, political antagonists, whether members of the Tory or Jacobite-inclined Country-party or Whig grandees, cherished Liberty as a watchword. The Country-party spokesman Henry St. John, Lord Bolingbroke, friend and patron of Alexander Pope and Jonathan Swift (Swift even owned a horse named Bolingbroke),[82] argued in 1734 in the *Craftsman* that the ever-present danger of political tyranny consisted in governmental invasion of the "Liberties of the People."[83] Bolingbroke's submerged metaphor for the people's just resistance to this tyranny was equestrian. Unless the people were "sunk into the lowest State of Corruption and Pusillanimity," he declared, "They will endeavour to shake off an Authority, so plainly levell'd at their antient Rights, and so contrary to its original Design."[84] Freeborn, liberty-loving Britons are like restive horses, who will shake off an unsympathetic or despotic rider. Christine Gerrard has shown convincingly how the appeal to Liberty among the Patriot Whigs opposed to Sir Robert Walpole's ministry was predicated on a notion of a freeborn "Gothic" British and Celtic past alien to the Hanoverian succession who occupied the throne.[85] Expressed in equestrian terms this opposition entails a preference for ancient Celtic snaffle bits and racecourses over the riding-house deployment of the Continental curb.

Justifying his use of a loose rein instead of strong contact with the horse's mouth, Samuel Chifney, the first celebrity jockey, claimed that "it puts a horse's frame all wrong; and his speed slackened where the horse has that sort of management to his mouth."[86] Note the pun on manage-ment, referring to the manège, with its intense discipline and collection of the horse. Although his reins appeared loose, Chifney insisted, this was no sign of artlessness or slackness of horsemanship on his part because his horse "had only proper *liberty*," which led to his "mostly running in the best of attitudes."[87] Stubbs memorialized the famous partnership between Chifney and the Prince of Wales's racer Baronet in 1791.[88]

The secret to this politico-equestrian liberty lay in riding in harmony with the actions and will of the horse rather than pulling against him, a relation Chifney described as riding with "manner." "The word 'manner,'" he added in a footnote, "is knowing, putting, keeping self and horse in the best of attitudes. This gives readiness, force, and quickness."[89] That Chifney felt he was still having to argue against the "take a strong hold and pull" school of riding is evident from his report of what remained the Newmarket catchphrase:

> The phrase at Newmarket is, that you should pull your horse to ease him in his running. When horses are in their great distress in running they cannot bear that visible manner of pulling as looked for by many of the sportsmen; he should be enticed to ease himself an inch a time as his situation will allow. This should be done as if you had a silken rein as fine as a hair, and that you was afraid of breaking it. (160–61)

Although his simile for riding with light hands became famous, and Chifney even offered to fashion for the Jockey Club for the sum of two hundred guineas a bridle "as I believe never was" to prove his point (161), the Jockey Club did not take him up on this sporting offer. Having paid £350 to a saddler to have the bridle made anyway, Chifney could not pay the debt and died in the Fleet Prison at the age of fifty-three.[90] He had been forced to retire from racing in disgrace after being accused in 1791 of "fixing" a race for the Prince of Wales, who had retained him as his jockey for life for the munificent sum of £200 a year. As Laura Thompson notes, Chifney's bridle would later be used all over the world, but it was a long time in gaining acceptance.[91]

The liberty-loving ideal of silken-thread contact with the equine subject took some time to catch on. Neither racing nor hunting in themselves assured that horses would be ridden sympathetically. Yet intimations of a light forward-going seat were appearing in sporting painting as early as the 1730s, as we have seen, and by the 1760s they were imbued with political significance.

As in James Seymour's painting of Mr. Peter Delmé's hounds, the equestrian ideal in Stubbs's *The Grosvenor Hunt at Eaton* (1762) is one of free forward movement (fig. 5). Stubbs represents the hunt followers as having good, light hands and aiming to ride on a loose rein, taking only the lightest possible contact with their horses' mouths, and then only with small snaffle bits. Their stirrups are up sufficiently for their knees to be bent, though not in an exaggerated way, and for their heels to be well down, with their feet forward. They are sitting in such a way as to appear to ride lightly, capable of getting their weight forward to save their

Figure 5. In *The Grosvenor Hunt at Eaton* (1762), George Stubbs was thought by contemporaries to have captured the English equestrian ideal so successfully that even horses themselves were said to have been delighted with the picture. His Grace the Duke of Westminster KG OBE TD DL and the Trustees of the Grosvenor Estate. Photo: Photographic Survey, Courtauld Institute of Art.

horses' strength or to negotiate an obstacle if need be. The horses themselves are clearly of Arabian and Thoroughbred blood, heads up and tails aloft. They appear delicate but strong, sinewy rather than robustly muscular, alertly interested in the stag and hounds, and, left to their own devices, making light work of carrying their riders.

Within Stubbs's circle of patrons and purchasers, this picture was said to be so successful at conjuring the pleasures of the hunting field that horses themselves approved of it. To the manuscript memoir compiled by Stubbs's friend Ozias Humphry in 1797, Stubbs's niece, assistant, and perhaps common-law wife Mary Spencer added a startling note concerning *The Grosvenor Hunt*, the "very large Hunting Piece" painted at Eaton Hall, Cheshire:

> Every object in this Picture was painted from Nature, and very successfully exe-
> cuted.—(when finished & hanging in his Show room) an old Hunter, that was stand-
> ing at rest for his Portrait, whenever he was roused from his dozing and looked to-
> wards this Hunting piece, began to Neigh and seemed very pleasantly agitated.[92]

Composed according to classical principles to elevate the hunt to grandeur, this picture also, according to Stubbs's companion and assistant, contained precisely detailed and affectionate portraits of each of the subjects, including Richard Grosvenor's horse.[93] This is not the only instance of equine testimony to Stubbs's successful mimeticism, as we shall see. As described by Mary Spencer, the old hunter's is a very Houyhnhnmlike response. The horse appears to take pleasure in an image of a hunt in which the equine participants are as individually portrayed as the human ones, and even come to dominate the scene. The hounds and dying stag are all muddled up together. The horses, gracefully poised on the brink, look on alertly, attentively. The very pleasant agitation on the hunter's part suggests that he was enjoying vicariously the painted horses' obvious interest in the stag's death. Basil Taylor has called this painting "the greatest of English hunting pictures."[94] It is entirely fitting, within the ideals of sporting culture, that this judgment of the painting's greatness should have been confirmed by a horse.

Riding lightly might be seen, I would argue, as a political allegory for the Grosvenor Hunt's attempt at self-representation as legitimate political leaders: as they ride their horses, so will they govern their fellow subjects, is the conceit. This is political ideology embodied on horseback, but in a complex way. According to Stephen Deuchar, the young Richard Grosvenor, who had been elevated to the peerage shortly before the picture was painted, displays in his association with the rather retro and royal stag hunt his "essentially reactionary—and socially pretentious—leanings very clearly indeed . . . But because those leanings were ones which in the early 1760s had some claim to political usefulness in the future (a strong neo-royal aristocracy was some old-style Tories' answer to the 'levelling' views espoused by the more radical among their opponents), the painting itself was far from anachronistic."[95] The defense of sport through sporting art, common to most decades of the eighteenth century in England, takes on a particular political configuration in the 1760s, with the sober and elegant gentlemen being featured in Stubbs's painting.

The Grosvenor Hunt's version of freeborn liberty for the landed classes and their servants may have appeared deliberately old-fashioned, but it was a version of liberty nevertheless, and one that Stubbs appears to have endorsed. Grosvenor, portrayed riding his favorite hunter Honest John, may not have been so thoroughgoing a reactionary Tory as Deuchar imples. Before identifying himself with William Pitt's interest, Grosvenor was one of the Rockingham Whigs, like a number of Stubbs's other patrons of the 1760s associated with Charles Watson-Wentworth, second Marquess of Rockingham.[96] Modern viewers may object to the horses' docked tails and, in two cases, cropped ears, to say nothing of the stag's death, as far from natural or benevolent. But Stubbs's picture, in its harmonious composition and attention to the horses' lively interest in the scene, affirms that Grosvenor and his party may not have been entirely wrong to have themselves painted thus if they wished to appear to be worthy governors of the people.

This self-representation is most profoundly figured as a partnership with intelligent, sensitive blood horses, who have initiative and ideas and will not be bullied into submission. That these horses were either imported or descended from horses imported from the Middle East—aliens within, foreigners who had to be naturalized—is one of the great ironies of English equestrian history. It is an irony very much in line with mainstream English history, however, in that the assimilation of alien but aristocratic horses could be compared with that of the originally Norman human aristocracy. The English self-definition was never that of a single homogeneous stock. As the racing historian Theodore Cook acknowledged, "The Norman put the finishing touch of breed to our old English nobles. In the same way the Eastern stock put the finishing touch to the English racer."[97] This comparison of mixed or hybridized ancestry, equine and human, would be disputed by certain arch-purists among Thoroughbred enthusiasts, who assert an entirely Arabian lineage for the breed, as we shall see in the following chapter. A debt to the East may be acknowledged, without being fully repaid.

Imperial Envy

Envy between imperial states has a long history. Trading partners, yet also imperial rivals, in whose wars the other was sometimes implicated, during the early modern period the long-established Ottoman and emergent British empires were sometimes emulative, sometimes admiring, sometimes dismissive of one another. What Gerald MacLean has characterized as "imperial envy" brilliantly describes relations obtaining between Europe and the Ottoman empire before the fully fledged discursive system of Orientalism, described by Edward Said, kicked in during the later eighteenth century.[98] In previous centuries Western commercial and cultural exchanges with the East were on a less dominative basis than developed subsequently. What is all too often forgotten is that between the sixteenth and eighteenth centuries, the Ottomans remained in a position of relative superiority in wealth, the arts, and military strength.

The purebred Eastern horse native to the Ottoman domains embodied in the flesh this cultural superiority. Both in the flesh and in artistic representation, Eastern blood horses belonged to that common currency of "objects and practices held in common between the Eastern and Western empires," that "repertoire of images recognizable to both Christendom and the Islamic world," as Lisa Jardine and Jerry Brotton have argued.[99] These "living, breathing luxury items," in Jardine and Brotton's phrase,[100] were ideal objects of what MacLean has called "imperial envy." Until well into the eighteenth century, it would have been a visiting Englishman or Scotsman consumed with envy of Ottoman power, splendor, or horseflesh, and hardly ever the other way round.

By the time of John Buchan's representation of the battlefield of the First World War, however, the British and their allies hold the whip hand over the Ottomans and the Germans, so that such a past relation recedes into ghostly obscurity. What is most ironic is that Sandy Arbuthnot, riding into Erzurum with "his firm English hunting seat," is wearing not "proper clothes,"[101] but the "green mantle" of the prophet of Islam he had been sent to find and had ended up pretending to be:

> He was turbaned and rode like one possessed, and against the snow I caught the dark sheen of emerald. As he rode it seemed that the fleeing Turks were stricken still, and sank by the roadside with eyes strained after his unheeding figure . . . Then I knew that the prophecy had been true, and that their prophet had not failed them. The long-looked for revelation had come. Greenmantle had appeared at last to an awaiting people.[102]

Beneath the turban and flying robes of the forward-going Islamic horseman lurks a Scotsman—himself a product of English cultural imperialism. The exquisiteness of this Orientalist fantasy lies in its reversal of a history in which the hunting field could be said to have been haunted by the specters of Eastern horsemen, as if inside every top hat or hunt cap and pink coat there lurked an Arab or a Turk. Hark to Sandy Arbuthnot.[103] That is to say, in the lingo of the hunting field, look to him, observe him closely, he signifies, he is showing the way.

And hark to the small, but fast and agile, "Turkish" horse that Sandy rides.

CHAPTER THREE

Steal of a Turk

• • •

Trafficking in Bloodstock

If Johnny Bellarmine had an idea of beauty, it was of cool horses
under green trees. He had seen them in 1981, at Newmarket races,
at a blistering July Meeting . . . He ignored the fashionable
blood . . . not because he could not afford it, but because its virtue
was all too evident: what he sought, in the antique crossings and
nicks of blood and progeny, was something miraculous . . . He
settled in the end for a Hungarian stallion, who had never won
a race, but who, at his eighth grandsire on the distaff side, had
a blank: an animal not recorded in the stud-books of Hungary,
Germany, England, Ireland, France, Italy, Russia or the United
States . . . The result, a bay filly foaled late in 1983 . . . won both
her starts at four. The second of these, a race at Ascot in Berkshire
in July called the King George and Queen Elizabeth Stakes, she
won by eighteen lengths, defeating the Derby winners of England,
France, Ireland and Italy and the winner of the previous year's
English and Irish Oaks. They came in like washing in a high wind.

—James Buchan, *High Latitudes*

How the English Thoroughbred came into existence remains a conten-
tious subject. Every tale about the origins of the breed is a partial story,
and usually a partisan one. Even recent genetic research, whether docu-
menting Y chromosomes inherited through paternal lines, or mitochondrial
DNA inherited through maternal ones, must be conducted and interpreted
within an archival and documentary framework fraught with potential errors and
the interests of previous researchers.[1] With the exception of famous and well-
documented Eastern imports—whose genes do still appear in the Thoroughbred

population today—the genetic mixture out of which this icon of Englishness was produced continues to be a matter for speculation. As Franco Varola observes, "The fact that present-day racehorses are recorded as descendants of the specimens bred in England from about the time of Charles II," and not "as descendants of specimens bred in Italy by the Duke of Mantua or of Milan, or, for that matter, by the Turkish sultans," is not "a genetic issue, but purely a political and sociological issue."[2] The question of origins is further complicated by the evidence of the eye, in that being able to deduce a horse's breeding as well as its abilities from its appearance, expressed as "having an eye for a horse," still remains a dominant way of thinking in the equine industry today.[3] Hence, not only stud books and racing calendars but also contemporary paintings and prints have been mined for evidence of the Thoroughbred's genetic origins.

It should be said from the outset that the question of the importance of genetic distinctions within horse-kind is both ideologically loaded and scientifically contested. Zoologically speaking, *blood horse* merely describes a geographical "cline"—a sequence of differences within a species—adapted to hot arid regions.[4] According to the zoologist Juliet Clutton-Brock, in northern latitudes and cold climates, "mammals tend to be large (a generalization that is often called Bergmann's 'rule')" and have "heavy bodies with short legs, while the extremities, such as the ears, are short and compact (Allen's 'rule')." In hot climates the same species tend to have "longer and finer limbs relative to the size of the body and longer extremities," as well as a "shorter and sleeker coat."[5] All domestic horses of the past and present are, however, "descended from the single ancestral species, *Equus ferus,* with the focus of its domestication being on the Scythian steppes, north of the Caspian Sea" (61). Therefore, while the taxonomy of "blood," or hot-blooded, horses—distinguished from cold-blooded ones or warmblood crosses between the two—may be "useful terms" for "the horse-breeder," Clutton-Brock concludes, such distinctions possess "no scientific credence" (61).

The archaeozoologist Sándor Bökönyi, arguing from the evidence left by Iron Age horse breeders, offers a different view from Clutton-Brock's rather categorical dismissal of the question of blood or breed distinctions. Bökönyi identifies an important difference between Eastern "Scythian" and Western "Celtic" horse types, finding "considerable difference—approximately 10 cm—of size between the two groups, quite unexpectedly in favour of the eastern group," so that it was in the interests of Western people to acquire these larger Eastern horses, who could carry heavier loads, move more rapidly with a rider of equal weight, more easily carry riders wearing armor, and cover longer distances.[6] The Scythian horses, Bökönyi claims, "owing to the Scythian expansion on the one hand" and "commercial connexions" on the other, "spread from North Iran and South Russia to Central Europe and North Africa and in Asia as far as the Altai Mountains."[7] Size mattered, and horses bigger of body were better from a breeder's point of view.[8] In conjuring this Eastern/Western difference, Bökönyi has recourse to the horse pictured on the electrum vase discovered in the kurgan at Chertomlyk (fourth century B.C.E.), which, Bökönyi opines, would be considered a "very fine" animal "even by present breeders' standards," which Bökönyi glosses as being "mostly reminiscent of Arab thoroughbreds."[9]

This chapter surveys the contours of the debate about the origins of the Thoroughbred and attempts to steer a reasonable course between alternative versions, accounting for the available evidence as much as possible. But it too is a partial and perhaps even partisan version of events. Against the current of recent genetic research, which has confirmed the continuing crucial role of Eastern imported bloodstock, pedigree researchers have been resuscitating the story of native British progenitors of the Thoroughbred, with Irish hobbies and Scottish and Yorkshire galloways reappearing from within the shadowy interstices of early modern sources dominated by Eastern imports.[10] Exactly what breeding distinguished the imported stock also remains frustratingly speculative. As a belief in the "prepotency" or genetic dominance of the Arabian over any other Eastern breed emerged during the eighteenth century, the early modern sources may themselves have become increasingly biased toward favoring what came to be described as an Arabian over a Turkish or Barbary origin.[11] Later, in the nineteenth and twentieth centuries, the anti-Ottoman sentiments of travelers and equine enthusiasts such as Wilfrid Scawen Blunt and Lady Anne Blunt may have compounded this prejudice.

What seems uncontestable, nevertheless, is that a potent infusion of Eastern blood transformed not only the equine gene pool in the British Isles but also ideas about horse breeding and record keeping, and, I would submit, ideas about equine abilities. So-called blood horses were a great gift from the East that statesmen, merchants, and country gentlemen sought to appropriate for themselves, and eventually on behalf of the nation. Appropriation, and sometimes theft, followed by a suppression or forgetting of foreign origins, has long been a part of the Thoroughbred's story.

Ironically, those keen genealogists, English horse breeders, first learned about equine pedigree keeping in the East. They imported the idea of a purified lineage and of written documentation to support it along with the horses themselves. Henry Blount observed in 1636 that there was a registry of purebred Egyptian horses kept in Ottoman Cairo where Mameluke influence could still be felt.[12] In

1667 William Cavendish claimed on the good authority of "many *Gentlemen* of Credit" and "Many-many *Merchants*" that the prices of Arabian horses of "One Thousand, Two Thousand, and Three Thousand Pounds a Horse" were "Intollerable," but their equine genealogy was impeccable—"the *Arabs* are as Careful, and Diligent, in Keeping the *Genealogies* of their Horses, as any Princes can be in Keeping any of their own *Pedigrees*."[13] The French diplomat Laurence D'Arvieux, who first traveled to Syria and Lebanon in the 1650s, provided an early eye-witness account of Bedouin record-keeping, confirming what Cavendish had been told:

> They know by long Custom the Race of all the Horses they or their Neighbours have; they know the Name, the Surname, the Coat, and Marks of every Horse and Mare in particular; and when they have no noble Horses of their own, they borrow some of their Neighbours, paying so much Money, to Cover their mares, and that before Witnesses, who attest it under their hand and Seal before the *Emir*'s Secretary, or some other publick Person, where the whole Generation, together with the Names of the Creatures, is set down in Form. Witnesses are likewise call'd when the Mare has Foal'd; and another Certificate is made, where they put down the Sex, the Shape, the Coat, the Marks of the Colt, and the time of its Birth, which they give to the Party that buys it.[14]

In the 1770s, George III's Gentleman of the Horse, Richard Berenger, and the zoologist Thomas Pennant both published translations of Arabic documents attesting to the purity of horses purchased in Syria by Englishmen.[15] The origins of that pioneering English work of animal pedigree-keeping, the *General Stud-Book*, lay in the Syrian desert.[16]

The very word *thoroughbred* or *through-bred* for a pedigreed horse is a translation of the Arabic word *kuhaylan*, meaning "purebred all through."[17] "Renowned for its physical beauty, endurance, intelligence and touching devotion to its master," the eminent Arabist Philip K. Hitti remarks, "the Arabian thoroughbred (*kuhaylan*) is the exemplar from which all Western ideas about the good-breeding of horseflesh have been derived."[18] English breeders had begun to adopt this usage by the second decade of the eighteenth century. C. M. Prior remarked in 1924 that this early usage of *thoroughbred* was no longer widely known:

> The term "thoroughbreds" as applied to horses supposed to be of pure blood, is of much older use than is generally supposed. We find the expression "bred horses" . . . as early as 1729, but a still earlier instance occurs in a letter of the first Lord Bristol, who, writing to his son in July, 1713, says:—"As thro-bred English horses are allowd to surpass most of ye same species," he offers to send him some from his stud for the Elector of Hanover, at whose Court his son, Carr Hervey, was at that time.[19]

So, from at least the second decade of the eighteenth century onward, some notion of a thoroughly known and documented pedigree as an assurance of purity, and thus of quality, had been taken on board by English horse breeders inspired by Bedouin example. Merchants, diplomats, country gentlemen, and military officers in both the Ottoman empire and imperially aspiring Britain recognized the value of bred or blood horses native to the Ottoman domains.

Mysteries of the Blood Horse

The term *blood horse* combines aristocratic mystery-making with empirical observation. "The term 'blood-horse,'" commented Major-General Tweedie (who describes himself as "for many years H. B. M.'s Consul-General, Baghdad, and Political Resident for the government of India in Turkish Arabia"), "may be merely a vestige of the primitive notion, that there is an essential difference between the red corpuscles of the 'quality' and the commonalty respectively. But the name also points to that beautiful swelling out of the veins after a gallop, in the racer and his descendants, by means of which the heart and lungs obtain relief."[20]

The horse breeders of the West and the Americas have, for several centuries now, divided the equine species into hot-, cold-, and warm-blooded varieties. The so-called blood horse is another name for the hot-blooded kind, traditionally regarded as representing a gene pool selectively bred for centuries by Asian nomads and thus serving as a potent resource for upgrading horses of lesser quality. What a zoologist such as Juliet Clutton-Brock would describe simply as a geographical cline becomes ennobled as a breed apart. Today's most perfect manifestation of the blood horse is the Thoroughbred racehorse, now dominantly a European and North American product, though of Eastern origins. As we know from Sándor Bökönyi, steppe migration of the Scythian people first diffused the ancestors of this type during the Iron Age both eastward and westward. The Islamic conquest of much of Asia and the Mediterranean, including North Africa and Spain, brought in its wake an even more extensive diffusion of Eastern breeding stock, especially steppe-bred Turanian or Turkmen horses from Central Asia and purebred Bedouin horses from the deserts of Arabia. The Arabian continues today to be regarded as the greatest fountain of genetic purity. The North African Barbary horse, or Barb, ostensibly a Berber horse, often contains some Arabian as well as Spanish lineage. The government stud farms of Morocco today stand at stud purebred Barb stallions, purebred Arabian stallions, and Arab/Barb crosses, regarded as the national breed, the Moroccan horse.

Formerly isolated by the Cold War from international attention, another horse has in recent years come to be globally recognized as a blood horse by horse breeders: the Turanian, Turkmen, or Akhal-Teke of the Central Asian steppe and Turkmenistan, which shares many features with the Arabian but is nevertheless of an observably different type. The Akhal-Teke is taller, more angular, more "on the leg," with a fine head but lacking the concave or "dished" face of the Arabian. What we might call proto-Akhal-Tekes formed the core of the so-called Turk, Turkmen, or Turcoman horses imported into the British Isles along with Arabians and North African Barbs.[21] One of the legendary three foundation sires from whom all Thoroughbred pedigrees derive—the Byerley Turk—was very likely a proto-Akhal-Teke. There is often a more striking resemblance between Akhal-Tekes and modern Thoroughbreds than there is between most modern Thoroughbreds and purebred Arabians or North African Barbs.

Horses of the indigenous Northern European type, whether native ponies or heavy cart and draft horses, are classified as cold-blooded, by contrast. Warmbloods represent a cross between the two. Germany and Central and Eastern Europe are especially known today for their warmblood breeds, suggesting how their relative geographical proximity to the East in the form of the Ottoman empire appears to have influenced the development of horse breeding.

Distinctions between Arabians, Barbs, and Turks represented new kinds of knowledge for people in seventeenth-century England. There was a tendency to conflate kind with point of embarkation, as Peter Edwards, following the advice of Daphne Machin Goodall, has shown: "It is difficult to know the origin of many of these Eastern horses as they came from a number of sources. Arabs, for instance, were often shipped through ports in the Turkish empire. The term 'barb,' moreover, was used in a general sense to denote a swift horse."[22] The origins of the Thoroughbred, consequently, can never be definitively determined, but much of the gene pool came from the territories of the vast Ottoman empire. As English people grew more familiar with imported horses from the North African Barbary states, Central Asian steppe, and Syrian and Arabian deserts, they began to label them more confidently as belonging to different lineages and physical types—Barbs, Turks, Arabians.

The belief that Eastern blood is superior and that "blood will tell," however unscientifically grounded, has dominated Western horse breeding since the late seventeenth century, and thus the whole Thoroughbred industry from its beginnings.[23] The modern international market in pedigreed Arabians continues likewise to be vexed by questions of genetic purity as an index of breeding prepotency and quality.[24] As early as 1756, William Osmer attempted to put racehorse breeding onto a more scientific footing by debunking the mystery of "blood" and substituting the scientific principles of mechanics in order to explain why one horse raced better than another. He nevertheless concluded that "he who has a fine female, and judgment enough to adapt her shapes with propriety to a fine male, will always breed the best racer, let the sort of blood be what it will, always supposing it to be totally foreign."[25] In the continuing debate about the origins of the Thoroughbred, Osmer was clearly on the side of those for whom ostensibly native horses played no part in the breed's evolution. The Thoroughbred for him was a perpetuation of pure Eastern blood on other shores and by other means. An even more restricted definition of purity than Osmer's, however, was possible. In the late nineteenth and early twentieth centuries, Wilfrid Scawen Blunt, Lady Anne Blunt, and their daughter Judith Blunt-Lytton, later Lady Wentworth, claimed that the Thoroughbred was not only entirely of "foreign" origin but of purely Arabian origin.[26] The Blunts were convinced that of the three so-called foundation sires, only the Darley Arabian, bred in the Syrian desert by Bedouin tribesmen, had had a significant impact on Thoroughbred genetics, a theory that has received some recent support from Patrick Cunningham, whose genetics and pedigree research has revealed that the Darley's Y chromosome is to be found in 95 percent of modern Thoroughbred stallions.[27]

Even those who defended racing traditions already well established in England before the first decades of the eighteenth century, by which time a critical mass of Eastern horses had been imported and begun to reproduce, appeared struck by the difference these recently arrived foreigners had made. At Bedale races in Yorkshire in the mid-1720s, the Londoner Daniel Defoe defended northern English horses against all comers, declaring with imperial triumphalist confidence that native gallopers, strong weight-carriers who could stay over "a deep country," with "not speed only, but strength to carry it," would "beat all the world."[28] Defoe's line has been seconded by subsequent Yorkshire mare enthusiasts.[29] Impressed as he was by native talent, however, Defoe sounded anxious about what he had heard regarding expensive imports:

> Let foreigners boast what they will of barbs and Turkish horses, and, as we know five hundred pounds has been given for a horse brought out of Turkey . . . I do believe that some of the gallopers of this country, and of the bishopric of Durham, which joins it, will outdo for speed and strength the swiftest horse that was ever bred in Turkey, or Barbary, taken them all together.[30]

Money talks, and a horse worth five hundred pounds must have something like speed to recommend it. Variations on the phrase "taken all together," which Defoe repeats, stressing "those words all together; that is to say, take their strength and their speed together," and "English horses, take them one with another, will beat all the world" suggest that only a broad sampling will make good on this assertion of English superiority (513). Yet ironically, in praising Yorkshire horsepeople for their attention to who actually sired whom, Defoe reveals the prevailing ignorance in England regarding equine heredity:

> The breed of their horses in this and the next country are so well known, that though they do not preserve the pedigree of their horses for a succession of ages, as they say they do in Arabia and in Barbary, yet they christen their stallions here, and know them, and will advance the price of a horse according to the reputation of the horse he came of. (512)

Even giving their stallions names seems to have been a departure from usual English practice, to say nothing of paying attention to equine paternity as helping to predict the next generation's talents. Regarding Yorkshire racehorse culture, Defoe's evidence is thus double-edged. He gives a good account of native racers, countering Osmer's later testimony in favor of entirely foreign origins, but he also acknowledges the influence of Eastern horses, prices, and breeding practices that was beginning to saturate English culture as early as the mid-1720s.

Extensive archival research undertaken by C. M. Prior in the 1920s and 1930s, moreover, has shown how even the apparently native English mares of Yorkshire and elsewhere, if traced back through several generations, usually derived from imported horses, including Spanish and Italian horses who were themselves of imported Eastern bloodlines. As Prior noted, a simple glance at the records of an important stud such as the Duke of Newcastle's at Welbeck demonstrated "how entirely of Eastern origin was the racehorse of the hundred years immediately after the Restoration, the Stud being virtually composed of pure-bred Arabians, Turks, or Barbs, it being impossible to differentiate between these various breeds."[31] Even those native Yorkshire and County Durham mares and stallions will have had some immigrant ancestors. Insofar as the archival evidence enables any nominal distinctions to be made, the proportion appears to be, for stallions at least, about 50 percent Arabians and about 25 percent each Turks and Barbs.[32] J. B. Robertson ascertained a similarly small pool of mares from whom the modern Thoroughbred is descended, observing that "the greatest possible number of ancestresses in the thirteenth remove—or even much further back—is fifty," that the "Barbs and Eastern horses" were "the long separated relatives of the native galloway," and that "there is every reason to believe that before the stud records commenced both the native racehorse and the imported Barb and Eastern horse were also intensely interbred."[33]

The bloodstock authority Peter Willett hedges his bets on the percentage of Arabian genes in the Thoroughbred's gene pool by remarking that the modern Thoroughbred appears to contain "some ingredient other than the pure Arabian": "while some strains . . . have the characteristic Arab quality, others have a distinctly coarser stamp."[34] He casts further doubt on the breed's purely Arabian origins by adding that "few of the Arab and other Eastern horses imported during the hundred years following the middle of the seventeenth century were used for racing, presumably because they were not good enough to stand a chance of winning."[35] For Willett, this evidence poses a question: Was there a genetic "'X' factor," independent of the importations of the seventeenth and eighteenth centuries, which would account for both speed and occasional coarseness—"Was there, in short, a native English element in the making of the thoroughbred?" (36) Willett concludes that although "an affirmative answer would satisfy a narrow kind of insular pride," "no case can be made for it" (36). Rather, as the entirely Eastern pedigree of Flying Childers, the first great racehorse (1714–41), demonstrates, the imported stock needed the addition of no mysterious genetic "X" factor; improvement occurred on the basis of changed climate, keep, and judicious selection for the purpose of racing. Speed had never been the sole criterion in the East.

According to Nicholas Russell, it was precisely the mingling of formerly separate Oriental strains—Arabian genes in combination with those of the "Turk" (Turkmen, Turcoman) and the North African Barb—that was the decisive factor in the creation of the English Thoroughbred. In his view, breeders and antiquarians have been inclined to exaggerate the impact of the late-seventeenth- and early-eighteenth-century influx of imports, and the breed's evolution was more gradual, occurring over many centuries. Russell believes that the importation of Arabian horses into Britain in small numbers dates back to the Roman occupation and the Crusades. Eastern horses appear in archival detail for the first time during the reigns of Henry VIII and Elizabeth I, as the sixteenth century witnessed much "multiracial cross-breeding" of imported Spanish, Neapolitan, and Barbary horses, who would themselves have contained Arabian or Turcoman blood.[36] By the late seventeenth century, English horses were the products of what Russell calls "massive mongrelisation."[37] However, Russell nevertheless acknowledges that something significant happened to horse breeding and horse culture in England between the late seventeenth century and 1750. Breeding for the turf incited "controlled hybridisations" between imported Oriental sires, considered "'pure' in the sense of unmixed in the local mongrel collection," and local mares (who by this time might themselves have some Eastern blood), creating a "local Oriental variant, modulated with North European genes" (219).

As Russell notes, a certain degree of magical thinking associated with pedigrees in a society with a ruling aristocracy like England's should be expected, since "the parallels between . . . the human obsession with title, hereditary position and social caste . . . and animal pedigrees, are too obvious to need emphasis" (19). Thus we should not be surprised to find claims of the supposed superiority of pedigreed animals to be grounded in "their descent from legendary ancestral beasts such as Bates's herd of Shorthorn cows or the famous trio of Arab/Turk horses in the pedigrees of all modern Thoroughbreds" (190). Russell assumes some genetic contributions from "cross-bred" racers and "Galloway saddle horses," a view that diverges from Peter Willett's and from that of the arch-purists—the Blunts and Lady Wentworth—but is in accordance with Mackay-Smith's and Nash's (219). However, Russell does not dispute that the so-called English Thoroughbred was essentially a product of imported Oriental bloodstock; in fact, he calls the breed "a variant of the Oriental horse, adapted to North European conditions" and benefiting from the mixture of previously separate "Oriental strains" or "races."[38] Russell's description echoes that of Franco Varola, that the Thoroughbred "is neither a pure nor an impure animal, but much more simply a hybrid, obtained by crossing different strains for racing purposes, and by keeping these strains isolated from the remainder of the species Caballus of the genus Equus within a register known as the *General Stud Book*."[39]

The obvious parallels between human and equine genealogy that Russell observes notwithstanding, there were differences in attitudes toward purity of lineage in humans and horses. What Russell calls "massive mongrelisation" in English horse breeding, culminating in the crossing and then in-and-in-breeding of previously separate Oriental "strains or races," was celebrated in 1810 in terms that would have horrified the great British public if applied to humans by that period, as Felicity Nussbaum has shown. In the most recent scholarly study of English ideologies of race in this period, Nussbaum argues that although racial categories, including attitudes toward racial mixing, were "highly adaptable within England in the eighteenth century," by the century's end "racialized fears" had become "most powerful and disturbing."[40] Corresponding with "increasingly public attempts to clarify black inferiority," Nussbaum observes, the "most vigorous attention to hybridity and mongrelization takes fire with the abolition of the slave trade in 1807 and with emancipation in 1833."[41] Once interracial progeny became likely on the home front, given the prospect of large numbers of "freed slaves who possessed only minimal skills," Nussbaum concludes, English attitudes hardened, and "the menace of impurity and degeneration" was seen to loom over an increasingly imperial England.[42]

In 1810 T. Hornby Morland enthused about equine miscegenation so rapturously that his rhetoric comes close to self-parody—but only close. He appears to have been deaf to the possibility of scandalous human comparisons or lascivious innuendo, preoccupied as he was with the "beauty of form, and every other valuable quality"—once again yoking beauty and utility—that emerged from mixing equine races:

> The advantages arising from *crossing the blood*, or *mixing races*, are so obvious to every man of experience, that I think it unnecessary to enter into particulars. I shall just briefly remark, that by *mixing races*, we obtain beauty of form, and every other valuable quality. It is from our attention to this particular for two centuries, that we have remedied the defects of conformation, united the essential qualities of speed and bottom in the same individual, and improved and perfected our breed so far, as to have acquired the credit of possessing the most pure, unexceptionable, and beautiful race of Blood Horses in the universe.[43]

In 1810, men of experience who understood how "mixing races" produced specimens of hybrid vigor would certainly have included plantation owners who fathered mixed-race children with their slaves, but Hornby Morland remained obsessively focused on horses. As did many of his countrymen. Righting genetic wrongs by correcting faults, uniting speed and stamina or "bottom," and purifying the resulting strain by subsequent inbreeding are all heralded by Hornby Morland as a collective project undertaken by fellow Englishmen over "two centuries." His periodization as well as his emphasis upon the inclusion of multiple "races" coincides with Russell's exactly.

Nicholas Russell's account appears to be the most adequate to date with regard to both the genetic and the early modern archival evidence. His model of hybridization of previously separate "Oriental strains" or "races," emblematized in "the famous trio of Arab/Turk horses" in all Thoroughbred pedigrees, not only acknowledges the genetic contribution made by so-called Turks or Turkmen horses but also a "modulation" of this Oriental mix by native North European genes. To this model of origin we should add the cluster of foundation mares, most of apparently "Oriental" lineage, whose genetic contribution is evidenced by recent mtDNA research. Thin-skinned representatives of a geographical cline, these ancestors of the Thoroughbred were highly likely to have made a show of blood after exertion, as General Tweedie put it.

Although exactly what Englishmen and Irishmen of the seventeenth and eighteenth centuries meant by a "Turk," as distinguished from an Arabian or Barb, will forever remain a matter of speculation, some distinction between "Arabians" and "Turkman" or "Turcoman" horses appears to have been emerging. As Heneage Finch, the second Earl of Winchilsea and Charles II's ambassador at Constantinople, reported in 1667 to the Habsburg ambassador Count Lesley, there was a shortage of Arabian horses ("they are all either at Court or going for Candia," referring to the Ottoman siege of Candia on Crete), so he was on the lookout for the larger "Turcoman" breed: "I intend to try for some of the Turcoman breed, for I despair of getting any Arabs from Aleppo, where my correspondent cannot even procure any for the King."[44]

There was no absolute prohibition on the export from the Ottoman domains of blood horses, whether of Arabian or Turcoman breeding, as has been recently asserted.[45] Rather, by the 1660s there had been a thriving Ottoman export trade in horses since Marco Polo's day at least, though in some cases export taxes were imposed and licenses were necessary, and in others political conflicts resulted in a ban on specific exports to specific purchasers.[46] The emerging distinction between breeds, Arabian and Turcoman or "Turkman," is in line with one drawn by Nathaniel Harley, an English merchant at Aleppo, several decades later:

> The Aga's who are Gentry of this Country Breed few or no Horses themselves, or if they doe tis of ye Large Turkman Breed wch serve 'em for presents and are most Esteemed at Court, By which means the Arab Breed is cheefly in the hands of the Villains or the Arabs themselves, and neither of 'em are duely carefull of the Size of their Stallions Their Cheef care being that they are of the true race.[47]

The earlier the importation, then, the greater the likelihood that the point of embarkation, rather than any assumptions about breeding, determined how the horse would be classified. As horsemen in the British Isles became more familiar with the Eastern strains on domestic turf, and began to imagine that they could distinguish between them on anatomical and other empirical grounds, *Arabian, Turk,* and *Barb* gradually became racialized rather than spatialized descriptive terms.

From the 1650s onward, the East increasingly became for the English upper classes a source of absolutely essential ingredients with which to concoct an identity that would advertize their cultural superiority at home as well as abroad. Horses were a crucial part of this phenomenon, as the English vied for position in the global marketplace. By the 1720s, among the essential accessories of the sporting aristocrat or gentleman were horses of indubitably Eastern breeding. The intermingling and hybridization or mongrelization of what had been formerly separate—and perhaps relatively genetically pure—Oriental "strains or races" would be translated into purity of lineage. At the same time, the very concept of equine genealogy as a predictor of identity was also imported from the East. By a Lockean logic, the very cultivation on English soil of what had been only an Eastern potency *in potentia* transformed the foreign into the rightful posses-sion of the imperial cultivator.

A Mercantile and (Long) Restoration Story

Between 1650 and 1750, English (and some Irish and Welsh and Scots) aristo-crats, mere upstarts in the world economy where Eastern blood horses had been traded for centuries, began shopping the world.[48] And their acquisitions, by fair means or foul, most prestigiously took the form of "his lordship's Arabian," or less often "his lordship's Turk" or "Barb," all trophies from the East, flaunting En-glish disregard for Ottoman authority and that of the Barbary states of North Africa. This is a story about English mercantilism, a chapter in Britain's grand narrative of "gentlemanly capitalism," and an episode in the creation of the fiscal-military state.[49]

It is also an episode in the history of the Stuart Restoration of 1660. The East-ern equine invasion that altered sporting culture in the British Isles has tradi-tionally been attributed to Charles II. As the editors of the Verney family mem-oirs remarked in 1907, the Restoration suited people such as Colonel Henry Verney "exactly; the world was once more fit for a gentleman to live in."[50] As a consequence of his "knowledge of horses and dogs, and his keen sporting in-stincts," they announce, the colonel was "ensured" a welcome from the king and the Duke of York at Newmarket and other races.[51] From the perspective of 1736, Alexander Pope did not disagree regarding the importance of equestrian sports to the cultural shift brought about by the Stuart Restoration:

> In Days of Ease, when now the weary Sword
>
> Was sheath'd, and *Luxury* with *Charles* restor'd;
>
> In every Taste of foreign Courts improv'd,
>
> "All by the King's Example, liv'd and lov'd."
>
> Then Peers grew proud in Horsemanship t' excell,
>
> New-market's Glory rose, as Britain's fell.[52]

In 1751 Thomas Warton characterized the Newmarketization of British culture—having Restoration origins but looking likely to continue in perpetuity—in sim-ilarly satirical terms:

> Go on, brave Youths, till in some future age,
>
> Whips shall become the *senatorial badge;*

Till *England* see her thronging senators
Meet all at *Westminster,* in boots and spurs;
See the whole House, with mutual frenzy mad,
Her Patriots all in leathern breeches clad:
Of *bets,* for *taxes,* learnedly debate,
And guide with equal reins a *Steed* and *State.*[53]

The standard history of the Thoroughbred horse echoes these assumptions. "It may not be extravagant to claim," announces Peter Willett, "that without" Charles II "there would have been no thoroughbred, no Jockey Club, no General Stud Book, no Racing Calendar, no Classic races, no betting shops—none of the ingredients of the system of horse-racing as we know it."[54]

That Charles II's court was often ensconced at Newmarket seems clear enough. That the king himself was a famous jockey and won some races cannot be denied, nor that the Rowley Mile was named after his favorite hack. Libertinism and sporting culture were as interchangeable metaphorically and as intertwined materially as a poem published in 1792 demonstrates: "THE LOVE CHACE. *Representing the going of a Pad.* An Highly Humourous Song. Written by King Charles the Second":

WHEN for air,
I take my mare,
And mount her first,
She walks just thus,   *Walk.*
And motion slow;
With nodding, plodding,
Wagging, jogging,
Dashing, splashing,
Snorting, starting,
Whimsically she goes:
The whip stirs up,
Trot, trot, trot;   *Trot.*
Ambling then with easy flight,
She wriggles like a bride at night,   *Pace.*
Her shuffling hitch,
Regales my breech;
Whilst trot, trot, trot, trot,   *Trot.*
. . . .
Just so Phillis,

Fair as lillies,

As her face is,   *Walk.*

Has her paces;

And in bed too,

Like my pad too;

Nodding, plodding,

Wagging, jogging,

Dashing, plashing,

Flirting, spirting,

Artful are all her ways;

Heart thumps pit, pat,   *Trot.*

Trot, trot, trot, trot.[55]

And so forth, until a galloping finish occurs in both sorts of riding. Whether or not Charles wrote these verses, which I have not been able to determine, they represent a popular idea of the Restoration court's addiction to sporting culture—whether sexual sports or equestrian sports. Even if the "Love Chace" was entirely retro, conjuring for a 1790s audience an imaginary Charles and his horsey court who enjoyed "the sport," in both senses of the term, the persistence of this idea tells us something about the myth-making inspired by the Stuart Restoration. More than a century after his death, Charles II was assumed by sportsmen to have had a hand in determining the proper idioms for both their favorite pursuits.

Yet reports of how profoundly the Restoration of Charles II changed English bloodstock and equine culture have been exaggerated. Even the supposedly authoritative *General Stud-Book* was sucked into the Charles-worshipping of eighteenth-century turf lore when James Weatherby wrote: "ROYAL MARES. King Charles the Second sent abroad the master of the horse, to procure a number of foreign horses and mares for breeding, and the mares brought over by him, (as also many of their produce) have since been called Royal Mares."[56] The king's desire for Eastern blood horses was undeniable, but the performance of his agents in the Ottoman domains was rather lacking, especially when compared with previous and subsequent successes by Levant Company merchants. In trying to correct such an erroneous impression as had been given by Weatherby of the king's personal responsibility for the number of imports who began arriving on British shores after 1660, C. M. Prior rather overstated the anti-Charles case in his second book, published in 1935:

> The King sent neither the Master of the Horse, or any other high personage, on such
> a mission, and there were no importations of horses of any moment during his

reign, the one or two that came to this country being merely presents from the East. It is true that the King told Lord Winchilsea, our Ambassador at Constantinople, to try and get him some Arabian horses, but he did not succeed in obtaining them.[57]

In his 1924 book, as we have seen, Prior had unearthed archival evidence of the difficulty during the 1660s of locating and securing in Aleppo suitable Arabians, as distinguished from the Turcoman breed. He had also provided evidence for the successful importation of at least one Arabian for Charles II in 1663. By 1935, Prior had either forgotten or thought it advisable to downplay this evidence. Charles's ambassador, the Earl of Winchilsea, had written to the king in August 1663 that he was sending to England "an Arabian horse," the best that could be procured, in the care of his secretary. The ambassador's secretary, Paul Rycaut, gleefully reported to his master from London:

> This weeke I presented his Majestie from your lordship with the 'cemyter' and horse . . . The King was much pleased with the cemyter, and highly delighted with the horse; for I tooke such care of him, to get him into a good condition, that hee looked as well in St. James's Parke (where his Majestie came downe to view him) as hee did at Adrianople; and the horse was commended by all for a curious shaped horse, and thought strange that after so long a voyage hee should retaine his flesh with so much vigour and comelinesse. The horse is ordered to bee sent to New-market, for the King hath a great opinion that hee is very fleet.[58]

What became of this "curious"—excellently, even exquisitely, shaped—horse remains obscure.[59] One documented import does not a bloodstock revolution make. However, Charles II's acquisition of Eastern horses, though less important than many once assumed, was not so thorough a failure as Prior was to assert in 1935.

Cromwell, Horseman and Connoisseur

What Prior's 1935 book did establish was that Oliver Cromwell might have succeeded rather better than Charles II in the acquisition of Eastern, and even of Arabian, horses. The Levant Company had written to Sir Thomas Bendish, ambassador at Constantinople, on 10 September 1657:

> His Highness wants some good Arabian horses, to furnish England with a beed of that Kind, and we have written to Aleppo to supply us with 2 of that sort. We desire you to procure two at Constantinople, and send them to England, but let them be of the best kind. If a licence is necessary at Aleppo, pray furnish the consul therewith.[60]

Arabians are specified, but only good examples are wanted, and of the best kind, indicating that the Lord Protector wished to be highly discriminating in furnishing the nation with bloodstock. To Henry Riley, the consul at Aleppo, the Levant Company wrote on the same day:

> His Highness, on our late address to him, expressed a desire to be furnished with certain Arabian horses, which we have promised to try to procure. We pray you enquire after two of the best breed, and, if possible, send them to us in England; the ambassador will give you a licence. We have written to Constantinople for 2 more.[61]

Thus the Duke of Newcastle's complaint of 1667 that the Interregnum was responsible for the poor state of English equine bloodlines stands revealed as partisan prejudice:

> There were, afore the Warrs, many good *Races* in *England*, but they are all now Ruined; and the many New Breeders of Horses comn up presently after the Warrs, are (I doubt) none of the Best; for, I believe, their *Stallions* were not very Pure, because the *Men* that did Govern in *Those Dayes*, were not so *Curious* as the Great Lords, and Great Gentry were Heretofore, neither would they be at the Cost; and besides, they have not *Knowledge* of Horses as in other *Countries:* For, though Every man Pretends to it, yet, I assure you, there are very Few that Know *Horses,* as I have heard the KING say: Since whose RESTAURATION, the Probability of getting Good Breeds again, is very Great.[62]

Far from proving guilty of this charge, that, not being a proper nobleman or gentleman himself, Cromwell had taken no care of pedigrees or horse breeding, the Lord Protector had shown the foresight to purchase Neapolitan as well as Arabian horses to contribute to the nation's equine gene pool. Cromwell paid 2,832 dollars for six horses from Naples, two stallions and four mares.[63] He had commissioned Charles Longland, in the diplomatic service at Leghorn, to obtain them, and on 18 June 1655, Longland had reported success, adding, "I know not yet, whether I shal speed in the commission I gav to Aleppo for a horse; but if I do, I am confident the world has not better horses than that place affourds."[64]

Although four horses were ordered, only one may have been obtained from the environs of Aleppo. Cromwell's Gentleman of the Horse, Nicholas Baxter, traveled to Rotterdam to collect an "Arabian" horse for the Lord Protector, which was shipped on board Captain Richard Rooth's ship *Dartmouth*, arriving at Gravesend by 3 November 1657.[65] This horse is most likely to have gone into the keeping of Rowland Place, Cromwell's Stud-master, at Hampton Court, and, after Cromwell's death in 1658, to have become Place's property, known as Place's

White Turk. Unlike Charles II's possible imports, this horse features as an important name in Thoroughbred pedigrees.[66] Prior speculates further that Place's White Turk, standing at stud at Dinsdale in Yorkshire, and James D'arcy's White Turk, standing close by at Sedbury, are likely to have been the same horse, "it being extremely unlikely that at the same time there should be two 'Turks' of this colour standing within a few miles of each other, when an Arabian was indeed a *rara avis in terris,* in this country."[67]

Prior may well have been correct in speculating that at this early date, the substitution of Turk for Arabian in the horse's English name would have had more to do with his having come from Aleppo, in Ottoman territory, than with any knowledge of how he was actually bred. However, it is also case that Prior, like the Blunts, would have assumed that the genetic influence later exerted by the horse signified Arabian breeding. In recent years, in the light of post–Cold War interest in Akhal-Teke horses, Alexander Mackay-Smith has argued that Place's White Turk should be regarded as a Turk, that is, as a Turanian or Turkmen (a proto-Akhal-Teke), though Mackay-Smith hedges his bets by asserting that this horse, like the Godolphin "Barb," would also have had Arabian crosses in his pedigree.[68] Either determination is grounded in an ideology of Thoroughbred origins—an aristocratic preference for a more purely Arabian lineage, emphasizing the supposed purity of Bedouin horse-breeding practices, or a more democratic preference for a greater genetic admixture that admits of other Eastern breeds derived from the Ottoman empire as well as native British contributions. The specific genetic heritage represented by Place's White Turk will, however, remain forever undecideable.

What we can say with some certainty is that, with regard to the Eastern equine invasion, any periodizing of a "Long Restoration" beginning in 1660 needs to begin further back, at least with Cromwell in the 1650s. One result of the Interregnum experiment was the dispersal of the royal stud at Tutbury in 1649, which, like the sale of the late king's art collection, as Jerry Brotton has shown, disseminated royal possessions among the public in the 1650s, with some benefits to the nation.[69]

There was a shortage of horses of quality in England in this decade, as shown by the correspondence between Cardinal Mazarin and Monsieur de Bordeaux, who had been sent from France to England to purchase horses and art objects from the dispersal of Charles I's effects. The letters repeatedly report that there were scarcely any handsome horses to be found, and Cromwell's own family were looking for foreign imports. In February 1655 the Lord Protector's eldest son, Richard, offered "to exchange a very fine gelding, which however, will only walk;

for a Barbary horse," and, Bordeaux wrote to Mazarin, "if Your Eminence has such a one in his stable, young and handsome, I would accept his offer."[70] Mazarin appears to have been keen to comply, and one Barbary horse might indeed have been sent to England, as Bordeaux cautions in his next letter that sending *more* than one would probably not be worthwhile, "attitudes of mind here not seeming to me to be such that civilities would have any result."[71] A simple exchange, a horse for a horse, was what the English understood, according to the French envoy; excessive politeness, such as sending additional Barbary horses, would fail to produce the desired results by improving diplomatic relations.

Once again the desire for free forward movement, and for Eastern bloodstock of a racing bent, dominated an Englishman's taste in horseflesh. Richard Cromwell was eager to swap a good-looking but one-paced gelding for a stallion with Barbary speed. The French cardinal, on the other hand, liked the idea of "a patent safety," a laid-back gelding whose best pace was a walk.

One further aspect of the Interregnum needs to be noted, since Irish success on the turf arguably dates from this period. The dispersal of the royal stud at Tutbury in 1649 led to six horses being presented to Lieutenant General Michael Jones, Commander-in-Chief in Leinster, in recognition of his services in Ireland on behalf of the Parliamentarian government.[72] Five of these "royal stud barbs" were acquired by the Earl of Thomond, and they may well have accounted for the subsequent success of the O'Briens on the turf in both Ireland and England.[73]

The Shipping News

After Cromwell, who else succeeded where a king himself might fail? Levant Company merchants such as Nathaniel Harley take the prize, but acquiring horses and exporting them successfully was far from easy even for Company factors. Horses had to endure arduous if not life-threatening conditions when shipped to England.

Even in ancient times, when ships were rarely specialized, the *hippagogoi*, ships for transporting horses, comparable to the *huissiers* of the Middle Ages that were used for the same purpose, were a notable exception.[74] As Jean Rougé observes, "There was probably a door on the side of the ship that served as a gangplank when opened, allowing the animals to be put on and taken off the ship."[75] Lisa Jardine and Jerry Brotton mention a sixteenth-century "heavy, round-bottomed" Portuguese ship of thirty guns designed to carry horses in its hold "as humanely as possible for long voyages," but they also note that this was the kind of ship "infamously used to transport African slaves across the Atlantic."[76] Jardine and Brotton comment that the customary equation for the low value placed on slaves' lives was that one horse equaled eight slaves, corresponding to the "space allocation in the deep hull of a ship: eight slaves could be stowed in the space required for a single horse."[77] Horses are not mentioned as cargo in Ralph Davis's study of the trade with Asia Minor and Syria, the essence of which was the exchange of English woollen cloth for Turkish or Persian raw silk:

> The valuable silk cargoes were supplemented by cheaper bulk cargoes of cotton, mohair, galls (a dyestuff) and later currants; and in the eighteenth century, sometimes, by the even cheaper potash.[78]

However, horses could easily have helped make up the weight on return voyages from Iskenderun, the port for Aleppo.

Horses would thus most likely have traveled in the hold of the ship, rather than on deck, as smaller animals such as pigs and sheep sometimes did. They may have been supported in slings. On her journey to the Crimea in 1854, at the beginning of the war with Russia, Frances Isabella Duberly, who was accompanying her husband Henry to the front, reported after nine days at sea:

> The slings begin to gall the horses under the shoulder and breastbone; and the heat and bad atmosphere must be felt to be understood. Every effort to alleviate their sufferings is made; their nostrils are sponged with vinegar, which is also scattered in the hold. Our three horses bear it bravely, but they are immediately under a hatchway where they get air.[79]

Despite this care, five horses died on the passage to Istanbul from Plymouth, including Mrs. Duberly's own horse. At Malta, where her horse was "lowered to his rest among the nautili and wondrous sea-flowers which floated round the ship," Mrs. Duberly wondered that a "small French brig, containing a detachment of the *Chasseurs d'Afrique*," a vessel of 150 tons, "had twenty-eight horses on board, and had lost none, although they provided no stalls for them, but huddled them into the hold as closely as they could stow them away."[80]

Horses had a better chance of surviving a sea voyage if there were only a few of them on board.[81] The survival rate of Levant Company–exported horses, such as those shipped by Nathaniel Harley—which amounted to at least nine horses besides the shipments that included the Dun and the Bloody-Shouldered Arabian[82]—was certainly improved by only one or two having been shipped at a time.

Provisioning at sea was always a major concern for both men and horses. M. Horace Hayes advised in *Horses on Board Ship: A Guide to Their Management* that the safest food was green fodder of some kind, most conveniently hay, and un-limited quantities of drinking water.[83] Concentrated food such as oats and barley was heating, according to Hayes, and idle horses on board could not digest it prop-erly; hay was the best grass substitute.[84] Water supplies were always a problem on board ship, requiring regular reprovisioning. Hay in sufficient quantities for a voyage of from four to six months, even for one horse, would have required a very large storage area. Military calculations during the sixteenth century allowed for fourteen pounds of hay a day per horse.[85] Reprovisioning of grass or hay may have happened along the way, along with water reprovisioning. But initial sup-plies of fodder must have been obtained from the Syrian plain in January or Feb-ruary, and inconspicuously at that, so as not to arouse suspicions of valuable horses being exported. Based on horse-keeping practices in the territories of the former Ottoman empire today, I would hazard that the basic fodder was most likely to have been what is called in Turkish *saman,* chopped hay, or a mixture of chopped hay and straw, which could be mixed with barley for horses in work, but need not be, and is often fed by means of a nosebag.[86] One advantage in shipping Arabian or Turkmen horses was that they were accustomed to being deprived of plentiful water supplies and of regular grazing for months at a time, and could survive on such meager fare as *saman,* or dry barley, locusts, dates,[87] or even such an unnaturally low-bulk diet as high protein grains mixed with mutton fat.[88]

Surviving the voyage might still mean reaching England in a very reduced state, requiring summer grass to recover their condition. Horses who arrived dur-ing October or November, as a number of Nathaniel Harley's horses did, were fed "corn," at least after landing. Thomas Pulleine, son of the Master of the Stud to William III, wrote to Robert Harley about the horses who had arrived with Cap-tain Charles Cornwall of the *Burford* at the Downs in October 1711, conveying his father's praise of these horses—"in his Opinion they are the most Hopefull as well as beautifull Horses he ever yett Sett his Eyes upon, & yt they have all the Symptoms of good Blood yt Can be requir'd"—and advising that these "Turkish horses" not be given any "Purges" such as the London farriers might suggest, "for by many repeated experiences he always found yt Method utterly spoild and ruind the Turkish Horses, but instead of yt to shred a Large Carrott every day for abt 6 Weeks amongst their Corne for each Horse, but Care must be taken not to use any yt have been frozen or wormeaten."[89]

Shipping horses was expensive because awkward and labor intensive. It was not always easy to find passage for a horse on homeward-bound English ships out of Iskenderun, and captains who agreed to taking horses on board expected to be well paid for the inconvenience. Between 1660 and 1760, captains in the East India trade, which was more lucrative at this time than the Levant trade, expected a high return on their voyages. K. N. Chaudhuri reports:

> With judicious management in the Indian Ocean, the capital stock of £1,500 exported by the commander of a 500-ton ship might easily double and on return home he stood to make a gain of £5,000 to £10,000 from a voyage. Such an income from a life of sea voyages and trade would have put the East India commanders on a level with the upper ranks of the landed gentry.[90]

The captains who brought over horses from Istanbul or Iskenderun would not have had the same reliably high rate of return on capital stock. Instead they expected large payments from the horses' new owners in England. Robert Harley, then Secretary of State, paid Captain Thomas Stepney £53 15s. for bringing two horses from Turkey in November 1706.[91] He also paid £3 4s. 6d. to the "Person who had ye care of ye Horses in ye Voyage," £8 12s. to "Mr. Wm. Thomas towards ye Charge of Landing Horses from Turkey," and £10 4s. 6d. to one Simon Chapman "upon account of a Journey to Deal to fetch up two Horses."[92] In November 1713 his son Edward, Lord Harley, complained to William Thomas regarding a new shipment of horses that "Capt Gare's demand for the charges since the Horses landed very unreasonable considering the ill care yt was taken of them," and "When you do pay him, you will let him understand how little he deserved so much when he abused the Horses at that rate."[93]

Diplomacy, War, Trade, and Theft

Precious cargo, who might nevertheless be neglected on their voyages, horses arrived from the East in various conditions and by various means, not all of them entirely above board. The stories of the Big Three foundation sires—the Byerley Turk, Darley Arabian, and Godolphin Arabian or Barb—taken together represent the three most popular avenues by which Europeans might acquire Eastern horses: war (Byerley Turk, ca. 1680–1714); trade, including the odd dodgy transaction (Darley Arabian, foaled 1700; imported 1704); and diplomacy or diplomatic gifts (Godolphin Arabian or Godolphin Barb, 1724–53).

The Godolphin Arabian, whose story has generated more speculative ink and more romantic Orientalist tropes than the other horses' stories combined, was, according to the views of modern Thoroughbred historians, most likely to have been a Jilfan Arabian from the Yemen, shipped to the Bey of Tunis via Syria, and sent by him as a gift to the King of France. The horse was purchased by Edward Coke in France, and imported into England by him in 1730, becoming the property of the second Earl of Godolphin after Coke's death in 1733.[94] Unlike the other two foundation sires, the Godolphin did not retain a consistent identity in the *General Stud-Book* but kept being differently represented, volume to volume, with sensational stories of his having drawn a water cart in Paris (presumably having been despised by the French) or of having been a "teaser" stallion before fighting to cover the famous mare Roxana. Opinion even varied as to the likelihood of his having been an Arabian or a Barb. Richard Nash has recently speculated that the insistence on the Arabianness of the horse in the 1730s, later supported by Richard Wall's and William Osmer's otherwise differing accounts from the 1750s, was part of a campaign by Thoroughbred fanciers in southern England to shift the center of Thoroughbred breeding and racing from Yorkshire to Newmarket.[95] By the 1730s the Arabian had emerged as the most prestigious, because believed to be the most purely bred, and thus the most genetically potent, of the three Oriental breeds. The Godolphin's story reached its mythic apotheosis in Eugène Sue's romance of 1838.[96] In its association with diplomatic gift-giving, and specifically with the English wresting away from the French of an undervalued Eastern gift, this horse's story encapsulates the British/French rivalry characterized as imperially formative by Linda Colley.[97]

The Byerley Turk, an Ottoman charger, and thus likely to have been a Turkmen, has traditionally been thought to have been a spoil of war captured at the siege of Buda in 1686. C. M. Prior does not dispute this story of origin, comparing the horse with the Stradling or Lister Turk, brought over by the young Duke of Berwick who, according to Prior, "had joined Charles of Lorraine's forces in wresting Buda from the invaders."[98] Alexander Mackay-Smith claims that the Byerley Turk was not imported but foaled in England of Turcoman stock,[99] an origin story in keeping with his argument debunking previous exaggerations of the importance of imported horses, especially Arabians, in Thoroughbred pedigrees. Jeremy James, having failed to find any evidence of Captain Robert Byerley, of Middridge Grange, County Durham, ever having left the British Isles to fight in Europe, speculates that it was Edward Vaudrey who brought the horse back from Buda in 1686 and sold him to Byerley.[100] In any event, there is documentary evidence that Byerley took his Turkish-bred charger (however obtained) with him on campaign to Ireland in 1688–89.[101] Prior comments: "At the Battle of the Boyne he was so far ahead reconnoitering the enemy that he narrowly escaped capture, owing his safety to the superior speed of his horse."[102]

The exotic foreign horse as spoil of war materializes a capturing of Ottoman power and splendor that may not have been outright theft but was still an appropriation of desirable goods from the Eastern empire. John Evelyn recorded seeing "three Turkish or Asian Horses, newly brought over" in St. James's Park in December 1684 that had been "taken from a Bashaw at the seige of *Vienna* in Austria."[103] Evelyn spectacularly exemplifies MacLean's thesis about imperial envy:

> & with my Eyes never did I behold so delicate a Creature as was one of them, of somwhat a bright bay, two white feete, a blaze; such an head, [Eye,] eares, neck, breast, belly, buttock, Gaskins, leggs, pasterns, & feete in all reguards beautifull & proportion'd to admiration, spiritous & prowd, nimble, making halt, turning with that sweiftnesse & in so small a compass as was incomparable, with all this so gentle & tractable, as called to mind what I remember *Busbequius* speakes of them; to the reproch of our Groomes in *Europ* who bring them up so churlishly, as makes our horse most of them to retaine so many ill habits &c: They trotted like Does, as if they did not feele the Ground; for this first Creature was demanded 500 Ginnies, for the 2d 300, which was of a brighter bay, for the 3d 200 pound, which was browne, all of them choicely shaped, but not altogether so perfect as the first. In a word, it was judg'd by the Spectators, (among whom was the King, Prince of Denmark, the Duke of Yorke, and severall of the Court Noble persons skilled in Horses, especially Monsieur Faubert & his sonn & Prevost, Masters of the Accademie and esteemed of the best in Europe), that there were never seene any horses in these parts, to be compared with them: Add to all this, the Furniture which consisting of Embrodrie on the Saddle, Housse, Quiver, bow, Arrows, Symeter, Sword, Mace or Battel ax a la *Tur<c>isque:* the Bashaws Velvet Mantle furr'd with the most perfect Ermine I ever beheld, all the Yron worke in other furnitur being here of silver curiously wrought & double gilt, to an incredible value: Such, and so extraordinary was the Embrodery, as I never before saw any thing approching it, the reines & headstall crimson silk, covered with Chaines of silver gilt: there was also a Turkish royal standard of an horses taile, together with all sorts of other Caparison belonging to a Generals horse: by which one may estimate how gallantly & <magnificently> those Infidels appeare in the fild, for nothing could certainly be seene more glorious, The Gent: (a German) who rid the horse, being in all this garb.[104]

Envy of one imperial nation-state by another aspiring to emulate such power and splendor is exquisitely palpable in this passage. Evelyn's admiration of the Turkish horses suggests how patently unfair he found the circumstances that enabled infidel foreigners to possess a monopoly on such extraordinary creatures. Not only their beauty but their characters and temperaments appeared superior to those of European horses, in Evelyn's view. He recalled what the Habsburg ambassador Ogier Ghiselin de Busbecq had reported of Turkish grooms and horses, that nowhere in the world were horses more kindly treated than in the Ottoman

Figure 6. This portrait of an Ottoman groom with a *Yedek* (led horse) captures something of Evelyn's description of the beauty of Ottoman turnouts. From an Ottoman costume book, ca. 1720s. © Copyright the Trustees of the British Museum.

empire, and as a consequence, no horses were fonder of their masters or more obliging: "There is no Creature so gentle as a *Turkish* Horse; nor more respectful to his Master, or the Groom that dresses him. The reason is, because they treat their Horses with great Lenity."[105] The "churlishness" of European grooms, by contrast, produced intractability in spirited horses.

Evelyn's horseman's eye also registers the military potential presented by the horses, caparisoned as they were in such beautifully fashioned but warlike "furnitures." An ironic touch is lent by the exhibition rider's being a fellow European—a German—although he is dressed like a Turk. The Westerner successfully disguised by his Oriental kit is a trope that recurs throughout British writing on the East, perhaps most powerfully realized in the closing pages of John Buchan's thriller *Greenmantle,* as we have seen.

So much for horses as spoils of war: most imported bloodstock entered the country by way of mercantile connections.[106] English families with a merchant or consular official on the spot in Aleppo were likely to be the most successful, though ambassadorial appointments at Constantinople proved fruitful too. The ambassadors William, sixth Lord Pagett, in 1703 and his successor, Sir Robert Sutton, in 1709 shipped Eastern horses to England,[107] as did Lady Mary Wortley Montagu and her ambassador husband Edward Wortley Montagu on their return journey in 1718. "Took aboard four our embasadors horses," wrote Nathaniel Morrison, the Master of the *Preston,* in his log for 2 July 1718.[108]

Most famously, the merchant and consul Thomas Darley exported the Darley Arabian from Aleppo to his father Richard at Aldby Park, Buttercrambe, near Leeds, in 1704. The circumstances of his acquiring the horse remain a matter of dispute, but some high-handed or under-handed dealing may have been involved. In 1791 the *General Stud-Book* reported that Thomas Darley had become "member of a hunting club, by which means he acquired interest to procure this horse."[109]

Certainly Aleppo merchants went hunting; it was their chief outdoor pastime and took them into the deserts and mountains where they would be likely to meet local tribesmen. Nathaniel Harley did not mince words regarding the importance of equestrian pursuits for Levant Company members—it was their only recreation, and it provided them with a vicarious sense of home, especially if they could supply their horse-fancying, huntin'-mad families in England with Eastern bloodstock. As Nathaniel wrote bluntly to his brother Edward "Auditor of the Imprest" Harley in 1710, "We have no other Diversion here but on horse back & therefore You may easily imagine how we value & esteem our Horses wch are hard to be got, yet for my part whenever it is my fortune to meet wth one thats good, the better he is & the more I like him, the more I wish he were wth you."[110] Hoping for fresh company from England, Nathaniel offered his (great) nephew Robert Harley, then a pupil at Westminster School, the chance, if he made the voyage to Aleppo, to "go a Hunting twise a weeke Hawking and Coursing as often as You Will, and what is more you Shall always ride Such Horses as my Lord Harleys Dun."[111]

Thomas Darley wrote to his brother Henry at Aldby in North Yorkshire, 21 December 1703, concerning the Darley Arabian's importation. The letter suggests how tricky such shipments could be. For a year and half, while awaiting a chance to send him home, Thomas Darley had kept the colt, who would soon be four years old and was "of the most esteemed race amongst the arrabs both by syre and dam, & the name of said race is call'd Mannicka":

> The only fear I have at present about him is that I shall not be able to get him aboard this war time, tho I have the promise of a very good & intimate friend, the Honble & Reverend Henry Bridges, sonn to the Lord Chandos, who imbarkes on the Ipswich Captn William Wakelin, who I presume will not refuse taking in a horse

for him since his Brother is one of the Lords of the Admiralty, besides I designe
to go for Scandn [Scanderoon] to assist in getting him off, wch if I can accomplish
& yt he arrives in safety believe he will not be much disliked for is esteemed here
where could have sold him at a considerable price if had not designed him for England.[112]

According to Lady Anne Blunt, there remained at the end of the nineteenth century "a tradition" among the Anazeh Bedouin regarding horses "of the Managhi
strain, having been purchased by a 'Gonsool Franji' (English Consul), one Daali
or Daalia (Darley) of Halep (Aleppo), 'min Zeman' (long ago)."[113] Such was the
reputedly unbroken continuity of oral history in the desert where horses' pedigrees and fortunes were concerned. William Youatt mentioned in 1831 that the
horse had been "bred in the neighbouring desert of Palmyra."[114] At what point
Thomas Darley's hunting club's interest with the locals gave way to the motif of
theft remains unclear, but in the most recent recitation of the Darley Arabian's
story, Rebecca Cassidy remarks that the horse:

> was owned by Sheikh Mirza II [of the Fedaan Bedouin] when British consul Thomas
> Darley caught sight of him and arranged to buy him for 300 gold sovereigns. Ap-
> parently the sheikh backed out of the deal and so Darley arranged for British sailors
> to steal the horse and smuggle him out via Smyrna.[115]

British sailors stealing from Bedouin tribesmen and then transporting a horse
hundreds of miles from Aleppo to Smyrna (Izmir)—by sea or overland? history
does not relate—may sound implausible, but some credence may be lent to the
theft motif by the evidence of Nathaniel Harley of the Levant Company.

As we have seen, Nathaniel Harley's letters home from Aleppo offer detailed
evidence of early eighteenth-century horse dealing and the sharp practices necessary to exportation from under the very noses of the Ottoman authorities. Finding the sort of horses that would be liked in England was not easy, and certain
horses could be subject to a prohibition on export if they might be destined for
the sultan's stables or fancied by a local Ottoman official. Nathaniel wrote a
Christmas letter to his brother Edward in 1705, remarking that he was confident
of achieving the shipping end of things if the right horse or horses could be located. He had been in Aleppo for nearly twenty years, since December 1686, and
found the equine shopping left something to be desired:

> I will do what I can to find both a Horse & Mare of the true Arab race, but I almost
> despare of meeting such as will please in England Having seen very few Since I have
> been Abroad, that I could think worth sending home, It being almost impossible to

find a just Horse, There being something always wanting Either before or behind, Or else ye Limbs; Could I meet wth such as I desire I should think I could not purchase 'em too dear, and would contrive some way or other to Send 'em you.[116]

When they could be found, purebred mares fetched high prices: "[F]ive Hundred even to a Thousand Dollars is as common a price as twenty or thirty Bunds [i.e., pounds or punts (silver ingots); *OED*] is in England, And the difference in their Shapes not so great as perhaps you may imagine."[117] The English ambassador Sir Robert Sutton also reported from Constantinople on 27 May 1708 that "the difficulty of finding handsom Arab mares is incredible."[118] The Arabs, who were "all robbers," according to Sutton, depended on their mares for their livelihood, and these mares were shared among "five or six people, and valued at most extravagant rates, 3, 4, or £500 sterling being a common price for them, and when a Frank appears to buy them, the price is always most unreasonably enhanced."[119] *Frank* was a general term for Europeans; the export market was booming.

Nathaniel did indeed contrive to find, as well as to send home, likely horses. Between 1706 and 1715 he successfully shipped at least three cargoes of horses to his family in England.[120]

By 1715, Harley was congratulating himself on having found a truly superior example of what the East could produce. Writing to his brother regarding the horse that would become known in England as Lord Harley's Dun, Nathaniel congratulated himself on being the only Englishman capable of master-minding such a stunning achievement as the exportation of this celebrated stallion:

Wanting fresh Letters from Scanderone I know not whether there will go more then one Horse, If there Should I am Sure you will admire and with a great deal of reason Laugh at me for being at the Expence of Sending such a poor Scrub as the Little Arab, But besides that he is something of a Favourite, I must Inform You that under the Pretence of Sending him a way I hope to get off the Dunn or Cream Colt, which is a Horse that has made more Noise and been more taken Notice of here then I desired, And has had the honour of being Visited by the Turke Himself incognito—who would have had him for the Grd. Sig.'s own Stable, So that 'twas no longer in my Power to keep him, and I believe 'twould not have been in the Power of any body else to have sent him away, for upon the first notice of it Three Expresses have been sent after him, and all the passes of the Mountains between this and Scanderone Ordered to be watched, and ye Marine Strictly guarded to prevent his being Ship'd off I have heard of his being got Safe to the place where I ordered him, But Shan't be easy till I hear He is got a board the Ship, for till then I can't think him Safe. Notwithstanding he has many Faults which I could wish were mended, Yet if he has the good fortune to come to you safe I believe few such Horses have ever come to England, Twould be too tedious at this time to give you the whole History of him and his Race, which I shall reserve till I am so happy as to See you.[121]

Faults or no, the Dun was a smash-hit in England. Nathaniel's nephew Lord Harley reported gleefully that the horse was "thought by all that have seen him to be the finest Horse that ever came over."[122]

What exactly was this horse's breeding? "The whole History of him and his Race" is never related in the Harley correspondence. Like other imports from Aleppo, he is often referred to by contemporaries and, later, by historians of the Thoroughbred as "the Harley Dun Arabian." However, dun or cream is an unusual color among purebred Arabians. The artist Bridget Tempest, who specializes in portraying today's Turkmen horses, Akhal-Tekes, speculates that, based on the evidence of John Wootton's portrait and Nathaniel Harley's letter, with its mysterious omission of the horse's "Race," the Harley Dun might well have been a Turcoman or Turkmen. Tempest observes of the Turkmen that they sometimes "have a distinctive shimmering golden coat, just like that of the horse in Wootton's splendid portrait."[123] Lord Harley's Dun sired the Harley or Oxford Dun Mare, from whom many good racehorses, including West Australian, Wisdom, Flying Fox, and Persimmon descended.[124] In the Harley Dun, then, we might find further evidence, to add to the example of the Byerley Turk, that the Ottoman empire contributed Turkic as well as Arabian bloodlines to the richly hybrid mixture known as the Thoroughbred.

Five years after shipping the Dun, Nathaniel Harley would engage in further anxious correspondence regarding the shipping of the Bloody Shouldered Arabian, as we shall see. There could hardly be more telling evidence of imperial envy expressed through the trade in equine bloodstock. This letter exemplifies how stealing or appropriating as much as learning from Ottoman culture was a *modus operandi* by which "his lordship's Arabian" or indeed "his lordship's Turk" came to England.

The rise of the English Thoroughbred as the supreme exemplar of that geographical cline, the blood horse, has traditionally been told as a Restoration story, beginning in 1660. The more particularly we inquire into the origins of the Thoroughbred, however, the further back we need to go, both in terms of the actual importing of horses and in terms of the mingling of Eastern strains with so-called English stock. The Englishness of the famous English racers was as much a fiction of national identity as was the consumption of coffee and tea as quintessentially English drinks. Cromwell was at least as interested in the fabled horses of Turkey and Arabia as was Charles II. The century between 1650 and 1750 was the crucial period of trading in imported Eastern bloodstock, including stealing horseflesh away from the lands of the Grand Signior. By 1750, the Arabian had achieved "the zenith of its success."[125]

After 1750, and the founding of the Jockey Club in that year or in 1751,[126] the concerted effort to import horses from the Levant began to dwindle. From mid-century onward, the equine gene pool dominated by the progeny of multiple generations of Arabians, Turks, and Barbs was considered sufficient in itself, no longer in need of refreshment from desert or steppe. By 1782, horses sired by Arabians were in some races, such as the Cumberland Stakes held during the First Spring Meeting at Newmarket, allowed to carry weights lighter by three pounds than horses got by English stallions.[127] Imperial envy of the Ottoman empire was also on the wane, and the Levant trade had been superseded by the trade with India. English mercantilism and imperial aspiration achieved a new global assertiveness and sublime confidence. This new identity would often be exhibited on the back of the "through-bred English horse," the English *kuhaylan*, whose equine superiority owed its very existence to the Long Restoration romance with the East.

CHAPTER FOUR

About a Horse

• • •

The Bloody Shouldered Arabian

The Arabian is worth his weight in gold.

—Isaac Hobart to Lord Oxford, 1728

On a chilly February day in 1717, Nathaniel Harley once again found himself with a likely horse on his hands. And once again, orchestrating a safe passage for the horse from Aleppo to England presented Nathaniel with a logistical conundrum, beginning with the watchfulness of the Ottoman authorities, who were at that moment pursuing a policy of prohibiting such exports with some vigor. A willing captain and suitable ship could also be hard to organize, but Nathaniel was confident he had made the proper arrangements. Timing and stealth were of the essence. Nathaniel wrote to his brother Edward "Auditor" Harley as follows:

> This being only to Acquaint you that I have Sent downe to Scanderowne a Horse to be ship'd aboard the Onslow, But can't tell whether He can be got off or not, The prohebition being very Strict at present. If he comes safe He will arrive in a very proper time to recover his Voyage. He is a Gordeen Horse and of the best breed among 'em, I bought him from under a Beg, (or Lord) of the Mountains when He was only Two Years and a Half Old; And He's now only ffive next Grass, He's smal & besides other falts, His Ears are large and ill set on, And only One of his Testicles yet come down, But he has got divers Colts, and the Gordeens would fain have him again for a Stalion, the Breed being so well known & so much Esteemed.[1]

It was Nathaniel's way to emphasize a horse's faults rather than broadcast his good qualities. Even after years of horse-dealing and exporting from the Levant, he was still uncertain of the reception these Eastern creatures would find back home. It was better not to excite undue expectations, in his experience. The dun colt shipped five years before had been a tremendous success, regarded upon arrival in England, according to his nephew Edward, Lord Harley, later the second Earl of Oxford, as "the finest Horse that ever came over."[2] He was far from certain that the gray stallion would meet with such immediate approval. And yet he had great hopes for this horse, so well thought of by the tribesmen who had bred him, and of such a rare and highly valued breed. The Arabs were extremely fastidious about breeding, about maintaining the purity of antique lineages. This horse was considered extremely desirable as a sire by the "Gordeens," the Jedran tribesmen.[3] He was strong, he was intelligent, he was finely made, if rather small, and he was very fertile, in spite of having only one descended, visible testicle. What mattered that his ears were rather long? They were not coarse or common ears; they were the finely wrought ears of a blood horse.

Still, it was better not to be fulsome. The gray would have to prove himself once he had survived the voyage to England. Although life among the expatriate merchants in Aleppo turned, sometimes maddeningly, around horses, their spirit, their speed, their boldness in hunting, their ability to pass on these qualities to their progeny, and, inevitably, the expense and worry of their upkeep, a horse was only a horse. To an Englishman in England, with estates to manage and a nation to lead, a foreign-bred horse was an exotic being, but still only a horse. Nathaniel added a slightly deflationary turn to the closing of his letter to his brother, reminding everybody, including himself, that horses were commodities, if rather special ones:

He goes recommended to Mr. Kingstone, As dos also a Barrel of Ciprus Wine, Both which he will take Care to Deliver to You.[4]

In spite of Nathaniel's ingenious strategizing, the horse arrived in Scanderoon (Iskenderun) too late to catch Sir John Williams's ship the *Onslow,* and so Nathaniel endeavored to get him another passage immediately. On 15 May he wrote to his brother to this effect, for the first time venturing to elaborate tentatively on the horse's good qualitites:

Nor indeed should I have sent him but that he is of a Celebrated Race among the Gordeens, From whom 'tis difficult to procure a Horse, the Race being in a manner lost among them, this Horse has no great Speed but is strong and would serve well for the manage being very easy to learn anything, you may please to dispose of him as you think fitt.[5]

Unfortunately, this effort too was foiled, this time by rough weather and rumors of war. The war in question, in which the Ottomans were frequently caught up, had been going on for years between Peter the Great of Muscovy (Russia) and Charles XII of Sweden, in alliance with other "Northerners," as Caroline Finkel observes. In this conflict, there had been truces between the Ottomans and both sides, but Ottoman aid was most frequently sought by Charles, and had it been refused, the Ottomans would have found themselves once again embroiled.[6] Nathaniel wrote to Edward on 18 May:

> The Horse I intended for you I sent to Scanderone in order to be put aboard the Ship, but he is this Morning returned hether again; the Sea as they tell me being soo Ruff to Ship him off, But I beleive the true reason is, The Apprehensions, of a Warr with Sweeden haveing made the Capt. unwilling to incomber his Ship with a Horse and the necessary provisions for him.[7]

It was not until 6 January 1720, three years after his first attempt, that Nathaniel finally succeeded in getting passage for the gray stallion, who had by this time matured into a very fine horse. Still Nathaniel was cagey, fearful of overselling the one he had chosen from among so many others, and of whom he had grown fond:

> By Capt. Oliver I Send a Grey Horse that I have had by me more than four Years, And have two or three times attempted to Send away but have been disappointed, And I think I wrote You of him before. He is of the Gordeen breed of which there's few now Remaining, And is the Chief cause of My sending him, He is of great Spirit but no great Speed, Wou'd Soon learn anything in the Manage, He has got Colts tho but One of his Testicles is come down, I bought him of a Beg of the Gordeens When he was only two Years and Half Old, And because you Will Observe A Redish Stain on One of his Shoulders, Which is now much wore Out but when I bought him was as red as Blood, I Will give you the Account the Owner of him gave me without afirming it to be true. The Owner, he told me, of the Mare that brougt this Colt was a Robber on the Road and being much Wounded he leant over his Mares Neck And his blood ran down upon her Shoulder And She being then with foale of this Colt, He had this mark on his Shoulder, Whether true or False I can't tel but the fellow answered very readily When I Demanded the cause of it. I Will say no more of Him But that He has a good Body, a fine Long Well Shaped Neck, A pair of Glistering Eyes, And Stands upon four good Leggs; Which I Hope may Make amends for any falts that may be found in him.[8]

Beauty and utility were exquisitely fused in equine form. Nathaniel did not expound upon the horse's promise as a racehorse, hedging his bets on that score. He emphasized his spirit, intelligence, beauty, soundness, and rational aptitude for learning the discipline of the manège. Fifteen years before, at the beginning

Figure 7. In John Wootton's portrait of *The Bloody Shoulder'd Arabian* (1724), the horse's Eastern origins are clearly represented, as is the connossieurship of his English owner. Wootton, inventor of the English equine portrait, painted the Bloody Shouldered Arabian at least nine times, more than he painted any other horse. Private collection.

of his search for horses to export, Nathaniel had cautioned his brother that "next to choosing a Wife for a man, The most difficult thing is to please him with a Horse."[9] In the case of the Bloody Shouldered Arabian, Nathaniel Harley need not have worried about his choice. He had proved remarkably successful in his horse-trading endeavors. Despite many plans and promises, Nathaniel never returned to England, dying in Aleppo of a fever on 17 July 1720, several months after the safe arrival in England of the gray stallion for whom he quietly harbored a strong affection and high hopes. And who bore on his shoulder a strange mark, the mark of romance, the mark of the desert-born, the mark of the fleet of foot, to whom the Arab raiders entrusted their very lives.

Precious Cargo

Within three years of his arrival in England, the Bloody Shouldered Arabian was painted by the country's foremost portraitist of horses, John Wootton (fig. 7). There he stands, bright-eyed, intelligent and noble looking, commanding the space around him. He champs softly on his bit, ready for action. In the many existing versions of his portrait, the Bloody Shouldered Arabian is always the same, though his circumstances and attendants vary. He is the still point of a turning world, timeless equine perfection. The horse's nobility is easily recognizable in the way his head is portrayed as higher than that of any of the human figures around him. The painter John Wootton (1682/83–1764) has here performed an ironic reversal of the code by which Sir Anthony van Dyck in his hunting portrait of Charles I, *Le roi á la ciasse* (1635), famously lowered the king's horse's head to near ground level so that the dismounted king, who was rather short, could stand above him.[10] Even when pictured with aristocrats and gentlemen rather than grooms, horses like the Bloody Shouldered Arabian are masters of all they survey.[11]

The Bloody Shouldered Arabian had arrived in England in the spring of 1720, destined for Nathaniel's nephew Edward, Lord Harley (1689–1741), who in 1724 would succeed his father, Robert Harley, and become the second Earl of Oxford. John Wootton painted hundreds of horse portraits—indeed, he pioneered the equine portrait in England—and he painted more versions of the portrait of this horse than of any other.[12] There would be more famous Eastern sires in eighteenth-century England, but the Bloody Shouldered Arabian became a cultural icon. The circumstances of ownership in which the horse found himself, Wootton's obsession with his likeness, and the horse's own peculiar qualities conspired to create a certain effective immortality.

Equine Commodities

A cultural biography of the Bloody Shouldered Arabian might stand as a first installment toward an eventual social history of Eastern blood horses as they came to dominate equestrian culture in early modern Britain. Ironically, it is only possible to write a cultural biography of this horse, insofar as it is possible, because of the multiple ways in which he was commodified. Arjun Appadurai's sense of the potential exchangeability of all entities, their eternal potential for commoditization, opens up a way of understanding the nature of the evidence we have regarding the Bloody Shouldered Arabian—in Harley family letters, in oil portraits, and in racing records and pedigrees.

Exotic foreign horses like the Bloody Shouldered Arabian were regarded in complex ways, as both fellow creatures and immensely valuable cargo, as beautiful animals and the inspiration for artistic representation. Both the horse and the picture of the horse are what Appadurai calls *"incarnated signs,"* goods whose "principal use is *rhetorical* and *social*," and which respond to a necessity that is, as well as aesthetic, "fundamentally political."[13] Drawing out the implications of Marx's model of the commodity form, Appadurai suggests a number of ways by which commodities become animated social agents—signs, rhetorics, aesthetic objects, and political counters—even as, according to Marx, human social relations become reified, de-animated, in their production and exchange.

A horse can never be a commodity in the way that entirely interchangeable objects such as consignments of wheat or copper are. Indeed, as Lisa Jardine and Jerry Brotton have argued, horses were traded individually, like precious works of art.[14] Bearers of precious genetic material, blood horses were given further "figurative meaning" by their representation in portrait medals, tapestries, sculptures, and paintings.[15] Moreover, as sentient beings, horses also required "a more complex response from, and relationship with," purchasers than did inanimate objects, however precious, and so cannot be classified as commodities in the strictest sense.[16] Yet horses were bought and sold, generated income through stud fees and the sale of progeny, and occasionally won money through races and wagers. Appadurai helps explore the complexity of the Eastern blood horse as simultaneously a traded commodity and an inspiration for sporting art, as a repository of precious genetic material and a recreational vehicle, as a valuable possession and a living creature whose health and well-being were of paramount importance.

It was because the Bloody Shouldered Arabian was commodified in so many ways that we know anything about him. He left a trail of evidence, verbal and visual, that was unusual for the equine kind.

Being and Well-Being

Most early modern horses appear only in lists. Before the Bloody Shouldered Arabian arrived at Welbeck Abbey, an account of the horses there had been drawn up in 1716. There were remnants of the Duke of Newcastle's stud, inherited by Lord Harley's wife, Lady Henrietta Cavendish-Holles, and the estate's other horses, under the care of two grooms.

Sixteen were kept in the stables and were "in pretty good order": "5 Stone horses" (three of them "fyne Stallyons"), "4 Geldings, 5 Mares," and "2 Stone Coults." Kept outside in "closes" were thirty-eight others: "11 brooding Mares, 4 foals, 4 Stone coults, 1 gelding, 1 Mare, 17 Hackneys." Like the stabled horses, these were under the care of the head groom Stephen Dickinson. A disturbing note is appended regarding the horses living out: "all of ym in a miserable condition, one of ym being blinde, & most of ye others are so bad yt they can Scarce Rise without help." It would appear that various equine pensioners who had been brood mares, riding horses, or carriage horses were kept alive at Welbeck, though in a less than salubrious condition.

Under the care of John Hancock were "About 1000 Sheep, 14 Cart, or Draught horses and mares, 3 Cows, 9 Also young foals"; here another anxious note of concern is sounded: "3 of ye Draught horses are blinde & 2 more are so old & so sake yt they can't live."[17] In the social hierarchy of horsekind, we notice, cart horses are classified with cattle and sheep rather than with riding and driving horses. Yet once again the old, ailing, and blind cart horses have been pensioned off and kept on in retirement. This provides some idea of the context in which the Arabian would be cared for and regarded.

The Arabian's welfare was always a cause of acute concern, and sometimes, clearly, of social tension among the stable employees. In July of 1727, for instance, John Cossen, Lord Oxford's steward at Wimpole, complained bitterly that the young under-groom Michael was not looking properly after the stallion during haymaking. We might detect a note of resentment on the groom's part that such special efforts needed to be made for the benefit of any horse. Cossen then asked another farm servant, Henry Flanders, to provision the horse properly; Flanders refused point blank. Nobody wanted to be bothered with providing the Arabian with the best of fresh provisions during such a busy time. Cossen wrote to his lordship, obviously disgruntled:

> A Week agone in very fine weather Michael the young Groom came in very hastily in ye middle of the day for Hay to be laid in the Stable for the Arabian, I told him the Carts were all at Work, so it coud not be done withal it woud be best for ye Horse to have a little of ye best Hay fresh every day and advised him then to bind & carry a small Bottle and so every day wch woud take up but a very little time He told me he woud not do it: I also bid Henry Flanders, he answered it were not his business since that I repeated it but to no purpose and told Michael I have known his Mother go near 2 Miles for a Bottle of Milk to help to bring him up. This morning I went into ye Stables and asked wt hay were given to the Arabian and answered of ye old rough Hay that had lain some time in the Stables. Had Mich: had any Love for the Horse or Duty to his Trust he woud not have neglected him so long, neither shoud he have done it twice had he mov'd readily at ye first tho not unreasonable to have such method continued. Early this morning I directed the House Laborer to carry to ye Arabian a Bottle of ye best Hay and so on for 3 or 4 times a Week.[18]

Only by directing a house servant, and not a stableman, could Cossen see to the horse's need for good fresh hay while standing in the stable. As we hear nothing further of the matter, presumably after haymaking had finished the stablemen returned to their routines.

"The Arabian is well" or "The Arabian is very well" was a postscript that ended many letters written to Lord Harley, later Lord Oxford, by Isaac Hobart, his steward at Welbeck Abbey, during the 1720s.[19] In 1722 Harley had requested a weekly update of his most treasured equine dependent's health whenever the horse was at Welbeck rather than at Wimpole, his preferred country seat, or at his London house in Dover Street. In the early years at Welbeck the horse contracted periodic eye inflammations attributed to colds and distemper, the remedy for which was to let blood.[20] During August 1727, while at Wimpole, the steward John Cossen reported that the Arabian was suffering from "Scabs" or "Knots" about the head and neck, perhaps caused by "being kept too much in Cloaths" during hot weather.[21] He was treated at least twice for an ailment that left his "Codd" or genital sheath enlarged, in the winter of 1724/25 and the summer of 1725.[22] Perhaps because he had been ill that year, he was suspected of having failed to get mares in foal during the 1725 breeding season. Since his popularity as a stallion remained undiminished, however, this may have been a groundless fear. Not having wintered well, in May 1726 the horse was described as having "fallen off very much,"[23] but requests for his services continued. The presence of only one visible testicle often gave cause for concern regarding potency, but the Bloody Shouldered Arabian reliably covered mares and produced foals throughout the 1720s.

Since most of the Welbeck horses suffered from lameness with dismaying regularity, it may seem surprising that there is no mention in Isaac Hobart's letters of the Bloody Shouldered Arabian ever being lame. His "four good Leggs" proved to be as Nathaniel Harley had promised, the hard, dry limbs of the desert-bred horse, with that extra density of bone that had impressed the Duke of Newcastle decades before. The duke had written (in his French treatise of 1658, translated into English in 1743), "I have experienced this difference between the bone of the leg of a Barbary horse and one from Flanders, *viz.* that the cavity of the bone in one shall hardly admit of a straw, whilst you may thrust your finger into that of the other."[24] As William Osmer opined, this greater density of bone was complemented by a greater size of tendons in relation to the dimensions of the leg, and the greater number, length, and fineness of the fibers in every muscle.[25] As a "Gordeen" (Seglawi Jedran)[26] the Bloody Shouldered Arabian clearly represented that most desirable geographical cline known as the blood horse.

Horses for Courses

Did the Bloody Shouldered Arabian ever race in England? The art historian Walter Shaw Sparrow finds him appearing as if part of a racing string in Peter Tillemans's *George I at Newmarket*, painted in 1722.[27] But there is, unfortunately, no definite evidence of his racing, and by the time the earliest racing calendars were being compiled by John Cheny in 1728, he would already have been retired to stud. Perhaps he raced, perhaps not, but he was certainly ridden. According to Hobart, whenever the time came for shifting between Welbeck and Wimpole or Dover Street in London, he had to be "rid,"[28] since he was likely to have been too much of a handful if led by a groom on foot or ponied from the back of another horse. Long before the horse's departure from Aleppo, Nathaniel Harley had recommended him as a riding horse, describing him as having "no great Speed" but as "strong," and predicting that he "would serve well for the manage being very easy to learn anything"; he later repeated that the horse was "of great Spirit but no great Speed."[29]

The question of speed in imported Eastern horses remains something of a puzzle. Obviously it was desirable, and some Eastern horses possessed it, or were thought to possess it. But very few imported horses actually raced and won in England. The fulfillment of their genetic capabilities appeared only in their offspring. Why Nathaniel Harley assumed that the Bloody Shouldered Arabian had no "great speed" we can only guess; perhaps he raced him in Syria.[30] The proof of the genetic pudding, as it were, appeared generations later in the racing calendars, which provide ample evidence that famous winners were increasingly bred from Eastern horses, including the Bloody Shouldered Arabian.

There is no doubt that the Bloody Shouldered Arabian was a popular sire. By 1723, three years after the horse's arrival in England, Hobart urged Lord Harley to send him to Welbeck as soon as possible since he was "very much wanted"; there were already mares belonging to other owners awaiting his services.[31] In 1726 there were requests for "leaps" or services from the fourth Earl of Berkshire and from Sir Gervas Clifton, in both cases on behalf of friends with likely mares.[32] If there had been a question about the horse's potency during the previous season, it seems to have proved a needless fear; his reputation remained unaffected. Mares belonging to the Duke of Bridgwater and the Duke of Ancaster were bred to him in 1729.[33] In one of the most intriguing moments of this correspondence, Hobart wrote to his lordship in April of 1728, "The Arabian is worth his weight in gold."[34] Hobart was presumably defending the gray stallion on the grounds of the excellence of his progeny, and perhaps also the income from his stud fee. Ironically, this letter was written one year after Lord Oxford had announced that he no longer intended to have any Welbeck mares covered by this horse.

Although the Bloody Shouldered Arabian proved to be both popular and potent, the size of his offspring remained a perpetual concern, especially as Lord Oxford himself became heavier and more difficult to mount. Oxford slowly grew disillusioned with the young horses he was getting by the stallion out of Welbeck mares, many of whom were not themselves of any size or particularly good producers. As Isaac Hobart lamented, "[O]ur Mares are Most of them old and Slight, nothing but Strong Mares can produce usefull Horses."[35] In 1727, Oxford announced that he no longer intended to cover any of his own mares with the horse, and he hoped to sell off most of the stock at Welbeck, "except the young Arabian mare and the old Dunn Pad Mare."[36]

However, as we shall see, certain events during the breeding and foaling season of 1728 and then later at the racecourse that summer may have caused a change of heart, and Oxford ordered a "grey mare," presumably the young Arabian mare, to be covered by the Bloody Shouldered Arabian at Wimpole in March 1729, before selling the stallion on.[37] Just before his departure from Wimpole that spring, the horse was serving as a tourist attraction for young gentlemen who came out from Cambridge to view the estate. On 8 April, John Cossen reported that two Mr. Foleys, the eldest son of the Duke of Montrose, and another man had a very enjoyable day out, having seen

> the Chappel, Library, were all over the house, spoke in ye praise of every thing but most of the 2 first viz ye Chappel and Library: They see the Gardens Somerhouses and ye Arabian, afterwards drank a Glass of White Wine eat some bread & some very good Cheese (and I gave their Servants some Strong Beer), they refusing any other eatables, as the hours being late made away for Cambridge being very well pleased abt. 2 a Clock.[38]

"His lordship's Arabian" remained a rarity, a curiosity, and a notable presence in the countryside.

Despite his success at stud, the Bloody Shouldered Arabian did not end his career in Oxford's ownership. The horse was sold to Charles Seymour, sixth Duke of Somerset, in the spring of 1729. The Duke wrote to Lord Oxford that he gave a hundred broad pieces, or £115, for his "old Arabian stallion called Bloody Shoulder," and expressed a wish that Oxford would "give orders to his servant at Wimpole to deliver the horse to a groom he will send from Newmarket to receive it, and to ride, or lead him away for Petworth, according as the horse hath been most used to."[39] John Cossen reported to Lord Oxford from Wimpole, "Fryday last came the Duke of Somersets Servants for the Arabian wch Michael delivered upon their producing Your Lordships Order they went for St Albans that night and next day (I am told) onwards for Petworth."[40] A casualty of the decline of Welbeck as a breeding establishment and of Lord Oxford's increasingly severe financial cramp, the horse was embarking on a new stud career, where he would embody a famous eighteenth-century literary trope, as we shall see.

Decades later, the Bloody Shouldered Arabian, far from being forgotten, had become a proverbial name in racing circles, as a letter in *The Connoisseur* of 1755 somewhat archly suggests:

> The pedigrees of our race-horses have been always preserved with as much care and exactness as the Tree of Descent among the family of a Spanish grandee or Polish nobleman; nor does the Welchman derive greater honour from proving himself the fiftieth cousin to Cadwallader or Caractacus through a long line of David Ap Shenkins, Ap Morgans, Ap Powells, Ap Prices, than the horse by being half-brother to the *Godolphin Barb,* or full cousin by the dam's side to the *Bloody-shoulder'd Arabian.*[41]

Pedigree mania, joked Mr. Town's Cambridge correspondent, was all the rage. In the thirty years since Defoe visited Bedale races, laxity and ignorance had been replaced by genealogical obsession. The fact that imported horses' pedigrees, and empirical knowledge of the horses included in them, remained a mystery possessed only by their Eastern breeders rather than their English owners, adds to the absurdist comedy. Yet it is significant that the Bloody Shouldered Arabian sprang to mind in 1755 as a suitable complement to Lord Godolphin's horse, who was the most famous racing sire of the day and had died only two years before.

Thus far the written evidence, meticulously recorded in spidery eighteenth-century hands, and the evidence of painted images. Understanding what this evidence might *mean*, however, requires investigating more fully than we have done so far the status of "Arabians" as both equine commodities and sentient beings in England during the eighteenth century.

The Harleys as Patrons and Collectors

English horse fanciers fancied not only horses but horse pictures and sporting art. Portraits of Robert Harley, first Earl of Oxford, and his son Edward, the second Earl, now grace the vestibule outside the Manuscripts Room of the new British Library, where a great deal of the family's massive personal archive, the Portland Papers, is housed.[42] And through the many boxes of the family's correspondence runs an ink and paper trail of devotion to, obsession with, and vast expenditure upon horses as well as historical, literary, and artistic artifacts, some of them featuring horses.

The Harley family, who enjoyed political favor and high office under the Stuarts but were marginalized by the Hanoverians during Sir Robert Walpole's regime, appear to have been the most archivally minded of English peers. Robert Harley, the first Earl, one of Queen Anne's ministers, was imprisoned in the Tower for possible treachery when the Hanoverian succession came to power. He it was who began the famous Harleian collection of manuscripts and rare books, as the diary of Humfrey Wanley, the family's librarian, testifies.[43] Today the Harleian collection enriches the holdings of the British Museum and British Library. In 1713, Edward, Robert's son, married Lady Henrietta Cavendish-Holles, an heiress, sportswoman, and descendant of the Duke of Newcastle, who brought to the marriage the estates of Welbeck and Wimpole as well as some five hundred thousand pounds.[44] Edward spent her cash lavishly on collecting until funds ran out.[45] By 1734 he faced bankruptcy.[46]

Between 1714 and the late 1720s, when Edward started to find himself in straitened financial circumstances, partly as a consequence of his collecting, Wootton painted more than forty pictures for him. Twenty of these were still owned by the family in 1936 when Harley's descendant, the sixth Duke of Portland, had the collection catalogued.[47] Many are sporting pictures, some portraits of dogs, but the most spectacular are portraits of horses, some of them life-sized. Although there is no record of how much Wootton was paid for the Bloody Shouldered Arabian's portrait, other horse portraits were billed at rates between ten pounds fifteen shillings and forty guineas.[48]

Equine Portraits between East and West

By the second decade of the eighteenth century, a new genre, the equine portrait, had begun to appear on the walls of country houses and as popular prints. Equestrian portraits were traditional, but equine portraits, though not without precedent, were a revolutionary idea. Newmarket racing first inspired English horse portraiture, following the Restoration of Charles II in 1660.[49] Between 1710 and 1730, horse portraits became common, with Wootton the leading exponent.[50] The most notable European models were the frescoes commissioned from Guilio Romano by Federico Gonzaga (ca. 1527–30), for the Palazzo del Te in Mantua, featuring Barb stallions who had won races.[51] Racehorses were thus the first horses to be figured and heroized as individuals in Italy, as well as England. But there had been Oriental precedents for equine portraits as well, in sixteenth-century

Persia and, within a few years, in Mughal India.[52] And the first English equine portraits were painted of imported Eastern horses—Arabians, Turks, and Barbs—and their racing progeny.

Examining horse portraits for evidence of what the horses actually looked like, and hence of how they were bred, is a risky business. There is a high degree of painterly stylization, and many of Wootton's horses look alike. Yet, I would argue, there must also have been a degree of realism, since Wootton's patrons and audience were often practically minded horsemen, country gentlemen as well as aristocrats, who viewed the pictures as representations of horses to be judged, as the horses themselves were often judged, according to empirical, pictorial criteria. That is to say, the aesthetic of horse portraiture in Wootton's pictures combined practical with decorative elements and considerations.

The importance of the horses as winners is conveyed through their emphatic superiority to all that surrounds them. As Walter Shaw Sparrow observed of Wootton's portrait of Bonny Black, painted in 1715, "There is a contrast so emphatic between the great filly and her environment that . . . [a]ll is accessory to Bonny Black"; she "dominates with the immense vigour of a black silhouette."[53] Sparrow went on to distinguish decorative art from exact portraiture, a distinction with which I wish to quibble. "Here is decorative art," he concluded, "not exact portraiture."[54] However decorative they may be, Wootton's paintings were also precise renderings of the ideal to be sought in equine flesh in the early eighteenth century, and that equine ideal was a decorative as well as an athletic and intelligent one.

Wootton appears to have been fond of the Bloody Shouldered Arabian, of whose likeness he kept a copy and to which he often returned as a subject. Those who could not obtain the stallion's services at stud might still hang his painted image on their walls. The version commissioned by Edward, Lord Harley in 1724, the year in which he succeeded his father as Lord Oxford, shows a groom wearing a turban (fig. 7). In 1914 the sixth Duke of Portland purchased an almost exact replica of the Harley-commissioned portrait, signed by Wootton and dated 1723, bringing the total of Wootton's pictures in the 1936 catalogue to twenty-one.[55] Painted a year before Harley's version was painted, the 1723 version is likely to be the earliest of Wootton's multiple portraits of the horse, unless both derive from an earlier—and currently unknown—original.[56] Apart from the groom's headdress, the two portraits are nearly exact replicas of one another. The making of copies from an original portrait was standard practice for Wootton.[57] It was a more lucrative alternative to engraving, and very few of Wootton's pictures were engraved—only one set of prints appeared during his lifetime, and not more than a dozen have since.[58]

"Speed on legs" might be the theme of Wootton's portraits of this horse, embodying the equine ideal that held sway at Newmarket and elsewhere. This is particularly ironic, given Nathaniel Harley's assumptions about the horse's capabilities. He had tried to avoid disappointing his relations by not talking up the horse too much before his arrival in England, and by mentioning his faults in advance—that he had only one descended testicle, possessed no great speed, and that he was "smal & besides other falts, His Ears are large and ill set on." But there is no evidence of these characteristics in Wootton's portraits. Rather, the "good Body," "fine Long Well Shaped Neck," "Glistering Eyes," and fine upstanding appearance upon "four good Leggs" are emphatically featured. The eyes particularly suggest high spirits, keenness, and intelligence, the qualities of a clever as well as good-looking, athletic, fast horse. Learning anything in the manège, we should recall from Cavendish's strictures, required not only spirit and intelligence but also a high degree of rationality and a willingness to be taught and to learn. These qualities will follow the Bloody Shouldered Arabian all the way to Petworth and beyond.

As portrayed by Wootton, the Bloody Shouldered Arabian conveys a tension between the foreign and the naturalized that encapsulates the paradox of the English Thoroughbred horse produced from imported predecessors. In one sense the horse's Eastern origins are very much on the surface, and yet a certain Englishing of him has taken place. Not only does a horizontal strip of water appear in the multiple versions of the portrait, reminding viewers of the stallion's importation in 1720,[59] but the horse is usually accompanied by a man in Turkish or Arab dress and by a saluki, an Eastern greyhound. Nathaniel Harley had, in the winter of 1715, shipped home to his brother Edward "Auditor" Harley a saluki intended for his nephew Edward, Lord Harley.[60] The Ottomanness of the groom, in these versions complete with drooping Turkish moustache and turban or conical dervish hat, insists that the horse is not English. And yet the pictures represent the horse precisely as an English acquisition, as a sign of his aristocratic English owner's good taste and imperial acquisitiveness. If the Oriental atmosphere and antique ruins suggest a certain antiquity of background appropriate for figuring the horse's ancient lineage, an English audience would also be highly conscious of the lands governed by the Ottomans as trading partners and imperial rivals, for both good and ill.[61]

Thus some of the particulars of the horse's conformation and personal qualities may have been stylized away by Wootton, but others have been emphasized. When the horse portrayed is the Bloody Shoudered Arabian, his distinctive shoulder marking is always present. Bearing upon his shoulder this mysterious mark, a sign of the violence but also of the romance of the East, the Bloody Shouldered Arabian should be read as he was in his own day, as simultaneously foreign, exotic, and "of quality"—bearing the mystery of blood—and as a fine specimen of mechanical excellence, a poster child of the English agricultural revolution.

Not Blood but Keep

Decades before Robert Bakewell's experiments at Dishley, English and Welsh horse breeders were engaged in selective breeding.[62] Recent scholarship has suggested that not only should the agricultural revolution be understood as a much longer, more gradual process than its eighteenth-century publicists so energetically claimed, but that Bakewell's actual achievements have been exaggerated.[63] As Harriet Ritvo puts it, "Even the renowned Dishley sheep might come in retrospect to seem more a triumph of public relations than of applied science."[64] Even if we remain skeptical of the patriotic spin surrounding the production of the Thoroughbred, something did happen to horse-breeding in the British Isles between 1650 and 1750, and especially between the 1710s and the 1750s, producing what was branded as an iconically English horse. Like Robinson Crusoe, whose father's surname was originally "Kreutznauer" (he came from Bremen),[65] the progeny of Eastern imports were naturalized as English subjects within one generation, ready for reexport to other countries as English produce.

The "Englishness" of the Thoroughbred originated not in nature but in nurture, not in blood but in keep. "[C]areful attention to feeding on the new grasses," according to Joan Thirsk, gave size and substance to the imported desert stock.[66] For there was a sense that if the roots lay in Eastern empires far older than the *arriviste* island nation, the full flowering of the tree could only happen in the British Isles. With size and substance added by the more nutritious fodder of a northern European climate—pasturage and cereal crops that had themselves been improved by agrarian experimentation—the scene was set for the emergence of a super-horse. Paralleling John Locke's argument for colonization—namely, that labor invested in land gave one the right to claim that land—the new producers of the Thoroughbred horse claimed not only proprietary but originary rights. They were caring for the root, cultivating the potential latent in the original stock, and enabling it to flourish. Nature as such was subordinated to human manipulation, an important shift in relations with animals that occurred between the seventeenth and nineteenth centuries, as has been argued by Harriet Ritvo.[67]

Yet Blood Will Tell

A shift also occurred during the eighteenth century in the means of explaining why one horse raced better than another, to which the difference between Eastern horses and European ones was crucial. Genetic potential was encoded as "blood" in the seventeenth and early eighteenth centuries, signifying a mystery by which innate qualities were handed down from generation to generation. Horses were considered homologous with humans in a hierarchy of rank according to their birth. Such thinking, however, would be challenged during the course of the eighteenth century once anatomical investigations and the study of mechanics produced new ways of viewing the bodies and pedigrees of horses.

It had been known since the mid-seventeenth century that the bone density of the Eastern breeds known as blood horses was much greater than that of the heavier northern European breeds. William Osmer went further in distinguishing the mechanical excellence of "foreign" horses. For his chief example, Osmer dwelt at length upon the merits of the Godolphin Arabian, whose "shoulders were deeper, and lay further into his back, than any Horse's ever yet seen," while the "muscles of his loins rose excessively high, broad, and expanded, which were inserted into his quarters with greater strength and power than in any Horse I believe ever yet seen of his dimensions."[68] It was this mating of well-shaped racing machines with the proper proportion, symmetry of parts, elegance, and "texture," he insisted, that would produce winners; there was no mystery at all to "blood."[69]

Nevertheless, the notion that "Blood tells" would remain a maxim at Newmarket, and persists even to this day.[70] And it certainly applied to his lordship's Arabian during the Bloody Shouldered Arabian's lifetime. The popularity of portraits of the Bloody Shouldered Arabian doubtless owes something to the iconic status of his coat and markings in addition to the equine ideal represented by his fine shape. Scientific explanation would today call such a shoulder mark either the remains of a red chestnut foaling coat that had faded unevenly, or a concentration of marks known as "fleabites" that developed later, a rare effect usually found only in Arabians but that could occur in any breed that possesses the graying gene, since gray is not a color but a loss of pigmentation. But because this marking is normally only found in Arabians, it continues to serve as proof of purity of pedigree today, as evidenced by the many websites retailing stories of "bloody-shouldered Arabians" now available online.

In the 1590s, when Eastern horses were still rare in England, Gervase Markham presciently proclaimed that Arabians were infinitely superior to other horses, a breed apart, because of their purity of lineage. Markham's conceit for capturing the Arabian stallion's high breeding was to represent him as in himself constituting a "staine" on all other horses. His paces, athleticism, valor, and, naturally, purity of blood showed up what others lacked:

> Nowe to come to the true Stallion, who for his braue trot, and pure vertue of valure in the fielde, is a staine to all other Horses: whose comely and easie amble, may be an eternall instruction to all Aldermans Hackneyes, howe to rocke their Maisters into a sound sleepe, whose wonderfull speede both in short and long courses, may make our English Prickers hold their best runners but Baffles, who by nature hath all things perfect, nothing defectiue: him I hold a fit Stallion to breed on, and a fit beast for his Maister to hazard his life on, and this is onely the Courser of Arabia.[71]

"It is impossible to be chivalrous without a horse," the medieval historian Noël Denham-Young opined while investigating tournaments as preparation for war.[72] Markham gives us the Arabian as himself chivalrous, as a worthy companion in battle, worth wagering one's life on or entrusting one's life to. The true Arabian was not only without defect but showed up the "stain" of impurity in all lesser breeds. The Bloody Shouldered Arabian's "stain" might be understood within this discourse to signify both the pure blood of the desert and inherited noble character—after all, his dam had loyally borne away that bleeding robber.

The association of gray horses with pure blood and noble character also has an Islamic resonance that nowhere registers in the early modern English discourse but nevertheless contributes to the horse's signifying capacity as an "incarnated sign" on a more global scale.[73] In Shi'a Islam, the death in battle of Imam al-Husayn, grandson of the Prophet Mohammed and third Imam of the Shi'a, is memorialized on the occasion of Ashura, the tenth day of Muharram, the first month of the Islamic year. Popular plays known as *Ta'ziya* reenact the battle of Karbala, which took place in the Islamic year 61 (680 C.E.), and the suffering and death of al-Husayn at the hands of agents of the Umayyad caliphat.[74] The iconography surrounding the event's theatrical reenactment includes images of gray Arabians with bloody shoulders who represent al-Husayn's loyal steed, Zuljenah.[75] As recently as March 2003, on the eve of the U.S.-U.K. invasion of Iraq that would soon lead to another bloody battle of Karbala, posters appeared in the back streets of the old city of Istanbul, near Istanbul University, featuring a gray

Arabian stallion with a bloody shoulder and arrows protruding from his body, advertising a performance of the *Ta'ziya*. Once again the horse is loyal to and figure for the noble man, a religious martyr in this case.

The English view of breeding and equine character tends to see being a loyal servant to a human master as a rational choice rather than a sacred mystery. "We may not, perhaps, believe all that is told us of the Arabian," remarked William Youatt in 1831, "yet it cannot be denied that, at the introduction of the Arabian into the European stables, there was no other horse comparable to him."[76] The breed's distinction hinges on stories of loyalty and devotion, including Bishop Heber's report that his Arabian in India "is so fearless, that he goes, without starting, close to an elephant, and so gentle and docile that he eats bread out of my hand, and has almost as much attachment and coaxing ways as a dog."[77] The bishop concluded that this seemed to be "the general character of the Arab horses," who are not "the fiery dashing animal I had supposed, but with more rationality about him, and more apparent confidence in his rider, than the majority of English horses."[78] The Arabian struck many English people as such a reasonable being that he might be considered a confidante or friend as well as a loyal servant. Youatt records the traveler Major Denham's account of the "degree of derangement" he suffered at the death of his Arabian in Central Africa, an emotion akin to "grief," of which he felt "ashamed," but justified because the horse had been his "support and comfort,—nay, I may say, companion, through many a dreary day and night."[79] Such an exceptional horse transformed the notion of "companion species" into "second self."

Winner Take All

In England and Ireland, but also for a few peers and well-heeled gentlemen in Wales and Scotland, this special relationship could be best experienced not so much with a faithful hunter or riding horse as with a winning racehorse. Nothing could be finer than to appear at the races as the breeder of a winner or the owner of the sire of winners. Although the Bloody Shouldered Arabian did not found a line of racehorses that can still be traced through the male line, as was the case with the Byerley, Darley, and Godolphin stallions, he regularly appears in important Thoroughbred pedigrees. As Prior notes, among his offspring were Sir Nathaniel Curzon's horse Brisk, winner of several Royal Plates; and a mare, the granddam of the Old Tartar Mare, from whom was descended Queen Mab, dam of many winning horses bred from her by Lord Strathmore at Streatlam Castle, County Durham. He also sired the Duke of Bolton's horse Sweepstakes, who got the dam of Lord Rockingham's Whistlejacket, the subject of Stubbs's famous portrait now in the National Gallery in London.[80]

Besides Brisk, Sir Nathaniel Curzon also bred and raced a chestnut mare by the Bloody Shouldered Arabian; she came sixth out of a field of thirteen in the One Hundred Guineas King's Plate for five-year-old mares at Black-Hambleton in 1729.[81] The Welsh gentleman Watkin Williams Wynn, of Carnarvanshire, also had a racing mare, a gray, by the Bloody Shouldered Arabian, who came second out of seventeen in the same Royal Plate at Black-Hambleton in 1730.[82] These were taxing races with heats of four miles, carrying ten stone (140 pounds).

Lord Oxford never had the pleasure of such racing luck with the produce of his own Welbeck or Wimpole mares, but he appears in John Cheny's racing calendars as a racing patron during the years 1729–30. Although by now he was nearing bankruptcy, he no doubt basked in the reflected glow of good performances by certain of the Bloody Shouldered Arabian's progeny.[83] Indeed, Isaac Hobart's delight in April 1728—"The Arabian is worth his weight in gold"—appears to have been incredibly prescient.

That summer of 1728, the chestnut stallion Sweepstakes, foaled in 1722, owned by the Duke of Bolton and bred by the late Mr. Snell, went on to win race after race, beginning with the Hundred Royal Guineas at Salisbury on 4 June, for six-year-olds carrying twelve stone (168 pounds), which was "yielded to him upon his winning one Heat; there started against him only a Bay M. of Mr. *Grevil's,* call'd here *Creeping Molly* being the same that came 11th for the Mare's Plate at *New-Market,* in *April.*"[84] At the next King's Plate, held at Winchester on 15 July, Sweepstakes won again; this time his reputation preceded him, and he started alone.[85] At Lewes on 8 August he came second to the Earl of Halifax's gray horse Goliah in both four-mile heats of the King's Plate.[86] The climax of the season was the King's Plate at Newmarket. John Cheny reported:

> On the third of *October* the following four started here, for the twelfth and last King's Plate of the Year, consisting as usual of an Hundred Guineas, and free for six Year Olds, carrying 12 *st.*[87]

Sweepstakes was second in the first heat, but once his blood was up, he won the two following heats. This must have been an exciting race, with Sweepstakes's former conqueror, Goliah, coming third at best, in the final two heats, and the Duke of Hamilton's Victorious beating Sweepstakes in the first heat, and then coming second in the last two heats, giving him a run for his money. The only mare, the Irish sportsman Sir Edward O'Brien's Polly-Peachum, was distanced, or left behind by the field, sufficiently to be withdrawn from the race after the second heat. Sweepstakes had lived up to his name by making a nearly clean sweep of the summer's hundred-guinea races, and he went on to sire the dam of Whistlejacket, about whom more later.

Three seasons later, in 1731, Nathaniel Curzon's gray horse, Brisk, had a hard but exciting summer, coming second in the Royal Plate at York on 16 August, winning the 6 September Royal Plate at Lincoln, and then being lamed and distanced in the Royal Plate at Newmarket on 7 October.[88] Brisk put Nathaniel Curzon on the racing map, and nine years later, in 1740, Curzon was racing another gray horse, Young Brisk, perhaps a direct descendant.[89]

The evidence for the Bloody Shouldered Arabian's ability to endow his off-spring with speed and stamina is considerable, and compelling, whatever Nathaniel Harley might have thought of him in his youth. The Duke of Somerset must have been pleased with his purchase of 1729, since people throughout the racing classes were undoubtedly talking about the Bloody Shouldered Arabian during these years.

Winning Ways—Houyhnhnms?

The superior character of horses like the Bloody Shouldered Arabian may well have contributed to Jonathan Swift's notion that Houyhnhnms were rational animals and idealized English selves. The last eyewitness report we have of this horse dates from October 1729, after he had arrived at Petworth. His sterling— or golden guineas—qualities were still apparent. Those "Glistering Eyes" that had impressed Nathaniel Harley in Aleppo continued to suggest innate equine intelligence long after the horse's arrival in England. The Reverend James Bramston, a close friend of Swift and Alexander Pope, wrote to Lord Oxford:

> I lately saw your Lordship's old friend the bloody shoulder'd Arabian, & have the pleasure to inform your Lordship that that Right Honourable Stallion enjoys a comfortable state of health in his old age, I have a shrewd suspicion that that bright animal came originally from the HOUYHNNMS land, & that he has the address at this time actually to find a means through his interest with the pretty mares of great Britain to transmitt advertisements of consequence to Edel's land, Lewins land, & Nuyts land: He is undoubtedly a horse of great quality and fine parts. I am promised a leap next Spring & have nothing to do but to look out for a Mare of Some considerable family that may not be an un fit mistress for a horse of his birth and education.[90]

The original Houyhnhnm, or "whinnying one," may well have been an Arabian, and no Arabian was more likely to have been on Swift's mind in the 1720s than his friend Edward, Lord Harley's new acquisition of 1720, the Bloody Shouldered Arabian.

Swift was conjuring the Houyhnhnms into being between January 1722, when Henry St. John, Lord Bolingbroke, wrote "I long to see yr travels," and the end of 1723, by which time Part 4 of *Gulliver's Travels* had been written, as Swift indicated in a letter to Charles Ford of 19 January 1724.[91] Swift's creation of the Houyhnhnms during the very years that Lord Harley and other horse fanciers were seeking to improve their studs, often at vast expense and with mixed success, may well have obliquely satirized this obsession with superior equines and ideas of equine superiority. Given the racecourse as the test of equine nobility, as we shall see in the next chapter, Houyhnhnms, the "whinnying ones," may also be a pun on "winning ones."

Swift had been a member of the Harley circle from Queen Anne's reign and his friendship with Robert Harley, the first Earl of Oxford—Chancellor of the Exchequer and later Lord Treasurer—onward.[92] Swift and Wootton the painter were friends as well as members of the second Earl of Oxford's circle. Swift sought advice from Wootton regarding the illustrations for *Gulliver's Travels*.[93] Nathaniel Harley in Aleppo was also in touch with Swift through his brother Edward "Auditor" Harley, recommending a young man as suitable for the choir at St. Patrick's in Dublin.[94]

Swift frequently complained of horselessness himself.[95] Although he depended for his health regimen on having a good trotting horse, he appears to have been difficult to please.[96] Having been offered a horse from the Harley family stud in 1714, Swift must have been aware of the family's importations and efforts to improve their breeding stock.[97]

Three years after the publication of *Gulliver's Travels* in 1726, the story of the Bloody Shouldered Arabian's importation could be read as a journey from one island to another, from Houyhnhnmland to Great Britain. His progeny appear destined to be sent back to the very mainland that lies nearest the Houyhnhmns' island nation, according to the map that accompanies Part 4 of *Gulliver's Travels*. These "advertisements of consequence" sound remarkably like the documented exports of Arabs, Barbs, and Turks, only one generation removed from their Eastern origins, to Continental Europe under the name of English Thoroughbreds. The Dutch names "Edel's land, Lewins land, & Nuyts land" signal Dutch East India Company possessions in southeast Asia,[98] but they also sound the sense of a trip across the Channel to the Low Countries.

In Bramston's formulation, Islamic difference has been erased by Protestant sameness, just as Anglo-Dutch differences had been effaced by a common Protestantism in the Glorious Revolution of 1688–89. A begetter of advertisements for Britishness, the Bloody Shouldered Arabian became a naturalized foreigner and a patriot, just like William of Orange. Since his "great quality and fine parts" were indisputable, his "birth and education" had to be assimilated. After all, Arab blood was only the *root* of the finest breed in the world. And the Williamite conquest of Great Britain in 1688–89 might yet be rectified by infiltrating the Low Countries' equine culture and advertising English superiority to those heavy Dutch horses and Flanders mares. This is clearly a Tory fantasy that would appeal to Swift, in line with anti-Dutch jokes identified by Linda Colley.[99] Lest I be accused of over-reading the political context, Bramston, I might add, goes on in his letter to tell Lord Oxford that he had made a few alterations to his new poem, *The Art of Politicks,* a Harleyite Tory satire, and was about to publish it.[100]

If Houyhnhnms had been inspired by Eastern bloodstock, they became in turn a figure for representing the superiority of Arabians and other Eastern horses. Houyhnhmns would remain figures for civilized, rational equines for decades to come. So great had been the influence of horses like the Bloody Shouldered Arabian that plain old English stock would never look, or be, quite the same again. Nor would the English return to the manège for their imagery or equestrian inspiration.[101] Riding short, like steppe and desert horsemen, they would seek it in open spaces, on the turf and hunting field, where the legacy of horses such as the Bloody Shouldered Arabian could best be experienced.

CHAPTER FIVE

The Noble Brute

• • •

Contradictions in Equine Ideology, East and West

Instead of being obliged to drag through the dirt after the most
sluggish, obstinate, and despised amongst our animals, I was
mounted on the noblest that the earth contains, had him under my
care, and was borne by him over hill and dale, far outstripping the
wings of the wind.

—Thomas Holcroft

There is no Creature so gentle as a *Turkish* Horse; nor more
respectful to his Master, or the Groom that dresses him. The
reason is, because they treat their Horses with great Lenity . . . This
makes their Horses great Lovers of Mankind; and they are so far
from kicking, wincing, or growing untractable by this gentle usage,
that you shall hardly find a masterless Horse among them.

—Ogier de Busbecq

lthough they might at first seem entirely incompatible, nobility and brutality were the defining characteristics of his lordship's Arabian in early
modern England. No other animal except the human laborer suffered
from such a contradictory identity. Breeding for improvement from Eastern
bloodstock, in the light of Eastern ideas about horsemanship and relations with
animals, helped produce an imperial discourse in which humans and horses became increasingly interchangeable. One of the richest results of this discursive
convergence is Part 4 of *Gulliver's Travels*. Jonathan Swift's satire stands revealed
in the light of the transformations accompanying the arrival of Eastern horses as
even more brilliantly and presciently critical than it has previously been thought
to be. Its targets are imperialism, colonialism, mercantile capitalism, the agri-

cultural revolution—as manifested in intensified extraction from land, beast, and human laborer—and instrumental reason more generally.[1] Without explicitly saying so, Swift appears to be participating in the comparison of imperial styles of rule that arose in discussions of horse-keeping in this period, and in which European brutality was contrasted with Ottoman leniency.

The production of the Thoroughbred from Eastern stock in a mongrel mix of formerly separate Oriental strains parallels and prefigures the breeding of slaves and the proletarianization of servants and colonial subjects within the British empire. The human laborer, whether an African slave or a white British or Irish servant, was scrutinized and disciplined according to a racialized and genetically conditioned grid of valuation and judgment. Ironically, what counted as miscegenation among humans, and was deplored, could be celebrated within equine cultivation as producing perfection through an eclectic mixing of desirable characteristics, topped up with hybrid vigor. Those "highly adaptable" racial categories of the eighteenth century, as described by Felicity Nussbaum, continued to dispose of the equine species in ways that combined a sanguine view of racial mixing for the good of the English stock as a whole with a complementary emphasis on purity, signified by the *General Stud-Book,* beginning in 1791.[2] By the early nineteenth century, with regard to both human- and horse-kind, a more "vigorous attention to hybridity and mongrelization" had emerged, with a consequent hardening of racial prejudices against Africans and other subjugated peoples (heightened by the abolitionist legislation of 1807 and 1833), and a nationalist obsession with the purity of the Thoroughbred's by now imaginatively anglicized gene pool.[3]

Swift's representation of imperial logic and colonial damage both reflects and predicts the itinerary of British imperialism. *Gulliver's Travels* remains both prescient of things to come and highly topical, replete with booty from the venerable, and vulnerable, Levant trade, especially those equine imports. Once upon a time, the Houyhnhnms, so polite, mannerly, reasonable, and obliging, may have been more immediately attractive to the reading public than they have become with the arrival of the internal combustion engine.[4] Morally sensitive and ever tractable himself, Swift's Gulliver tries desperately to refashion himself to fit in with the civil society of equines upon whose shores he finds himself in Part 4 of *Gulliver's Travels.* Gulliver reflects that since horses "were the most generous and comely Animal we had," who "excelled in Strength and Swiftness," their fate was all too often a despicable one.[5] Uplifted by Houyhnhnm influences to the point where he cannot bear people, when Gulliver returns to England he takes refuge in the stables, purchasing two young "Stone-Horses" (stallions) and hiring a groom to look after them. Conversing with them for at least four hours a day, he is pleased that his horses understand him "tolerably well" and that, "Strangers to Bridle or Saddle," they live "in great Amity" with him and "Friendship to each other."[6] Thus Gulliver attempts to repair the damage done to Houyhnhnmkind in Britain and Ireland.

Common Brutality

Swift embeds within Gulliver's reportage to the Master Houyhnhnm a miniature indictment of contemporary horse-keeping practices, anticipating Anna Sewell's *Black Beauty* by more than a century. If horses happened to belong to "Persons of Quality," Gulliver recounts to his Houyhnhnm audience, and they were thus "employed in Travelling, Racing, and drawing Chariots,"

> they were treated with much Kindness and Care, till they fell into Diseases, or became foundered in the Feet; but then they were sold, and used to all kind of Drudgery till they died; after which their Skins were stripped and sold for what they were worth, and their Bodies left to be devoured by Dogs and Birds of Prey.[7]

To add insult to injury, Gulliver continues, appealing to Houyhnhnm sensitivities, these are the lucky horses. The others, the "common Race of Horses,"

> had not so good Fortune, being kept by Farmers and Carriers, and other mean People, who put them to great Labour, and feed them worse. I described as well as I could, our way of Riding; the Shape and Use of a Bridle, a Saddle, a Spur, and a Whip; of Harness and Wheels.[8]

Master Houyhnhnm wonders why the horses tolerate such treatment, and do not throw or roll on and crush their jockeys, who are mere "Brutes."[9] The dapple-gray Master Houyhnhnm is the only figure of governance and authority in the text, apart from the King of Brobdingnag, to show any interest in the outside world. The gray horse and the king, neither of whom is human, ironically "show the real humanist's eagerness to learn from strange experience."[10] Gulliver explains how horses were "trained up from three or four Years old to the several Uses we intended them for," that most of the "Males" were castrated "to take down their Spirits, and make them more tame and gentle," and that in any case these horses "had not the least Tincture of Reason any more than the *Yahoos*" did in Houyhnhnmland.[11] Swift takes a scholastic commonplace from his undergraduate days at Trinity College, Dublin, that man was *animal rationale*, with the property of reason, while horses were only *animal hinnibile*, with the property of whinnying, and inverts it.[12]

Appealing to his imagined equine audience, while reversing his human readers' presuppositions about human reason and animal irrationality, Swift makes
the familiar strange. He excoriates the injustice of class hierarchy, so thoroughly
infused within the body politic that it applies to horses equally with humans. In
the light of this de-familiarization, such common practices as the gelding of stallions to make them more tractable appear no longer to be mere matters of human convenience. They stand revealed from the Houyhnhnm point of view as vi-
olations of the natural order of things. In its brutality and unthinking use of living
beings as mere instruments of human convenience, Swift renders early modern
horse culture, like imperial mercantile culture more generally, repugnant.

Swift's was an early instance of what would become a staple trope of eighteenth-
century representation of animals, the exposure of human cruelty. In *The Adventurer* number 37 (1753), John Hawkesworth contrasted the lives of a donkey and a
horse to protest against both low and elite forms of abuse. The donkey, "the slave
of indigence," is worked and beaten to death, the horse, "the pride of greatness"
and "the favourite of caprice, avarice, and barbarity" suffers a more complicated
demise.[13] Once again, servitude has become slavery, and luxurious humanity ex-
ploits the living for profit. Having won a match race against a mare whose owner
offers double the stakes the next day for any gelding that can beat her, the racing
stallion is castrated by his greedy owner and immediately "mounted and spurred
on to the goal."[14] So great is his competitive spirit that the horse wins the race,
only to die at the finishing post. In the afterlife, the horse's ghost reports to the
donkey:

> Injured as I was, the love of glory was still superior to the desire of revenge: I de-
> termined to die as I had lived, without an equal; and having again won the race, I
> sunk down at the post in an agony which soon after put an end to my life.[15]

Overhearing this "horrid narrative" in a dream, the author "blushed that I was a
man."[16] In 1792 Hawkesworth's essay was reprinted to accompany *The Life and
Death of a Race-Horse* by Thomas Gooch, a series of prints modeled upon six paintings that had been exhibited at the Royal Academy in 1783. Like the series of four
aquatints after Thomas Rowlandson, *The High Mettled Racer*, of 1789, Gooch's illustrations graphically materialized Swift's exposé and Hawkesworth's.[17] The
Thoroughbred racehorse joined Hogarth's Rake and Harlot in a progress-to-
dissolution narrative. In the wake of Swift's prescient critique, a midcentury popular periodical discourse about cruelty to animals had become, by the abolitionist decades of the 1780s and 1790s, a visual program not only comparing but
connecting human and animal slavery as effects of empire and mercantile wealth

accumulation. The founding of the Royal Academy, though intrinsically linked to imperial aspirations, was also crucial to the dissemination of such images, as we shall see.

The gullible Gulliver, saturated with Houyhnhnm lore, turns the world upside down in a radical way, and in so doing reveals how animals, servants, colonial subjects, and slaves are all implicated in British imperial and mercantile aspirations. Swift has Gulliver, however absurdly, take it upon himself to rectify such injustices, reversing human-equine power relations. It is humans who will be trained to labor, horses will be kept and cosseted and do no work. Among the pacts Gulliver makes with himself after retiring from travel are (1) instructing his family in the Houyhnhnm virtues, insofar as he finds these particular Yahoos trainable or "docible Animals," (2) forcing himself to behold his own "Figure" in a "Glass," in order to accustom himself to bear looking at human bodies again, and (3) lamenting "the Brutality" of British and Irish Houyhnhnms while always treating "their Persons with Respect, for the sake of my noble Master, his Family, his Friends, and the whole *Houyhnhnm* Race, whom these of ours have the Honour to resemble in all their Lineaments, however their Intellectuals came to degenerate."[18] Here Swift distinguishes cruelty from brutality and returns "brutality" to its roots in brutishness or animal being. British Houyhnhnms—that is to say, actually existing horses—are cruelly treated because they are perceived to be mere brutes or animals. British Yahoos—actually existing humans—behave like brutes toward their fellow beings whenever they behave in cruel and unthinking ways, and that, for Swift, was most of the time.

In creating Houyhnhnmland, Swift reverses the intellectual capacities of horses and humans from the normativities of contemporary Britain. For his part, Gulliver hopes to "Houyhnhnmize" his little bit of England by treating horses with respect, in spite of their intellectual degeneration, and by continuing to value their noble lineaments as shared with the superior Houyhnhnm race. He will keep stallions, admire and talk to them, but never ride them. He will continue to smell of the stable, like his groom, whose company he prefers to any other human's, and his and the groom's conversation will be chiefly about horses. So far, so much like a racing stable or Thoroughbred stud. What this reversal reveals, ironically, is how, in spite of widespread abuses, there were little islands of Houyhnhnmland within the British Isles already. Gulliver is an affectionate parody of the horse-mad Englishman or Irishman, whether sporting aristocrat or professional horse-coper. The fraternity of Gulliver and his groom, bound together by their mutual obligations to the stallions in their keeping, is a microcosm of this highly masculinized world.[19]

In Gulliver's imagination, the bodies as well as the minds of horses and humans are counterpoised. Gulliver far prefers the "Persons" of horses to those of humans, forcing himself to stare in a mirror in order to break his imaginary identification with horse-kind. He has been fixed in a mimetic relation with horses for so long that he cannot bear his own form, or the sight of the image of his own form. Beholding his image forces him to confront his identity. His figure mimes the substance of his self. Swift would appear to agree with the psychoanalyst Jacques Lacan that the "mirror stage"—the moment of recognition by the young subject of his image in a mirror as a coming to consciousness of self-hood—is fundamental to the fabrication of identity. This trope will reappear in relation to blood horses, emblematized in the anecdote of how Stubbs's portrait of *Whistlejacket* was regarded by its subject as so lifelike as to *be* a mirror.

Houyhnhnms and the East

The complex web of geopolitical and comparative-imperial discourse about the superiority of Eastern bloodstock bears directly on Swift's conception of the Houyhnhnms, who are simultaneously noble and domestic, heroic and gentle, chivalrous and commonsensically rational. Astounded to discover the Houyhnhnms' intellectual sophistication and domestic manners, Gulliver in his first encounter with them parodies travelers' accounts of first meetings with native peoples in places remote from Europe. He then experiences a nice display of Houyhnhnm hospitality:

> The Horse started a little when he came near me, but soon recovering himself, looked full in my Face with manifest Tokens of Wonder: . . . We stood gazing at each other for some time; at last I took the Boldness, to reach my Hand towards his Neck, with a Design to stroak it, using the common Style and Whistle of Jockies when they are going to handle a strange Horse. But this Animal seeming to receive my Civilities with Disdain shook his Head, and bent his Brows, softly raising up his Left Fore-Foot to remove my Hand. Then he neighed three or four times, but in so different a Cadence, that I almost began to think he was speaking to himself in some Language of his own . . . I was amazed to see such Actions and Behaviour in Brute Beasts; and concluded with myself, that if the Inhabitants of this Country were endued with a proportionable Degree of Reason, they must needs be the wisest People upon Earth . . .
>
> . . . But I had no Time to pursue these Reflections; for the Grey Horse came to the Door, and made me a Sign to follow him into the third Room; where I saw a very

comely Mare, together with a Colt and Fole, sitting on their Haunches, upon Mats of Straw, not unartfully made, and perfectly neat and clean. The Mare soon after my Entrance, rose from her Mat, and coming up close, after having nicely observed my Hands and Face, gave me a most contemptuous Look.[20]

Swift's satire here operates by playing on the tropes that had entered discussions of horsemanship following the arrival of Eastern blood horses. These superior equines do not respond as expected to the English jockey approach. This time, it is the imperial gaze of the traveler, with an eye toward colonization, that has been reversed. These equine natives regard foreigners like Gulliver with an intelligent, seemingly human, look and converse among themselves in their own language. They epitomize domestication and, most miraculously from the stableman's point of view, keep their dwellings so conspicuously dung-free that they might just as well be human. They are above all rational, civil, hospitable to strangers unless provoked, and considerate of their fellow horses.

Houyhnhnms sound, according to Gulliver's account, remarkably like the Turkish or Arabian horses described by European travelers. Their political virtues of honesty and communitarian ideals—leading, with savage irony, to an ethnic cleansing of Yahoos—are accompanied by domestic virtues of the sort that were simultaneously attributed to the horses themselves and to the kindly care and attention they received from their Eastern grooms and owners. Such invocations of the superiority of the Ottoman system, whether of horse-keeping or other forms of governance, establish a contrast with European imperial ideology, the chief target of Swift's satire.

What the Habsburg ambassador to the Ottomans, Ogier de Busbecq, reported at first hand, William Cavendish reiterated from merchants' accounts. Both agreed that Muslim kindness toward animals trumped Christian harshness by producing astonishing results in equine behavior. Busbecq staved off melancholy by spending time in his stables among Ottoman horses and grooms. Here he discovered,

There is no Creature so gentle as a *Turkish* Horse; nor more respectful to his Master, or the Groom that dresses him. The reason is, because they treat their Horses with great Lenity. I my self saw when I was in *Pontus*, passing through a part of *Bithynia*, called *Axilos*, towards *Cappadocia*, how indulgent the Country-men were to young Colts, and how kindly they used them soon after they were foled; they would stroke them, bring them into their Parlours, and almost to their Tables, and use them even like Children . . . [A]nd the Grooms, that are to dress them, are as indulgent as their Masters; they frequently sleek them down with their Hands, and never use any Cudgel to bang their Sides, but in case of great Necessity. This makes their

Horses great Lovers of Mankind; and they are so far from kicking, wincing, or growing untractable by this gentle usage, that you shall hardly find a masterless Horse
among them.[21]

Anatolian countrymen, whether farmers or servants, treated their horses like
members of the family. Finding himself in an equine-centered state, where harmonious human-horse relations resulted in good behavior on both sides, Busbecq admired and learned from the Turks. Cavendish's account is Busbecq in
miniature, with a particular interest in Turkish horse-clothing:

The *Turks* are the most *Curious* in Keeping their *Horses* of any *Nation,* and Value
them, and Esteem them most: They have all the Wayes of Dressing them, and keeping them Clean, that can be Imagined. They Cloath them first with a Fine *Linnen
Cloth* and *Hood* next their Skin; then with a *Hair-Cloth* and *Hood,* Lined with Felt,
over their Linnen Cloth and Hood: And all these are made so Fit, as to Cover their
Breasts, and to come pretty low down to their Leggs. There cannot be a Better Way
than this for their Cloathing.[22]

More pragmatist than sentimentalist, the Duke of Newcastle passes quickly over
how the esteem of Ottoman grooms for their horses might lead to mutual attachment, and on to the usefulness of horse-clothing of the sort that would soon
play a major role in the training of racehorses in Britain. When Thomas Holcroft
described the elaborate horse-clothing in which stable lads like himself had to
dress their charges for sweating gallops, and when Samuel Chifney advocated
sweating horses to a razor-sharp leanness, both were describing practices inherited from the Turkic tribesmen of the Central Asian steppe.

Seeing Ottoman horses for the first time, John Evelyn, as we saw in chapter 3,
remembered how Busbecq had explicitly contrasted Turkish with European
grooms in terms of cruelty. Evelyn was perhaps thinking of the passage in which
Busbecq lamented how fear and physical force seemed the only resources of European grooms in their dealings with horses:

But, alas! our Christian Grooms treat Horses at quite another rate; they never think
them rightly curried, till they thunder at them with their Voice, and let their Club or
Horse-whip, dwell, as it were, on their Sides. This makes some Horses even to trem-
ble when their Keepers come into the Stable, so that they hate and fear them too:
But the *Turks* love to have their Horses very gentle, that, at a word of Command, they
may fall down on their Knees, and in this Posture receive their Riders.[23]

European horses, in the eyes of their European grooms, Busbecq recalls, must be
mastered by means of threats and punishments. Turkish horses, on the other

hand, serve humans willingly, even prostrating themselves on their knees from gentleness and love rather than fear. In Europe, brutality was everyday normality: Busbecq presents a chilling picture of European horsemanship. What Christian horse-keepers desired from their charges was cowed subservience: keeper here suggests the jailer or slave-driver. The Turks, by contrast, wished for an extremely close working relationship with their equine charges.

This contrast provided the basis for a comparative analysis of imperialisms and styles of rule, from which the European style came off badly. Ironically, images of the "cruel Turk" were refuted, or at least placed in uneasy proximity with this new idea about kindness toward animals as fellow creatures.[24] Europeans may have striven for nobility as against brutality in their self-governance and their discipline of the equine species. But brutality seemed to get the better of stablemen and their employers alike. The Ottoman way, so often characterized by the West as despotic whenever the power of the Sublime Porte was invoked, appeared suddenly both kindly and lenient in the light of the philosophy of horse-keeping.

The consequences of the "great Lenity" that Busbecq praised were a loyalty and willingness to serve that set apart Eastern horses from their European counterparts. The absolute attentiveness of Eastern horses to their riders' desires was legendary. This keenness to please often struck Europeans as a sign of great intelligence. Busbecq continued:

> They will take up a Staff or Club upon the Road, which their Rider hath let fall, with their Teeth, and hold it up to him again; and when they are perfect in this Lesson, then, for their Credit, they have Rings of Silver hung on their Nostrils, as a Badge of Honour and good Discipline. I saw some Horses, when their Master was fallen from the Saddle, that would stand Stock-still, without wagging a Foot, till he got up again. Another time, I saw a Groom standing at a distance, in the midst of a whole Ring of Horses about him, and, at a word of Command, they would either go round, or stand still. Once I saw some Horses, when their Master was at Dinner with me in an upper Room, prick up their Ears to hear his Voice; and when they did so, they neighed for Joy.[25]

This montage of images of cooperative dexterity, including horses circling obediently solely to verbal commands, and horses neighing with pleasure at their owner's voice, combines the discipline of the manège with what looks and sounds like equine enjoyment. These anecdotes from the Ottoman world are especially illuminating in their contrast with the tales of human cruelty and equine subjugation in Europe. The European, Christian regime of treating horses like brutes, even if in a noble cause, produced only cowed submission. The Ottomans, though regularly and reasonably accused of cruelty in some respects, were also something other: a source of alternative models for imperial rule over the colonized. Those silver rings in Ottoman horses' nostrils were at once a badge of servitude—indeed, slaves might be similarly accoutered—but they were also distinguishing marks of honor and affection.

Such tricks and gambols as Ottoman horses displayed, to use terms that the Duke of Newcastle might have employed, constituted the very repertoire of the horses who became famous in Europe for their superior intelligence, beginning in the 1590s with Bankes's Marocco, whose name hints at a Barbary origin.[26] All these horses had some association, however fanciful, with the East.[27] Gervase Markham explained in painstaking detail how Bankes could have got his "Curtall"—a horse with a docked tail—"to fetch and carry, either Gloue, Handkerchife, Hat, or any such like thing," to pick out particular people in the crowd, to count, and to guess correctly numbers whispered by bystanders to Bankes himself.[28] It was, Markham declared, "a rule in the nature of Horsses, that they haue an especiall regard to the eye, face, and countenaunce of their keepers, so that once after you haue brought him to know the helpe of your eye, you may presume he will hardly erre except your eye misguide him."[29] Or as S. R. put it in a pamphlet of 1614, what was important to note about Bankes and his horse was that "nothing can be done, but his master must first know, and then his master knowing, the horse is ruled by him by signes."[30] Long accustomed to humanizing contact that could be more intimate than European horses were used to, Eastern horses were thought to be particularly accomplished not only at reading such signs but at behaving with a willing compliance. Such methods of training, which could solicit from pupils such apparently happy engagement, might usefully be employed elsewhere, in governing far-flung territories.[31]

Once they arrived in Britain, however, Eastern horses and their progeny suffered a certain estrangement from the ideal of Eastern human-equine intimacy. Differences in fodder or "keep" and in "keeping" practices conspired to make the transition difficult for Eastern horses. In 1800, James Weatherby reported an Arab horse called Chillaby, belonging to the London riding master Charles Hughes, who had been taught to "fetch and carry, and perform divers other extraordinary feats, at command."[32] In the case of Chillaby, at least, a regimen of deprivation had to be followed in order to gain his full attention. It was "partly by diminution of his food, partly by keeping him from sleep, or working him in the night, and partly by lenient management," that "Mr. Hughes reduced him to that state of docility" necessary for him to perform these feats.[33] The fecund English countryside, with its lush and scientifically improved grasses and cereal crops, may often have gone to the heads of the imported horses, making them difficult if not completely unmanageable in their new circumstances. And it seems unlikely that without some trials and errors, the imported horses would have been able to persuade their English grooms to treat them differently from English horses. Learning from the Other that brutality did not pay was clearly the burden of Charles Hughes's "lenient management."

By the seventeenth century, European accounts suggested that Bedouin horse culture was, if anything, even more intimate with horses than was Turkic Ottoman culture. After Busbecq, the most often cited description of horse-keeping in the Ottoman empire was that of the Frenchman Laurence D'Arvieux, who had begun his diplomatic career in Syria in the 1650s. "Undertaken by Order of the late French King," D'Arvieux's account was first published in French by De la Roque and soon translated into English.[34] Fluent in Ottoman Turkish, Persian, and Arabic, D'Arvieux offered the first European eyewitness reportage of Arabian horses among the Bedouin. D'Arvieux's account was both as seemingly authentic a description as could be wished for by a European reading public, and the stuff of romance:

> The *Emir Turabeye* had a Mare that he would not part with for Five thousand Crowns, because she had travell'd three Days and three Nights without drawing Bit, and by that means got him clear off from those that pursued him. Nothing indeed was handsomer than that Mare, as well for her Size, her Shape, her Coat, and her Marks, as for her Gentleness, her Strength, and her Swiftness. They never tied her up when she was not bridled and saddled: She went into all the Tents with a little Colt of her's, and so visited every body that us'd to kiss her, make much of her, and give her any thing. She would often go over a heap of Children that were lying at the Bottom of the Tents, and would be a long time looking where to step, as she came in or out, not to hurt 'em . . . Those Mares are so us'd to live in that familiarity, that they bear any kind of Toying with. The *Arabs* ne'er beat 'em, they make much of em, talk and reason with 'em, and take the greatest Care imaginable of 'em.[35]

We cannot be certain whether Swift actually read either Busbecq or D'Arvieux. However, their works were very well known, much discussed, and frequently cited by other English writers. Swift is unlikely to have been unaware of reports of how matters equine and equestrian were differently organized in the East. In his imagining of Houyhnhnm manners and domestic arrangements, Swift appears to echo Busbecq's and D'Arvieux's accounts of Ottoman and Bedouin horsemanship.

Peculiar Nobility

Swift's imaginary equine civilization satirized the fantasy of civil equines that had become something of a vogue in the British Isles. From Gervase Markham onward, there had been, as we have seen, a growing strain of celebration in English writing of the noble qualities of the Arabian horse, other Eastern blood horses, and, by descent, the English Thoroughbred. Markham's hymn to his Arabian charger in the 1590s, when Eastern blood horses were still relatively unknown, had emphasized how the horse's character as well as athleticism showed up the faults in all other horses as if they were a blemish that bespoke impurity. The Arabian, "who for his braue trot, and pure vertue of valure in the fielde" was "a staine to all other Horses," had "by nature" "all things perfect, nothing defectiue." There was only one breed that Markham "did hold a fit Stallion to breed on, and a fit beast for his Maister to hazard his life on," and this was "onely the Courser of Arabia."[36] Parallel, though less celebratory, arguments would be made about the peculiar suitability of Africans for chattel slavery. Once Eastern bloodstock became better known in Britain, these characteristics of intelligent loyalty and willingness to serve, apprehended as purity of lineage, became part of popular discourse about those superior equines, horses of "quality."

Even the legend of the eighteenth-century highwayman Dick Turpin gained in romance when his gallant mare, Black Bess, was portrayed by William Harrison Ainsworth in the 1830s as "born of a desert Arabian, 'brought to this country by a wealthy traveller,' and an English racer, 'coal-black as her child.'"[37] Every detail of Black Bess's "make" in Ainsworth's description fulfills the promise of the blood horse as ideal partner in heroism—or romanticized crime (remember the robber on the road whose mare gave birth to the Bloody Shouldered Arabian): "'In make she was magnificent, every point was perfect, beautiful, compact'; 'look at her elegant little head'; 'she was built more for strength than beauty, and yet she *was* beautiful'; 'as to her temper, the lamb is not more gentle. A child might guide her.'"[38] Chivalry and Eastern blood were inseparable, as were Eastern blood and equine perfection.

Expectations of rationality among horse-kind were consequently on the rise during the eighteenth century, especially among the more enlightened sort. This is the cultural context within which we should read William Cowper's description of the traveler Misagathus and his horse in Book 6 of *The Task*, "The Winter Walk at Noon." The hot-tempered Misagathus, enraged by the piety of his fellow traveler Evander and determined to prove that he has no fear of death, attempts to leap his horse off a cliff. The horse very reasonably refuses to obey such an irrational command:

> But, though the felon on his back could dare
> The dreadful leap, more rational, his steed
> Declin'd the death, and wheeling swiftly round,
> Or e'er his hoof had press'd the crumbling verge,
> Baffled his rider, sav'd against his will![39]

The horse's survival requires distinct powers of reasoning as well as a defiance of human commands, according to Cowper. The horse's will is not to be thwarted here because the horse is in the right, and in his right reason. Not even the rider's brutal punishment can force this horse over the brink:

> . . . again he sought
> Destruction, with a zeal to be destroy'd,
> With sounding whip, and rowels dyed in blood.
> But still in vain. The Providence, that meant
> A longer date to the far nobler beast,
> Spar'd yet again th' ignobler, for his sake. (525–30)

Defying the implements of equine slavery, the whip and the spurs, which in Cowper's verse echo uncannily the implements of human chattel slavery, the horse emerges from this passage of *The Task* as distinctly nobler than the human brute treating him so cruelly. Cowper's investments in animal-kind will not allow Misagathus to escape unpunished from his own brutishness. Although the rider's rage is now quelled, and he resumes his journey along the road, forgetting his outburst, a storm is brewing, both in the atmosphere and in the horse's mind: "A storm was near, / An unsuspected storm" (544–45).

> His horse, as he had caught his master's mood,
> Snorting, and startling into sudden rage,
> Unbidden, and not now to be control'd,
> Rush'd to the cliff, and, having reach'd it, stood.
> At once the shock unseated him: he flew
> Sheer o'er the craggy barrier; and, immers'd
> Deep in the flood, found, when he sought it not,
> The death he had deserv'd—and died alone!
> So God wrought double justice; made the fool

The victim of his own tremendous choice,
And taught the brute a way to safe revenge. (549–59)

Cowper's moralizing gathers intellectual force from the idea that horses, particularly finely made and sensitive blood horses, were both rational and quick to respond to their riders. A contest of wills might then ensue. Cowper's poetic design celebrates the superiority of the traveler's horse while dramatically disposing of the rider. Misagathus has just too much of the brutal instrumentalist about him, too much of the cold rage that propels slave traders and overseers. He is morally inferior to a noble brute.

Newmarket Nobility

The world of racing epitomized equine nobility in close contact with servitude, both human and animal. As Thomas Holcroft, the radical writer who first earned his livelihood as a stable boy at Newmarket, remarked, racehorses represented "the noblest state of that animal's existence."[40] From being a poor and ragged shoemaker's son, Holcroft recollected, upon elevation to the post of Newmarket lad, he found himself "warmly clothed, nay, gorgeously, for I was proud of my new livery, and never suspected that there was disgrace in it." He was "voluptuously" fed, but most gratifyingly of all, he was "mounted on the noblest that the earth contains, had him under my care, and was borne by him over hill and dale, far outstripping the wings of the wind."[41] Holcroft worked for John Watson, the Newmarket trainer employed by Captain Richard Vernon. Between 1759 and 1763, aged fourteen to seventeen, Holcroft earned four guineas a year while learning to ride excitable horses during their four to eight hours a day of exercise. This exercise climaxed in what Samuel Chifney called "sweats" and Holcroft "brushing gallops," with the horses wearing body-clothing to sweat them thoroughly in the Turkish fashion. The entire regimen of care—mucking out, grooming, rugging-up, saddling, bridling, controlling the horses' food and water intake scrupulously—was designed to achieve a degree of hard fitness necessary for racing four-mile heats. Here was agency for the son of an itinerant artisan, aspirations fulfilled for a poor boy of the laboring classes. Except for the absence of intellectual stimulation, which eventually drove Holcroft to London and radical politics, Newmarket represented privilege and pleasure: "As far as I was concerned with horses, I was pleased; but I saw scarcely a biped, John Watson excepted, in whom I could find any thing to admire."[42] For Holcroft, Newmarket proved to be a kind of Houyhnhnmland.

However snobbish and hierarchical the racing world may have been in many respects, the racecourse also presented opportunities for cross-class exchanges. Professional horse-copers, from stable lads to jockeys, trainers, itinerant horse dealers, stud grooms, farriers, yeoman farmers who bred for the market, and hunt and other equestrian servants, regularly came from the lower ranks. That they mixed with the great on occasion could be part of the appeal of a world where those knowledgeable about horses, regardless of social station, were in demand. As Holcroft notes, before he grew tired of the lack of intellectual pursuits among his fellow stable lads—a trajectory that led to his eventual coming to political consciousness—he saw nothing wrong in wearing servant's livery. Like an Ottoman horse with a silver nose-ring, Holcroft wore his badge of servitude proudly. It was, for him, a sign of his belonging to the great world. Not surprisingly, Holcroft regarded *Gulliver's Travels* as his favorite book, though he admitted that, like the shoemaker who had lent the book to him, he failed to understand how much of it was not so much fantasy as applicable to the real world in which he found himself.[43]

Blood Horses as Partners in the Sporting Life

By the early nineteenth century, a certain self-congratulatory tone started sounding throughout descriptions of the by now thoroughly Anglicized blood horse. The English Thoroughbred had become a microcosm of all that was splendid and British, an imperial icon. However, rather than carrying a wounded rider to safety before expiring, in Arab or Ottoman fashion, the English Thoroughbred would be the willing partner of the British sportsman. The utility of blood had by now become primarily directed toward sporting pleasure, whether racing or hunting with hounds. The product of the equine agricultural revolution, the quintessence of enlightened improvement in breeding and management, was now a horse who actively enjoyed a partnership with sympathetic riders in such sports. In 1810, as T. Hornby Morland, an exemplary spokesman for this nineteenth-century attitude, rhapsodized:

> The Blood Horse, in grandeur and justness of proportion, surpassses all quadrupeds; neither ferocious nor carnivorous, he possesses the most engaging and admirable qualities: his noble spirit and native courage, attempered by his generous disposition, and attachment to man, entitle him to our particular attention; as of all animals, he seems best calculated to become the servant and associate of man. Although courageous and intrepid, he suffers not the natural vivacity and fire of his temper to carry him off with a furious ardour; but, from the generosity of his dis-

position, he regulates his motions, and kindly submits to the will of his master: he seems to participate of human pleasures, delivers up his whole powers when required, and encounters the greatest dangers, rather than disobey the mandates of his governor.[44]

The English Thoroughbred had, in short, become the tractable and yet vigorous beast of sixteenth- and seventeenth-century reports of Turkish and Arabian horses, only better. Morland particularized the Thoroughbred's distinctive combination of courage, competitiveness, and good manners as follows:

> When domesticated and familiarized with man, his manners become mild and gentle, his temper social: in the field, his force and ardour are conspicuous marks of emulation; he anxiously presses to be foremost in the course, he braves danger in traversing a river, or in leaping a fence or precipice; and it is remarked, that those which are most adventurous in these natural exercises, are the most generous, mild, and tractable, when reduced to a domestic state.[45]

These tropes—the horse being good-tempered rather than resistant "in a domestic state," and the horse behaving like a willing servant to man, manifesting nobility as much in tractability as in fiery spririts—hark back to early modern paeans to Eastern bloodstock. But now the blood horse had also proved himself on the racecourse and hunting field, T. Hornby Morland continues, anxiously pressing "to be foremost in the course," braving danger in "traversing a river" or "leaping a fence or precipice." Speed was of the essence as was bravery: both necessities for that spirit of expedition that characterized both the business and recreation of Britons. Attachment to humankind was now figured as natural, so long as the horses were enjoying those activities for which they had been fashioned, and at which they were bred to excel.

It was the thrill of being borne across country by a horse whose own pleasure lay in speed and displays of cleverness and courage that provided much of the appeal of modern fox hunting, which had evolved as a sport in tandem with the new breed of horse and new kinds of hound.[46] Blood horses, who could be ridden at liberty, and with liberty, and upon whom riders could entrust themselves to equine intelligence across difficult terrain, were the motors of the English hunting seat. Not everyone could pass muster as a racing jockey, but anyone who could muster a horse could ride to hounds. As John Adams would have it, "The system of riding adapted for racing, is exactly the same as the hunting seat, when rode in the stirrups."[47] If racehorses epitomized equine nobility, hunters popularized it. The hunting field democratized the English experience of a close partnership with a superior being who was nearly human in courage and intelligence. And all this appealed to a nation of people who had reason to believe themselves masters of the world.

The Contribution of Sporting Art to the Houyhnhnmization of Society

The equine obsession that Swift satirized in the 1720s, other writers and sporting artists, including John Wootton and George Stubbs, celebrated. Patronized by sporting aristocrats and gentlemen, Stubbs and other painters collaborated with their employers in a kind of horse cult. The racecourse and hunting field were seldom far from these people's imaginations. Their conversation was often chiefly of the stable. Even a chief minister might open letters from his huntsman before any other correspondence, as Sir Robert Walpole is said to have done.[48] Although there were satirical attacks by metropolitan intellectuals on Booby Squires—attacks that Henry Fielding found amusing enough to satirize in turn—elite culture in eighteenth-century Britain remained thoroughly saturated with horsiness, of necessity as well as by choice. And so long as artisanal and plebeian culture remained agrarian, or when urbanized, shared certain tastes with the more affluent,[49] it too was both horse-powered and horse-preoccupied.

The visual impact that "his lordship's Arabian" had on eighteenth-century painting proved a crucial measure of the influence of Eastern equine bloodstock on British culture and society. Between 1768 and 1772, just at the very moment when the Royal Academy was being founded, both Stubbs and Sawrey Gilpin in their different ways attempted to "houyhnhnmize" their horses, as E. K. Waterhouse observed some time ago.[50] "Perhaps Stubbs and Gilpin," he speculates, "were both trying to produce evidence that horse painters deserved equivalent ranking with face painters in the new foundation."[51] Fifty years after the Bloody Shouldered Arabian's importation, the blood horse of Arabian, Barb, or Turkish descent still offered the loftiest, most exalted image in the English horse painter's repertoire. Between 1768 and 1772, when Sawrey Gilpin painted scenes from Swift's *Gulliver's Travels,* he portrayed the Houyhnhnms as Eastern blood horses (fig. 8).[52] Compare Gilpin's horses not only with Seymour's and Wootton's (Figures 4 and 7) but also with Stubbs's *Mares and Foals in a River Landscape* (ca. 1763–68; fig. 9).

Consider the difference between the gray Master Houyhnhnm and the native, coarser-headed, rather hairy-heeled Sorrel Nag who befriended Gulliver and stands on his right. Gilpin's direct echo of an Eastern equine ideal in portraying

Figure 8. Gulliver's equine friends represent a range of types in keeping with the hierarchies of horse-kind in Houyhnhnmland, in Sawrey Gilpin's *Gulliver Taking His Final Leave of His Master, the Sorrel Nag, Etc., and the Land of the Houyhnhnms* (ca. 1768–69). Yale Center for British Art, Paul Mellon Collection. Photo: Bridgeman Art Library.

Figure 9. Notice the similarity between the gray mare on the right of George Stubbs's *Mares and Foals in a River Landscape* (ca. 1763–68) and the gray Master Houyhnhnm, a masculinized version with a larger crest, to whom Gulliver defers in Gilpin's picture. © Copyright Tate, London 2003.

Gulliver's Master reminds us that although Swift's satire ostensibly figured the land of rational equines and savage hominids as a land down under, Houyhnhnm-land was not necessarily so very far from England or its colony, Ireland.

The imperial aspirations of the Royal Academy of Arts were clear enough in the odes and songs performed at its founding feast in 1769. The "Triumph of the Arts," by the Reverend Dr. Franklin, made the comparison to Eastern empires explicit:

> Whilst Eastern tyrants in the trophied car
> Wave the red banner of destructive war,
> In George's breast a nobler flame
> Is kindled, and a fairer fame
> Excites to cherish native worth,
> To call the latent seeds of genius forth.[53]

A red Ottoman banner directly inspires George III to nurture amongst his countrymen arts as well as arms. The contrast with rival empires and the metaphor of the Academy's founding as an act of cultivation—the agricultural revolution troped upon again—also appear in Mr. Hull's song, sung by Mr. Vernon. And in this song, the global imperial ambitions are made even more explicit than in Franklin's "Triumph":

> No more to distant realms repair
> For foreign aid, or borrow'd rule,
> Beneath her monarch's generous care,
> Britannia founds a nobler school,
> Where Arts unrivall'd shall remain,
> For George protects the polish'd train.
>
> So shall her sons in science bred,
> Diffuse her Arts from shore to shore;
> And wide her growing genius spread,
> As round the world her thunders roar:
> For he, who rules the subject main,
> Great George, protects the polish'd train.[54]

Now Britain needs no raw materials, rules, or inspirations from the East. The home-grown variety of arts, like native arms and naval fleets, will prove the envy of the world. As Robert Strange argued in the voice of "Plain Truth, a Lover of the Arts," the arts were as crucial to "securing" imperial power as any military agency:

Who contributes to establish an academy, contributes as effectively to secure the liberty and independence of his country, as he who pays an army, or mans a fleet; for it will be found, that every state has been soon subverted, after learning has been neglected, and the polite arts suffered, to decay.[55]

From its inception the Royal Academy of Arts had both an imperial and a public pedagogical mission, broadcasting the superiority of British arts as well as arms.

Swift's text, replayed in Sawrey Gilpin's illustrations, also contained local, partisan allusions as well as imperial ones. It is politically significant that the Nag, "who always loved me," as Gulliver proudly declares, is a "sorrel."[56] The horse who trod in a mole-hill at Hampton Court, throwing William III with fatal results, was named Sorrel, and sorrel horses became a code for Jacobite and anti-Whig and anti-Hanoverian sympathies.[57] The color hierarchy in Houyhnhnmland also "follows contemporary equine authorities" for whom the white and sorrel were ranked below the bay and the black, and the dapple-gray was regarded as the best sort of horse.[58] The Master Houyhnhnm, an equine philosopher-teacher, might also allude to Bolingbroke, Swift's English horse brought over to Ireland in 1714, when Swift came over for his institution as Dean of St. Patrick's Cathedral in Dublin.[59] This horse was named for Henry St. John, Lord Bolingbroke, no friend of Dutch or Hanoverian monarchs, who famously recommended that the ideal monarch be a philosopher as well as a "Patriot-King."[60] What further ironies might attach to Swift's comment that although Bolingbroke was a fine horse, he "hated riding him"?[61]

Swift's reversals of contemporary normativities at once distance us from the norm and theatricalize it. Houyhnhnmland reflects ironically upon a nation obsessed with horses, but also one in which that obsession was increasingly focused on matters of breeding, with its overtones of race and imperial genetic mastery. Particular strains or races of horses were being glorified as superior to native sorrel nags, and even to the human masses. Swift's satirical evisceration of the aristocracy was considered too inflammatory by his publisher Benjamin Motte and was edited for publication in the first edition of *Gulliver's Travels* in 1726. It was only in 1735, with George Faulkner's Dublin edition of Swift's *Works*, that the following passage was restored, in which Gulliver explains that contrary to Master Houyhnhnm's flattering assumption that he, Gulliver, must be of noble birth, Gulliver is proud to be one of the "lower Sort, having been born of plain, honest Parents," and:

That, the Productions of such Marriages [among the Nobility, who marry solely for Money] are generally scrophulous, rickety or deformed Children; by which Means the Family seldom continues above three Generations, unless the Wife take Care to provide a healthy Father among her Neighbours or Domesticks, in order to improve and continue the Breed. That, a weak diseased Body, a meagre Countenance, and sallow Complexion, are the true Marks of *noble Blood;* and a healthy robust Appearance is so disgraceful in a Man of Quality, that the World concludes his real Father to have been a Groom or a Coachman.[62]

Motte considered this double-barrelled accusation of aristocratic debility and illegitimacy to be venturing too close to libel, if not sedition. It certainly sheds new light on the aristocratic propensity for genealogical fetishism of the equine kind.

An Imperial Obsession: Breeding and Barbary

Within British equestrian culture, the exact breeding of a horse, when it could be determined, was a compelling topic of interest throughout the eighteenth century. Like the origins of the Thoroughbred as a whole, the history or pedigree or type represented by a particular horse was endlessly discussed and debated. The difference of the Eastern blood horse from common horses continued to be reiterated, as were the differences between and among Eastern races or types. Categorical distinctions were drawn between Arabians, Turks, and Barbs, though horsemen frequently disagreed about the precise characteristics of each. The eighteenth-century terminological wrangling about whether Lord Godolphin's horse was an Arabian or a Barb, for instance, continues to the present day. This fixation on breeding or type is an aspect of the culture of the horse that frequently eludes most lay people, including art historians, but like the vehement views expressed both pro– and anti–fox hunting, it testifies to an enduring element of what makes the British British, and especially the English English.

Equine race-typing always signifies. At the 2005 *Stubbs and the Horse* exhibition at the National Gallery in London, a picture from a private collection was listed as *Brood Mares and Foals* (1767–68), although the owner's frame in which it was displayed bore the label *Barb Mare and Foal*.[63] The appearance of this painting in the exhibition was something of a coup. In 1984 the picture was reported to be in "a staunchly private collection" and had never been exhibited or reproduced.[64] The *Stubbs and the Horse* catalogue confirms this, adding that, since Stubbs showed it at the Society of Artists in the spring of 1768, and again on 30 September of that year, in a special exhibition in honor of the King of Denmark's visit, "it appears never to have been shown in public."[65] The picture, which Stubbs exhibited as *Brood Mares and Foals*, was known primarily through Benjamin

Green's mezzotint version of 10 May 1768, in which the composition is reversed.[66] The unauthoritative title on the frame—*Barb Mare and Foal*—directs our attention to the nearly white gray mare with a very straight profile—not a dished face like an Arabian—and a thickish neck with something of a crest, and her smoky rose-gray foal, who are indeed the primary focus of the composition and lighted accordingly. This title may have no authority from the point of view of Stubbs's own records but evidently reflects what some owners of the picture thought it represented. The curators of the exhibition, who were naturally more interested in classifying Stubbs's paintings according to recurrent subjects or themes, of which "brood mares and foals" is a notable example, ignored the frame's racial labeling in favor of generic labeling.

In this particular picture, the mares and foals are portrayed in front of Creswell Crags, a rocky landscape to which Stubbs returned repeatedly, especially in his "houyhnhnmizing" pictures—such as *Lord Rockingham's Arabian, and a Groom* (1766)—and in those depicting lions frightening or attacking horses in the wild. The mare might be an individual portrait, or she might represent a type—a Barb—or she might simply be a mare with a foal, like the others in the picture, though they do not stand out as she and her foal do. She might have been the pride and joy of whoever commissioned the picture, as its origins are unknown, although its first owner was Colonel George Lane Parker of Woodbury, Cambridgeshire, brother of the third Earl of Macclesfield.[67] Another version of this mare's portrait, entitled *A Brood Mare Belonging to Mr. Shafto*, appeared in a drawing manual of 1798; there may have been a connection involving horse ownership between Parker and Jennison Shafto, who lived at West Wratting, near Cambridge and Newmarket.[68] Or the mare might represent what somebody, admiring Stubbs's expertise in these matters, thought a Barb mare ought to look like. Is the fact that the gray mare might be a Barb significant? Is her presence before the sublime Creswell Crags meaningful? Might the picture be further evidence that Stubbs associated Creswell Crags not only with wild landscapes but with Barbary landscapes in particular?[69] Might he have done so after visiting Morocco and witnessing a lion attacking a horse there, as was reported by T. N. in Stubbs's obituary in *The Sporting Magazine*?[70]

Whatever the case may be, as late as 1767–68, identifying the mare as a Barb was considered worth doing. Today it is no longer considered to be worthwhile information by the exhibition's curators. The fascination with Barbary bloodstock, however venerable, appears no longer relevant. Might there be a fear of racism attached to this reticence? As a consequence, the Eastern origins of English horses are once again submerged, the trace of the Eastern Other within the

English same once again forgotten. This is particularly ironic since elsewhere in the exhibition the Arabian origins of Thoroughbred horses are regularly emphasized. Two pictures of "his lordship's Arabian" are present: *Lord Grosvenor's Arabian Stallion, with a Groom* (1766–70; catalogue entry 49) and *The Marquess of Rockingham's Arabian Stallion, with a Groom* (1766; catalogue entry 51). They are both stallions, neither of them ridden, both of them shown with their courteous, serious, English grooms. A particular line of argument is being implicitly followed: the acceptable face of the Eastern origins of the English Thoroughbred is an Arabian sire. This line would certainly flatter the Arab patrons of racing, such as the Maktoum family of Dubai, without whose considerable investments in breeding and racing, through the appropriately named Darley Stud and Godolphin racing operation, the U.K. Thoroughbred industry would be greatly impoverished.[71] Mares remain relatively anonymous: generic broodmares, whose precise types or origins may be obscure, or may have been, in some cases, deliberately obscured.

If we follow the *Stubbs and the Horse* curatorial line in looking at Sawrey Gilpin's illustrations to *Gulliver's Travels,* we will assume that the gray Master Houyhnhnm is an Arabian, just as we will assume that the gray mare who mirrors him in Stubbs's *Mares and Foals in a River Landscape* is an Arabian. But if we compare Gilpin's gray with the so-called Barb mare in Stubbs's *Brood Mares and Foals,* we might see enough resemblance—especially in the head, neck, crest—to conclude that Houyhnhnms could be Barbs as well. The difference this distinction makes in painterly terms may be minimal, but in terms of accuracy within a horse-breeding culture it is important. Seeing Arabians everywhere means colluding with an Arabianization of the heterogeneous Eastern lineage that produced the English Thoroughbred from already Easternized "mongrel" origins.

"His lordship's Arabian" may or may not have been an Arabian, but he was certain to have been a foreign horse with a racing shape, a thin skin through which the blood vessels showed, and hard dry limbs. These characteristics of quality among the equine kind were also, in painterly terms, Houyhnhnm characteristics, thought to be genetic predictors of superiority in spirit, if not mind, as well as body.

Stubbs's Portrait of *Whistlejacket*

No horse picture of the eighteenth century is more radical in its houyhnhnmization of its subject than *Whistlejacket* (fig. 10).[72] Purchased by the National Gallery,

Figure 10. It would have amused Jonathan Swift to learn that George Stubbs's *Whistlejacket* (1762), a portrait of a horse completely free of human contact or control, has become a national icon, perpetually among the top ten most popular reproduced images at the National Gallery, emblematizing a "shared national culture." The National Gallery, London.

London, with the support of the Heritage Lottery fund in 1997, this life-size picture of a rearing, fiery-eyed chestnut stallion with a silvery mane and tail, silhouetted against a honey-colored background of contextless space, overpowers many other (human-centered) pictures in the gallery.[73] Most probably painted in 1762, *Whistlejacket* is almost certainly earlier than the houyhnhnmizing pictures Waterhouse had in mind, and predates the founding of the Royal Academy of Arts by six years. What this suggests is that even before the Academy came into being, Stubbs was already committed to elevating his art, including his horse pictures, to the same status enjoyed by the highest genres—history painting, which surpassed all others, and human portraiture, the specialty of Sir Joshua Reynolds, whose *Discourses* admitted the genre's inferiority to history painting but argued that portrait painters should strive to elevate and universalize their subjects nevertheless.

Much of *Whistlejacket's* power derives from the Oriental character of the horse: closely Eastern-bred, and largely Arabian-bred, though with a "Turkish" stallion and a "Barb" mare figuring significantly as well.[74] In his day, with regard to his lineage, the stories told about the horses of the Ottoman empire or the desert applied to him. Yet this horse is now understood by the British public as a great English horse, as an icon of Thoroughbred Englishness. In his day he was of course also perceived as an English product of improvement, as a creature manufactured in the British Isles in accordance with the tenets of the agricultural revolution.

Whistlejacket became a celebrated racehorse.[75] In his breeder Sir William Middleton's colors, he raced at Newmarket in 1756 and was narrowly beaten for the Jockey Club Plate by the Duke of Ancaster's Spectator, also painted by Stubbs (1765–66).[76] Middleton sold him to Charles Watson-Wentworth, second Marquess of Rockingham, who commissioned the Stubbs portrait and other important pictures. In 1759, in Rockingham's ownership, he won a match at Newmarket for two thousand guineas against Mr. Turner's Brutus, each carrying nine stone (126 pounds) over four miles, after which he was retired to stud. William Pick of York reported:

> This was an exceedingly fine heat, being strongly contested the whole four miles, and won by a length only. Whistlejacket was rode by John Singleton, and Brutus by Thomas Jackson, who both shewed great skill in horsemanship, and so jealous were they of each other gaining advantage at starting, that they called one another back several times.[77]

Whistlejacket clearly showed the same competitive spirit so praised by T. Hornby Morland—"force and ardour are conspicuous marks of emulation; he anxiously presses to be foremost in the course"—and described by Hawkesworth's racehorse in the *Adventurer* as "love of glory."

Perhaps the most remarkable instance of equine emulation on the racecourse was recounted by Thomas Holcroft, who offered the following anecdote as deserving "the attention of the philosopher, as an instance of deep feeling, great sagacity, and almost unconquerable ambition among horses; and which goes nearly to prove, that they themselves understand why they contend with each other."[78] That is to say, Holcroft offered this philosophically interesting anecdote of equine feeling, sagacity, and ambition as a houyhnhnmizing intervention in the debate about animal rationality. Forester, who belonged to Holcroft's employer Captain Richard Vernon, was a "vicious" horse with "foundered" (laminitic) feet who could only be looked after, and would only obey, Tom Watson, brother of John Watson, the Newmarket trainer whom Holcroft served as a stable boy. Vernon decided to match Forester against Jenison Shafto's horse Elephant. Shafto rode his own horse, while Forester was ridden by Watson. Neither of them trusted to a hired jockey, in other words. Forester's fitness was a problem. The horse had been turned out at grass because he was unsound. He was taken up and immediately put into work,

> and kept in training a sufficient time to qualify him to run this match; but it was evident that his legs and feet were far from being in that sound state which such an exertion required, so that we concluded he must be beaten, for the reputation of Elephant arose out of his power rather than his speed. Either I mistake, or the match was a four mile heat over the strait course; and the abilities of Forester were such, that he passed the flat, and ascended the hill as far as the distance post, nose to nose with Elephant; so that John Watson who rode him began to conceive hopes. Between this and the chair, Elephant, in consequence of hard whipping, got some little way before him, while Forester exerted every possible power to recover at least his lost equality; till finding all his efforts ineffectual, he made one sudden spring, and caught Elephant by the under-jaw, which he griped so violently as to hold him back; nor was it without the utmost difficulty that he could be forced to quit his hold. Poor Forester, he lost; but he lost most honourably! Every experienced groom, we were told, thought it a most extraordinary circumstance. John Watson declared he had never in his life been more surprised by the behaviour of a horse.[79]

Elephant, the less emulative, and so less honorable, horse, required hard whipping, while Forester powered himself against the odds of bad feet and limited fitness. This anecdote sheds light on the spirit of rivalry that is one of the most striking features of the story of Stubbs's painting of Whistlejacket's portrait: the portrait would not be as it is, according to Stubbs's own account, had Whistlejacket not responded so fiercely to what he saw as a painted rival.

In Holcroft's mind it was impossible to separate equine sagacity—that is to say, a degree of reason—from deep equine feeling. Both manifested themselves in profound equine ambition, including rivalry to the death. Among prey animals, in whom the fight or flight impulse is endemic, competitive swiftness is about individual survival. Horses were and are quite likely to resist being the last in a group, the last being the first to be attacked by predators. But in the context of racing training and competition, this survival instinct appears to have been transmuted into something nobler and more rarefied: the horse's seeking the glory of winning for its own sake. And to win at all costs could mean biting and fighting one's rival, when the fleetness machinery failed. These horses are emblems of Britain's imperial aspirations, produced by imperial breeding practices, and they display the qualities suited to imperial agents: extreme competitiveness, aggression, but also intelligence, and a confidence in their own superiority, founded on myths of blood.

The stories told about the painting of Whistlejacket's portrait, and about the horse's uncannily sensitive recognition of the painted image of himself as a rival, suggest something of the complex signifying power attributed at once to Stubbs's mimetic artistry and to the blood horse's powers of observation and intelligence. In the story Stubbs told his memoirist Ozias Humphry, we have a story of a literal, material, flesh and blood horse, and a painted image of a horse, a representation of a horse, encountering one another as if they were Gulliver and the Master Houyhnhnm in the imperial contact zone. Or as if they were Gulliver and his much loathed Yahoo-like image in the mirror. So perfect is Stubbs's art as a mirror held up to nature that the painted image serves as a kind of mirror stage for Whistlejacket. But horses being horses, and stallions, stallions, it is as a rival that Whistlejacket apparently perceived himself.

Because this account of the picture's composition comes from the single most authoritative source for Stubbs's life, his friend Ozias Humphry's manuscript memoir, it is worth quoting the scene of Whistlejacket's being painted at length:

> On the last day this Horse stood, which was so remarkably unmanageable that it was dangerous for any one but the person accustomed to feed him, to lead him from the stable, and to this Man only that task was entrusted.—The picture was advanced to such a state that Mr Stubbs expected to have finished the last sitting or rather standing, at a given hour: when his feeder was desired to attend & take the horse back to his Stall; but it so happened that it was completed before the appointed time, and the boy who held the horse for Mr Stubbs to paint was leading it up & down a long range of stables.—In the mean while, Stubbs had placed the picture advantageously against the wall to view the effect of it, and was scumbling and glazing it here and there, when the Boy, cried out, "Look, Look, Sir, look at the Horse!" He immediately turned around, and saw Whistle Jacket stare and look wildly at the picture, endeavouring to get at it, in order to attack it.—The boy pulling him back & checking him, till at length the horse reared up his head and lifted the boy quite off the ground: upon which he began beating him over the face with a switch stick, and Stubbs like-

wise got up and frightened him with his pallette and Mahl stick: 'till the Animal, whose tail was by this time turned towards the picture with an intent to kick at it, but being baffled and his attention taken off, became composed, and suffered himself to be led quietly away.[80]

When confronted with *The Grosvenor Hunt*, the old hunter in Stubbs's London showroom neighed with pleasant agitation at the artist's mimetic gifts. Whistlejacket, on the other hand, was shocked at seeing in a painted image of himself another horse, and therefore a rival. Whistlejacket seems to have been a spirited horse, who, like Forester, would only obey the stable lad he had chosen to obey, and who presumably treated him in a way he found acceptable. He was a winning racehorse with an independent mind rather than "a managed horse of service," in the Duke of Newcastle's terms. He was in both colloquial and technical senses, then, "unmanageable." His character was notably emulative, to borrow T. Hornby Morland's phrase, or sagacious and ambitious, to apply Holcroft's. As a racehorse, he learned not to suffer competitors to beat him. Presumably as a studhorse he brooked no competition either.

What could better demonstrate the virtues of an eminently realist aesthetic than judgment from the horse's mouth? Both the anecdotes concerning equine appreciation of Stubbs's mimetic genius were offered to Ozias Humphry in perfect seriousness, it seems, one by Mary Spencer and one by Stubbs himself, so they should not be ignored, however apocryphal they sound. Stubbs was happy for these stories to be broadcast, in which his art was proved to be so replete with scientifically achieved verisimilitude that horses themselves approved of it. These anecdotes have classical antecedents: the grapes that were so realistic that birds pecked at them. Such famous classical precedents for Stubbs's claims to a mimetic mastery testified to by animals intensify the already complicated position he espoused when he insisted that he always took his inspiration directly from nature and never from previous works of art or other artists, not even from the classical masters whom Reynolds recommended. The story of Whistlejacket's portrait may well reveal not only Stubbs's sense of the historical ironies of his position as a mere horse painter who was also an artistic genius, engaged in furthering the merits of his art while marrying them to scientific knowledge, but also his subversive wit at the expense of Royal Academy orthodoxies.

Whistlejacket might have been designed to engage with and confound Reynolds's *Discourses*, those lectures to young painters that set the tone for artistic ambition and advancement. Reynolds insisted on the need for painters to consider their art in the light of universal beauty, striving as much as possible, given their abilities and the genres of painting within which they worked, for something of the grand or heroic style epitomized by history painting. Above all, they were to scorn mere mechanical imitation or copying of nature. In his third *Discourse* Reynolds boldly stated, "Nature herself is not to be too closely copied. There are excellencies in the art of painting beyond what is commonly called the imitation of nature."[81] More devastatingly, at least for those students of the Academy who were still striving to achieve a good likeness in painting, he added that "a mere copier of nature can never produce anything great."[82] What was required was a mastery of ideal forms. "The *gusto grande* of the Italians, the *beau ideal* of the French, and the *great style, genius,* and *taste* among the English, are but different appellations of the same thing," Reynolds argued. "It is this intellectual dignity, they say, that ennobles the painter's art; that lays the line between him and the mere mechanick."[83] Painting should be invested with the artist's intellect, in the hope of engaging the intellect of audiences, thus removing the taint of art's associations with manual labor and tradesmen: "The value and rank of every art is in proportion to the mental labour employed in it, or the mental pleasure produced by it. As this principle is observed or neglected, our profession becomes either a liberal art, or a mechanical trade."[84]

Successful mimesis of the natural world, therefore, presented something of a paradox. All art depended to some degree upon deception of the spectator, but the greatest painting sought something grander than mere illusion or deceit. For Reynolds, only the "meaner artist" was "servilely to suppose that those are the best pictures, which are most likely to deceive the spectator."[85] John Barrell has observed how Reynolds's appeals to minds "not servile," minds capable of "emulation" of the lessons of history painting, complicated the ideal of the public sphere as Reynolds envisaged it. For Reynolds acknowledged that to work upon spectators, to move them to emulation of worthy action, painting required the visual equivalent of verbal rhetorical persuasion—the deception implicit in a visual likeness successfully mimetic to move an audience to emulation—and that acknowledgment jeopardized the social exclusiveness of Reynolds's concept of the public sphere. Barrell formulates the paradox thus:

> One disadvantage of the rhetorical aesthetic was that it could make no clear distinction between the responses of the learned and ignorant, even to heroic painting, for a successful picture, like a successful piece of oratory, would move or persuade every member of its audience. True, the learned could judge of the principles by which a successful painting had been composed, but this act of judgment had to be imagined as being made only after the initial, involuntary response, for if they were

prompted to judge a work even as they were being moved by it, it would cease to move them. The paradoxical result of this was that the vulgar, who in some accounts could be included among the "ignorant," might be more persuaded to emulate acts of public virtue, which they could not however perform, than the learned, who could perform them.[86]

In glossing *Whistlejacket* with the horse's response to the picture, Stubbs appears to outmaneuver Reynolds's strictures regarding the appropriate audience to be moved to heroic deeds through emulation. If the vulgar mass could feel moved by a spirit of emulation to acts of public virtue but were incapable of performing them, and this complicated the theory of how art might participate in constituting the public sphere, what might we make of Stubbs's widening of the debate about mimesis and emulation to include equine audiences? The spirit of emulation, as we have seen, distinguished blood horses from their common colleagues. If a painting was so lifelike as to deceive a horse into acting in a rivalrous and emulative fashion, that painting's powers of persuasion were indisputably great. The picture had clearly exceeded mere mechanical competence or sevile imitation of nature by an extraordinary ability to deceive, parodying Reynolds's theory and hinting at the social contradictions within it.

Although Whistlejacket was led away quietly, "baffled" and "his attention taken off," we cannot help but be aware that the horse's reported recognition of his own image as a flesh and blood horse confirmed that art could indeed be a mirror held up to nature. Like Gulliver looking in a mirror to reaffirm his Yahoo-status, when Whistlejacket sees himself, he finds a truth in painting. What is the horse in the portrait looking at, if not at a rival stallion? Whistlejacket successfully read Stubbs's codes. Putting the nearly finished canvas in a situation advantageous to viewing it, Stubbs invited his subject to take a look at his work. High-spirited stallions on the lookout for a challenge—and no doubt bored by being kept walking up and down—might well use any excuse for acting up. In this case the painted image was already of a horse doing just that, rearing with a keen and fiery look on his face. The pose echoes famous equestrian portraits of kings and princes. It is a naturalistic version of the *levade*, one of the airs above the ground of the *haute école*. In this case, however, the horse is portrayed as free of human control—not only unmanageable but unmanaged. His gaze at the viewer represents a challenge by a knowing, feeling, energetic subject. He is equine power and beauty unleashed.

Thus, before he was belabored about the head by the stable lad and Stubbs, and his "attention" was "taken off," the horse exhibited a humanlike and even rational attention to painting. He both saw and did not see "himself" in the picture. The picture both was and was not a mirror. It offered something even more material and embodied than a mirror could—not simply a reflection of the subject but an image of another horse, an Other, if you will. In the absence of alternative senses, particularly smell, the image was nevertheless vivid enough to the stallion's sight to communicate life and to stir the emulative fibers of Whistlejacket's competitive being.

How did Stubbs achieve (in the first place) such a pose and expression, an image of a horse that would elicit such an attack on the part of his subject? There may be a clue in Humphry's *Memoir,* and it connects the portrait of *Whistlejacket* with Stubbs's pictures of horses frightened by lions, his natural-historical but also Gothicized and romantically primitivist masterpieces. In a marginal note, Humphry reports that in order to paint the white-horse-frightened-by-a-lion pictures, Stubbs borrowed, through Mr. Payne the architect, a white horse from the king's stables. Stubbs then achieved the look of absolute terror in the horse, not once but over and over again, by a simple means:

> The expression of Terror was produced, repeatedly, from time to time by pushing a brush upon the ground towards him, and this aided by his anatomical skill enabled him to give the sentiment to this Animal which the picture represents.[87]

Whether it was an artist's paintbrush or a stableman's grooming brush, the brush in question, when pushed across the floor toward the horse, was sufficiently mysterious, threatening, uncanny, and unknowable for the white horse to be baffled by it. Put another way, the white horse was the sort of horse to be upset and terrified by what he did not understand, even when it happened repeatedly. He never got the joke, as it were. If recent speculation about the political allegory involved in the lion and horse pictures is correct,[88] Stubbs not only pleased opposition patrons, such as Rockingham, with pictures in which the white horse of Hanover succumbed to the lion of Britain, but also had a bit of private fun at the expense of one of George III's Hanoverian white horses. The white horse may be magnificent as an image of terror, and sympathetic as having fallen prey to a ferocious predator. But this story reveals the horse also as a bit of a fool.

No such story attaches to Whistlejacket's reaction to the image of himself, or to how his attitude in the portrait was achieved in the first place. He is allowed the dignity of recognizing his own magnificence within Stubbs's art through misrecognizing himself as another. The anecdote might easily have been invented by the psychoanalyst Jacques Lacan to illustrate his theory of the split nature of the subject, the spectral image of the Other that is irreducibly necessary for the subject to recognize himself as such—the it within the I.

But the political allegorical dimension of the lion-and-horse pictures is not entirely absent from the scene of Whistlejacket's portrait, however. The decision to portray the horse entirely without any context or background has been the subject of much speculation and discussion. Once again Humphry's *Memoir* provides the official Stubbsian version of events. Rockingham had supposedly commissioned Stubbs to paint Whistlejacket for an equestrian portrait of George III that would hang as a companion piece to his equestrian portrait of George II by David Moriere. Stubbs was to supply the horse, the best portrait painter of the day would paint the king, and the best landscape painter would fill in the background. But upon hearing how Whistlejacket had reacted to Stubbs's picture, Rockingham was apparently pleased and ordered that the picture be left as it was. Humphry reported that Rockingham commissioned Stubbs to paint another of his horses, Scrub, to serve as the king's mount, though this commission was not, apparently, a success.[89] There has been speculation that Rockingham, having moved into the opposition camp (perhaps because of the king's high-handed colonial policies in America), had changed his mind about having a portrait of George III painted. In that case Whistlejacket's splendid isolation would also bear for those in the know, like the horse-and-lion paintings, the marks of anti-Hanoverian allegory, and could be aligned with Whig liberalism in its anti-imperial guise.

What the exhibition *Stubbs and the Horse* makes clear is how the backgroundless pictures painted for Lord Rockingham stand out among Stubbs's many other modes of horse portraiture. The smaller accompanying pictures painted for Rockingham during the same year, *Mares and Foals* and *Whistlejacket and Two Other Stallions, with the Groom Simon Cobb* (fig. 11), also adopt the backgroundless mode. In their linear design, these two pictures have often been compared with classical friezes. Coupled with the overwhelming power of *Whistlejacket* in the same room, these pictures form a group that comes across as far more innovative than any other pictures painted for any other patron. They are positively avant-garde in the context of all the other pictures, except the lion-and-horse pictures, with which they share conceptual novelty wedded to classical form. It is tempting to attribute some of Stubbs's artistic boldness here to the intellectual approval he must have received from Rockingham. Charles Watson-Wentworth, Lord Rockingham, was not only an eminent Whig politician but also the patron who appears to have encouraged Stubbs in his most daring departures from the horse-painting tradition.

Those departures take the form of an attempt at an absolute mimeticism rad-

Figure 11. In Stubbs's *Whistlejacket and Two Other Stallions, with the Groom Simon Cobb* (1762), Simon Cobb's dignity is matched by his sensitivity to the horses in his care. The Trustees of the Rt. Hon. Olive, Countess Fitzwilliam's Chattels Settlement, by courtesy of Lady Juliet Tadgell. Photo: Bridgeman Art Library.

ically devoted to the horses themselves. If we recall that Reynolds had famously insisted upon the superiority of the ideal form to any individual deviation from it, and upon the greater nobility of the general concept of the species compared with particular representatives of it, then *Whistlejacket,* and the other horse pictures painted for Lord Rockingham without backgrounds, might be seen to parody Reynolds's tenets about ideal form by applying them to horse portraiture. These paintings foreground the horses themselves as subjects while arranging them according to distinctly classical principles of composition. These horses are rendered not so much as status symbols, expensive possessions, brute beasts who could be beaten or whipped into winning or obeying, but as sentient beings in their own social groups and as objects of the painter's gaze and brush simultaneously. I use *rendered* here advisedly—a word from the abbatoir turned to aesthetic account. The individual characters of the horses are suggested by means of what we might call the horses' "speaking" looks. The young chestnut mare on the right of the picture of mares and foals, for instance, directs a fiery and withering glance at her fellow equines, just as the Houyhnhnm mare in *Gulliver's Travels* reduced Gulliver to a mere Yahoo with her contemptuous look. Their shapes or "makes" are studies in blood-horse refinement and embodied intelligence as well as opportunities to display painterliness for its own sake.

For the portrait of *Whistlejacket* to have achieved its iconic status within a national frame says a great deal not only about British culture and its enduring relation to horses but also about the paradoxical underpinnings of that culture, which link questions of national identity with attitudes toward the natural world and practices for controlling it by divisive and appropriative means. Whistlejacket is painted as a free and fiery being. He is possessed of energy worthy of William Blake's mythological Orc, but also of a fleshly solidity and powerful embodiment worthy of Reynolds. He is above all independent of human control yet at the same time produced and contained by it. This image satisfies human spectators' fantasies or wishes about the power and freedom represented by horses when that power and freedom serve their own interests and desires. If Keith Tester is right, and even animal rights activists are more concerned with what it means to be human, and with fantasies about human freedom, than with the species being of actual animals themselves,[90] Stubbs's picture allows those fantasies free rein. We can identify with Whistlejacket's beauty, power, and freedom while also feeling relieved that this horse appears, at least, to be neither enslaved nor subjected to human domination, at the same time that neither the horse nor the portrait could have existed without that very domination and ability to appropriate.

What would happen to the image and the way it functions in the public imagination if *Whistlejacket* were not Whistlejacket, but some other kind of horse, and not the product of Eastern blood and English breeding? A cart horse, for instance? Imagine a powerful, hairy Shire horse rearing. This would be a different sort of image altogether, one more suitable for picturesque treatment by a George Morland or a Rosa Bonheur. The sense of untamed energy in the rough, as it were, would, in the case of the Shire horse, also, as in the case of Whistlejacket, disrupt any smugness on the part of spectators regarding humans' instrumental use of horses. But the question of equine nobility, a nobility that justifies and transcends animality or brutishness, would be differently put.

The image of the blood horse, combining as it does beauty and power, utility and intelligence, aesthetic pleasure and triumphant athleticism, all wrapped up as a way of disguising Eastern origins, conveys a different message from the image presented by any other sort of horse. By definition a non–blood horse is a more "common" horse, a less superior member of the species. The English claim upon the blood horse represented by the Thoroughbred—that naturalized product of appropriations from the East—satisfies certain longings that we might label as the kernal or core of English identity. Slavoj Žižek might call this "the English thing." The liberty of the freeborn subject, despite hybrid origins, the nobility of the aristocrat (or the "natural" aristocrat, whether highwayman or stable lad), the finely tuned competitive longings of the racehorse for ultimate speed and the glory of winning: all these are emblematized in Stubbs's *Whistlejacket* and in the legacy of imported Eastern bloodstock more generally. These horses showed what horses could do and be, and even think and say. That they were naturalized foreigners was quickly forgotten. They became English by dint of familiarity, in partnership with sporting men and women.

"This riding and tumbling, this being blown upon and rained upon and splashed from head to heels with mud," Woolf wrote, "have worked themselves into the very texture of English prose and given it that leap and dash, that stripping of images from flying hedge and tossing tree which distinguish it not indeed above the French but so emphatically from it."[91] Here is national rivalry once again displaced onto differences in riding and writing. Here also is the appeal of fox hunting as both an adrenaline rush and an aesthetic experience. And such leap and dash, such thrusting riding, could achieve its most elegant form on the back of a Thoroughbred horse.

If *Whistlejacket* suggests something of equine freedom and power, as well as nobility of ancestry and innate intelligence, characteristics inherited from Eastern forebears, the picture might be read as bearing witness to a certain degree of equine agency detectable within eighteenth-century English culture. After his lordship's Arabian arrived on the scene, and only then, were horses considered worthy of painting, as subjects of portraits rather than objects in pictures about humans. There were Eastern—Persian, Mughul, and Ottoman—precedents for this equine portraiture. But in the British Isles, it was the arrival of these exotic horses themselves that inspired a new genre of painting. In *Whistlejacket*, Stubbs took that genre to a new level of significance and artistic importance. In its continued popular appeal, the picture is surely testimony not only to the value of images of horses within the United Kingdom today but also to the cultural impact made on British culture by equine importations from the East.

In racing circles around the globe today, the Thoroughbred remains uncontested as a breed. Yet among some equestrian sportspeople, the Thoroughbred has fallen from favor, even as the imperial legacy becomes a matter for national embarrassment rather than pride. Warmbloods, such as the white Hanoverian horse owned by George III probably was—horses produced initially by crossing blood horses with "common" cart horses, and thus eventually obtaining both the fine-skinned "quality" of blood horses and the calming influence, or more phlegmatic and manageable temperaments, of non–blood horses—are now preferred by some competitors in eventing and show jumping. Too hot to handle, too focused on speed and bold jumping, too inclined to shy or "blow up" before huge crowds, too independent-minded, too likely to have ideas about what line to take, what pace to follow, and what to do—the Thoroughbred's very sensitivities and signs of humanized and humanlike intelligence have come to be seen by some as potential liabilities in equestrian competition. And fox hunting, the emulative alternative to eventing, in which Thoroughbreds or near-Thoroughbreds have always excelled, is in disfavor, officially banned in England and Scotland, though various compromise forms of hunting appear to be continuing, regardless of the ban.

Have the Thoroughbred and fox hunting fallen from favor as part of the disintegration of imperial identity? It would appear that warmbloods such as George III's Hanoverian, who was a bit of a fool but very easy to paint, have become more valuable commodities in equestrian competition than Thoroughbreds. Recall the comments made recently by the chairman of the British selectors for the Junior European eventing team, Robin Balfour, who labeled dressage "our weak point for many years" and lamented that "we don't have the warmblood horses the Germans have."[92] So much for the unmanageable horse as hero! In racing, perhaps, the equine athlete with spirit and ideas might still be desirable, but eventing, once the closest to the hunting field or light cavalry maneuvers, would seem to be in the process of a European conversion to the virtues of the manège after some three centuries of greater equine liberty. The spirit of *Whistlejacket* may still be fashionable in Britain, but the reality of Whistlejacket appears to be dwindling in appeal for today's riders. The Duke of Newcastle, with his "mannaged riding," might have the last laugh after all, as dressage becomes ever more popular.

Servants Equine and Human

Stubbs may have gone as far as any painter could in houyhnhnmizing his equine subjects, but what of the Yahoo in the frame, as it were, the groom Simon Cobb, who extends his arm protectively toward Whistlejacket in Stubbs's picture of the three stallions? (fig. 11). Rockingham may have enjoyed the celebrity of owning successful racehorses, and taken pleasure in aiding and abetting an innovative painter of them, but what was in it for the servant class, this partnership with the noble brute? We have Thomas Holcroft's testimony that the stable lad at Newmarket basked in the glow of Thoroughbred superiority. So too does Simon Cobb here. He looks serious, intense, intelligent, and sympathetic toward the animals in his charge. It is hard to imagine him indulging in casual brutality toward them. Indeed, his gesture, the hand gently offered to the horse—rather than the hand patting the neck presumptively, the gesture of jockeys in England, according to Gulliver, which is resisted by Master Houyhnhnm—implies a respectful and sympathetic regimen like the Ottoman one described by Busbecq and Newcastle or the Bedouin one described by D'Arvieux.

Did Stubbs utopianize the little Houyhnhnmlands of English sporting culture in which he was patronized and his talents were celebrated? What of the charge that his idealization of horses in painting was inevitably compromised by the practices in which he engaged in order to produce his *Anatomy of the Horse*, the work that first gained him the attention of horse-owning patrons? His devotion to equine art cannot be questioned, but was his seeming devotion to the species as distant and instrumental as that of the harsher sort of horseman? His dissections for the *Anatomy* did involve his purchasing horses cheaply and bleeding them to death, by cutting their jugulars, while injecting them with a preservative fluid so that he might dissect and study them for as long as possible.[93] Stubbs's fellow-artist Petrus Camper had no doubts that Stubbs's devotion to horses was sincere and that he "loved" them.[94] But others have found in Stubbs's art a darker side, a revelation of the necessity of cruelty in animal husbandry, and of Stubbs's own implication in the more brutalizing side of horse culture, from abbatoir to hunting field. Matthew Reynolds has recently described this aspect of Stubbs's art, in which the artist who has "fed off horses all his life" exposes the "barbarity in the civilized world" which he "elsewhere painted naturalistically," as "a meditation on the cruelty of the scalpel and the spur."[95]

This is the aspect of Stubbs's art that has received the lion's share of representation in *Stubbs and the Horse*, while the aspect that has received the least is Stubbs's own immersion in sporting culture. Why, for instance, was Stubbs's self-portrait on horseback not included in this exhibition? In that picture, Stubbs sits his horse like a hunting man.[96] The horse is clearly well-bred, perhaps even clean-bred, showing a good deal of "blood," with a remarkably well laid-back shoulder and fine head and neck, promising cleverness, sensitivity, elastic paces, and speed. Stubbs has accoutered himself as nothing less than a sporting gentleman. If he did so with a mischievous glint in his eye, that is no reason to suppose he utterly despised the culture that inspired and nourished his art and provided him with a livelihood.

The status of servants and laborers in sporting culture was as ambiguous as the status of the horses they looked after. Abuses were common, but so were stronger bonds across the class divide than were to be met with elsewhere. Even Holcroft, from the vantage point of his subsequent political enlightenment, found much to praise about Newmarket in its treatment of men as well as beasts.

When he was injured in a fall from a filly he was exercising, he was most kindly nursed back to health, and far from suffering under any apprehension of social oppression, he gloried in his proximity to equine nobility. In Holcroft's own imagery, at Newmarket he was translated from a plowboy—the rural equivalent of his status as the son of an impoverished shoemaker—into a most exalted station. "[I]nstead of being obliged to drag through the dirt," he recalled, "after the most sluggish, obstinate, and despised amongst our animals"—the draft horse who pulls the plow, or the even more despised team of oxen—"I was mounted on the noblest that the earth contains, had him under my care, and was borne by him over hill and dale, far outstripping the wings of the wind."[97]

The livery Holcroft wore as a stable lad may have been the badge of servitude, but it was a servitude ennobled by his partnership with the blood horse, the noblest brute. As Lord Harley's steward Isaac Hobart wrote to his lordship in 1723, it was imperative to employ people who were not only knowledgeable horsemen but who loved their charges, and would look after them with a kind leniency that was rare in England: "And as to The future Management of the Studd, it is My Duty to represent to Your Ldp. the necessity of having alwayes upon the Spot A Groom that Knows, & love's, & will be carefull of a Horse, (If Such a one is to be had.)"[98] Contradictions terminological and social haunted both horses and the laboring poor equally during the eighteenth century. His lordship's Arabian, like Master Houyhnhnm, offered perpetual lessons in the nobility of brutes.

Her Ladyship's Arabian

• • •

Aftermaths

I have a little white favourite that I would not part with on any
terms. He prances under me with such fire you would think that
I had a great deal of courrage to dare Mount him, yet I'll assure
you I never rid a Horse in my life so much at my command.
—Lady Mary Wortley Montagu, Letter to Anne Thistlethwayte, 1717

W hen she lived at Edirne and Istanbul during her husband's embassy to the Sublime Porte, Lady Mary Wortley Montagu enjoyed riding. Ottoman horses were unparalleled, she reported, for their beauty and their sensitive responsiveness to a rider's wishes. Lady Mary gleefully commented that she presented an unusual spectacle to the locals because special saddles for women were unknown: "My Side Saddle is the first was ever seen in this part of the World and gaz'd at with as much wonder as the ship of Columbus was in America."[1] Montagu appears to have aspired to conquer a few Ottoman hearts and inspire some envious heart-burnings among the female population. Such fiery yet biddable steeds as her "little white favourite" showed off a lady's horsemanship to perfection. Lady Mary's letter of 1717 presages things to come.

His lordship's Arabian, the fount of genetic excellence, during the course of the eighteenth century became a lady's mount. The evolution of the Thoroughbred meant that after about 1750, the fashion for imported bloodstock waned. A sufficient concentration of Eastern blood had been gathered in the British Isles for breeders not to look any further afield. Bred and reared under English and Irish conditions from the synthesis of formerly separate Eastern strains, fed on the new and improved grasses, Thoroughbreds emerged as larger, stronger horses than their desert and steppe antecedents. Thoroughbreds were more suitable mounts for larger, heavier Englishmen than were imported desert-bred horses like the Bloody Shouldered Arabian or most of his progeny.

Even Lord Oxford, with the remnants of the Duke of Newcastle's Welbeck stud at his command, had difficulty mounting himself from his own home-produced horses. In 1723 his steward Isaac Hobart reported that of the young stock at Welbeck, "not any will be fit to keep for Your Ldps. Service but The chestnut Stone horse got by Snake, & the gray Stone horse by Dimple."[2] In 1727 Lord Oxford was still hopeful of having his own breed at his service: "[W]hat are the Betty Filly and the Levinz Filly like to prove the Arabian colt & Careless colt I hope will prove good for Service."[3] To which query Hobart replied that although the Bloody Shouldered Arabian's progeny appeared serviceable enough for lightweight riders, they would never be up to carrying his lordship: "The Levinz & Betty filly's prove very well to their Sire, but neither of them are strong enough for your Ldps. riding; The first is better then fourteen hands-Three Inches high, has a great deal of Speed & will carry twelve Stone very well, The other is but a Galloway, well temper'd, moves finely & is handsom as her Mother."[4] Like many mature Englishmen, Lord Oxford rode at more than twelve stone (168 pounds).

The eighteenth-century actress George Anne Bellamy was thus understandably chuffed at being able to present her darling Lord Granby with an Arabian horse who could easily carry a man's weight. Her natural father, Lord Tyrawley, had originally given her this paragon of Eastern abilities, shipped from Gibraltar:

> I had some time before made Lord Granby a present of a very fine horse, which Lord Tyrawley had sent me from Gibraltar. It was one of the swiftest of its species Arabia ever produced; and was able to carry any weight, which rendered it invaluable. The happiness I received from being able to make such a present to *such* a man, equalled the value of the gift.[5]

By the second half of the century the number of Eastern imports was in decline. Clearly, speed remained a prerogative of Eastern blood horses. But with a few exceptions, such as Bellamy's Gibraltar Arabian, desert horses were neither tall nor strong enough for English horsemen. The British-born progeny derived from immigrant ancestors was beginning to seem a genetic resource sufficient unto itself, so far as size was concerned.

Not only weight-carrying ability but also conformation was at issue in the Thoroughbred's difference from Arabian and other Eastern forebears. The Thoroughbred was often a leggier, longer-backed, more raking sort of horse than the short-coupled Arabian. The influence of the Turanian or Turkmen strains might be detected here. For a long-legged Englishman, a horse with a more sloping, well laid-back shoulder than was often possessed by Arabians had a great deal to recommend it. As Thomas Lister, Lord Ribbesdale, remarked in 1897, "Arab shoul-

ders seldom carry an English saddle becomingly. I don't say that they are necessarily bad, but they are often thick and inelastic; the wither wants line and drawing, and very few Arab horses lend their forehand to your seat and horsemanship."[6] Cutting a dash on horseback was as important at the turn of the twentieth
century as it had been in the sixteenth or seventeenth.

William Cavendish's stricture, that without a beautiful seat, one could never
be a good horseman (or woman), still held. A free-moving and graceful, but short-
coupled, horse was ideal for carrying ladies side-saddle. One of Wootton's pictures
of Lord Oxford's wife, Lady Henrietta, hunting at Wimpole, portrays her riding a
gray horse very much like the Bloody Shouldered Arabian. Lady Henrietta was
painted most often riding her favorite cream-colored mare, sometimes described
as a dun, who had been a wedding gift from "Cousen Harley."[7] But the horse she
rides in *Lady Henrietta Harley, out Hunting with Harriers* (ca. 1720s) is not the
cream mare.[8] Whether or not the Countess of Oxford rode the Bloody Shouldered
Arabian to hounds, Wootton, who clearly liked painting this horse, may have fancied that she should have done. Could this painting have presciently projected the
image of things to come?[9]

By the time of Robert Smith Surtees in the mid-nineteenth century, the "Arab
palfrey" had become the favorite mount of lady riders in the hunting field. Perhaps most famously, Lucy Glitters in *Mr. Sponge's Sporting Tour* rides her hostess
Lady Scattercash's Arabian White Surrey to hounds, showing up the pretensions
of her ladyship's other guests and demonstrating the equestrian superiority of an
otherwise dubious background. Lately a performer of "flag-exercises" at "Astley's
Royal Amphiteatre" in London, Lucy mounts White Surrey and handles him so
gently but confidently that the pair show the way over treacherous obstacles to the
rest of the hunting field. Lucy's understanding of a sensitive horse is apparent to
the Arabian from her first moments on his back:

> Taking the horse gently by the mouth, she gave him the slightest possible touch of
> the whip, and moved him about at will, instead of fretting and fighting him as the
> clumsy, heavy-handed [Mr. Orlando] Bugles had done. She looked beautiful on
> horseback, and for a time riveted the attention of our sportsmen.[10]

The question of good hands, always important in treatises on horsemanship, was
perhaps even more crucial for women riders, who depended more on intelligent
contact with the horse's mouth than did men, riding astride, with a leg on each
side of the horse for communication and control.

The more well bred the horse, the more sensitive the mouth was likely to be,
and thus the more delicate the lines of communication necessary. The ideal lady's

horse, according to John Lawrence, should "have a considerable show of blood" and not exceed fifteen hands, going easily at a canter with "the neck gracefully curved, and the mouth having pleasant and good feeling."[11] Treatises directed at women riders, such as Mrs. J. Stirling Clarke's *The Habit & the Horse* (1860), while regretting that the majority of women seen riding in London parks "have no hands at all," argued nevertheless that although the "essential of a perfect hand" ("exquisite sensibility, and power of immediate adaptation to the peculiarity of any horse's mouth") was a "natural gift" and could not be taught, the means for "forming a good hand" could be imparted.[12] Readers of Jane Austen's *Mansfield Park* may recall the scene in which Edmund Bertram teaches Mary Crawford to ride, "directing" her "management of the bridle."[13] We are led to suspect that what the intrepid Mary possesses in athleticism, she lacks in "sensibility, and power of immediate adaptation" not only to the "peculiarity of any horse's mouth" but to the peculiarity of any person's character, especially the moral delicacy of the clerical Edmund's.[14] Lucy Glitters, notwithstanding her low-born circus-performing background, has exactly the touch, the natural gift of a perfect hand, and the Arabian White Surrey responds to her delicate touch brilliantly.

The infusion of Eastern blood that produced the Thoroughbred manifested itself not only in sensitivity and speed but also in horses with ideas. Mainly the ideas had to do with going as fast as possible, whatever the terrain. But even ideas about going fast implied an impatient intelligence at work and some notion of equine agency. Surtees may well have been the first English novelist to represent a horse as a fictional character who exercises plot-determining agency. And, significantly, the horse is of Arabian breeding. For the first time in English fiction, a horse—Leotard in *Mr. Facey Romford's Hounds* (1865)—explicitly asserts his authority in the plot and makes things happen. "[I]f Leotard's mental qualifications had been as good as his bodily ones," we are told,

> he would have been a very nice horse, and well worth a hundred pounds. But, like many bipeds, he could better bear adversity than prosperity, and as soon as ever he got his condition up a little, back came all his bad qualities. He then would not do anything he didn't like, and if coerced, resented it. He then either kicked the party over his head, or, in the language of the low dealer, "saluted the general"—that is to say, reared up on end.[15]

Thus, after being sold to the low-born but upwardly mobile Countess of Caperington, who fancied herself a good rider—although, the narrator declares, she was not one (411)—Leotard "began to exercise a judgment of his own" (409). One day, when the Countess wanted to canter across the grass sidings of the Rosendale road, to meet the overladen market coaches, Leotard insisted on taking her to Tewkesbury instead:

> Not that he had any acquaintance at Tewkesbury—indeed, we dare say if she had pulled him up for Tooksbury, as she called it, he would have insisted upon going to Rosendale. It was just a spirit of contradiction—a sort of equine awkwardness that nobody could account for. (409)

Surtees's anatomization of the hunting field, with its rigorously satirical classification of landed and trading society, includes animals—most notably horses and foxes—among its agents because hunting is above all a theater of animal actions and psychology. The difference between the "very nice" horse and the "vicious" (410) one is that the very nice horse tolerates human incompetence. The Leotards of this world have the breeding to excel but will only respect skilful, knowledgeable horsemen and women such as Facey Romford and Lucy Glitters.

Such idiosyncrasies gave the blood horse, whether small (Eastern) or large (English Thoroughbred), a formidable reputation. "Within certain obvious limits the whole success of the thoroughbred, or nearly thoroughbred, as a hunter, depends on the person who rides him," advised Lady Diana Shedden and Viola Bathurst, Lady Apsley, daughters of the sporting Duke of Beaufort.[16] "Essentially a highly strung, responsive horse, he must be ridden by someone possessing symnpathy, tact, courage, and confidence before he can give of his best."[17] Not to ride a blood horse was unthinkable for competent horsewomen like the Somerset sisters. They admitted, however, that others, less skilful or intrepid, might not be convinced of this: "Possibly those who do not care for the thoroughbred, or nearly thoroughbred, as a hunter, are unable to get the best out of him, by reason of their own temperament."[18] Yet the advantages of the blood horse they listed revealed the indispensability of the Thoroughbred as a sporting partner:

> But there is no doubt that the habitual rider of blood horses enjoys several things denied to others.
>
> (1) There is that feeling of serene elation when one's horse responds to the lightest touch of land and leg to our call for effort at the big, black, uncompromising place, compared to the "wonder if he'll do it" sort of feeling and the necessary "reminder" administered to the "common 'un" under like circumstances.
>
> (2) Secondly, there is that glorious confidence of reserve power in a quality hunter galloping well within himself on an eight-mile point with hounds racing ahead flinging but an odd note here and there, instead of that stark care that one's com-

moner will be going through things, getting hopelessly tailed off and making one long secretly for a check.

(3) There is the delight in the blood horse who is also a good hack, the springy tread, the play of steel thread muscles under satin skin that make the long way seem so short.

(4) There is the real pleasure of our visits to the stables, where fine lean heads turn with prick-eared alertness to greet us, moving delicate feet out of our way.

(5) The real common horse invariably treads on us in the stable, and out hunting if we fall surely he's on us heavily, while the well-bred one will be up in a second and will avoid treading on us all he can.[19]

Blood will tell, even in the instant that the hoof glances off our prone bodies rather than pinning us to the ground. It is still part of the myth of blood that the Thoroughbred or other horse of extreme quality will do everything in his or her power not to tread on human beings. Whether a throwback to the culture of great leniency or a predisposition to avoid something treacherously soft underfoot, this delicacy has empirical evidence to support it. Characterised thus, the blood horse is surely the noble reflection of the self that every horseman or woman ought to desire.

That such a combination of utility and beauty might require genetic refreshment to ensure its preservation became a preoccupation in the later nineteenth and twentieth centuries. Women were in the vanguard of this latter-day infusion of Eastern blood. As British interest in the Middle East sharpened, along with imperial rivalry with France and Germany, it occurred to travelers who were also keen horsepeople, such as Wilfrid Scawen Blunt (1840–1922) and his wife, Lady Anne Blunt, née King-Noel (1837–1917), that if whatever was good in the Thoroughbred stemmed from Eastern blood, it might be an idea to return to the pure desert stock for replenishment of the English breed. After horseback expeditions in Spain, Anatolia, Algeria, and Egypt, the Blunts embarked on desert expeditions in Syria and Saudi Arabia, and brought back stallions and mares to found the Crabbet Stud in Sussex. They would eventually produce a world-famous breeding program with outposts in Egypt as well as England, and Crabbet-bred horses would be exported all over the world.

The pleasure that Lady Anne took in riding her horses enhanced the pride she took in successful dealing and breeding. Late in life, separated from Wilfrid, fluent in Arabic, and living permanently in Egypt, in 1907 Anne abandoned her side-saddle for the first time and felt that she had truly come home:

Up to the hills, only a short trot and short canter as this was my first astride expedition. However I think there is great *repose* in the position, a relief to me not to be on the twist, one's inside spirally arranged, and the three hours seemed to me nothing.[20]

As companions of her most treasured moments, Lady Anne's Arabians continued to challenge her capabilities as a rider and give her unsurpassed pleasure:

My lesson was a somewhat rough one as I had to keep *"riding"* even at a walk, [Ghádia] being fresh after Sunday's gap. I was afraid to let her canter lest she should be too much for me, but trotted her in circles and then on the straight when suddenly she took advantage of me and bolted—I not being quick enough to catch hold by the curb, for I was riding on the reshmeh [Arab bitless bridle] (she will not stand a bit except when going fast)—and I quite lost control for a moment, however it was only perhaps for 100 yards when I stopped her. The pace felt like being shot out of a gun! It however gave me confidence afterwards, finding myself still on her back . . . The afternoon heavenly the sun set in a blaze of fire followed by that strange return of a brilliant radiance. My ride was so delightful, I feel as if I had never really ridden before! What joy to have such a pleasure before I die, I am so endlessly thankful for it![21]

The romance of the desert, and the companionship of horses, continued to enthral Lady Anne until her death in December 1917. Even when feeling "sorrowful," she wrote in her diary for May of that year, the sight of her "4 legged friends" was "most soothing"; they outclassed human companionship in combining honesty with beauty, offering "an affectionate welcome in which no guile and then the contemplation of extreme beauty and distinction!"[22] The useful and the decorative, the practical and the beautiful, continued to define what was most desirable in the Eastern blood horse.

The Blunts' sojourns in the Ottoman empire and the Arab world revived interest in the Eastern origins of the Thoroughbred. Convinced of the superiority of the pure or *asil* Bedouin-bred horse of the Syrian and Arabian deserts, the Blunts and their daughter Judith Blunt-Lytton, later Lady Wentworth, argued, however tendentiously, for the entirely Arabian lineage of the Thoroughbred. Wilfrid and Anne initially went to Syria because of their belief in the genetic importance of the Darley Arabian. The Darley was the only definitely desert-bred horse of the three most famous foundation sires, they insisted, which explained why he had shown such prepotency in the male line of Thoroughbred breeding. The prepotency of the Darley is a line of argument that has been, as we have seen, recently revived, with supporting chromosomal evidence, by Professor Patrick Cunningham and others of the Smurfit Institute of Genetics at Trinity College,

Figure 12. In *The Arab Tent* (1866), Sir Edwin Landseer conjures a Houynhnhnm-like paradise among the desert tribes, with elegant, intelligent, extremely well mannered mares and foals dwelling in tents, along with salukis and monkeys: a peaceable kingdom with mutiple species, and the human presence largely absent. The Wallace Collection, London.

Dublin.[23] The Blunts were not alone in their preference for desert-bred horses. Roger D. Upton, in *Newmarket and Arabia*—the title says it all—argued similarly for a return to Eastern origins if the Thoroughbred were not to degenerate.[24]

Victorian Orientalism also helped to revive older notions of Arabian superiority. The idyllic vision of Bedouin society, first represented by D'Arvieux in the seventeenth century, enjoyed a revival in Sir Edwin Landseer's painting *The Arab Tent* (1866; fig. 12). Nearly 150 years after the Bloody Shouldered Arabian's importation, the Arabian still offered English painters an ideal of equine exoticism, beauty, and reasonableness, a paragon of gentility on the hoof. The mare and foal in this picture could have stepped from the pages of Part 4 of *Gulliver's Travels*. Is it too far-fetched to presume that Swift's Houyhnhnms, who were themselves fantasy products of the Levant trade and the romance of Eastern bloodstock, had some influence on the production of subsequent fantasies of the equine exoticism to be found in the East?

In his authoritative treatise on the horse published in 1831, William Youatt expressed suspicion about the romantic stories of Arabian superiority in circulation in England, but even he acknowledged the breed's profound influence on equine culture in the West. "We may not, perhaps, believe all that is told us of the Arabian," he cautioned, "yet it cannot be denied that, at the introduction of the Arabian into the European stables, there was no other horse comparable to him."[25] As we have seen, Youatt's stories of the Arabian's loyalty to human masters, such as Bishop Heber's report that his Arabian in India was "so fearless, that he goes without starting close to an elephant, and so gentle and docile that he eats bread out of my hand, and has almost as much attachment and coaxing ways as a dog," confirmed earlier travelers' accounts. Such stories were bound to excite curiosity among those able to travel east to see for themselves. The bishop hazarded the opinion that this combination of sterling qualities seemed to be "the general character of the Arab horses," who are not "the fiery dashing animal I had supposed, but with more rationality about him, and more apparent confidence in his rider, than the majority of English horses."[26] Gentle beings, confiding and affectionate beings, and above all, reasonable or rational beings, the blood horses of the desert could function, for those who learned how to deal with them, as idealized English selves.

Yet calling so much of the imported foundation stock "Arabian" was probably misleading. The influence of North African Barbs and, especially, so-called Turks, should not be underestimated. Youatt argued confusingly that, although "Arabians" were the origin of genetic superiority, they were in fact latecomers to Arabia:

> In the fourth century two hundred Cappadocian horses were sent by the Roman emperor, as the most acceptable present he could offer to a powerful prince of Arabia. So as late as the seventh century, the Arabs had few horses, and those of little value. These circumstances sufficiently prove that, however superior may be the present breed, it is comparativeley lately that the horse was naturalized in Arabia.[27]

It was Arab stewardship of bloodlines from elsewhere, Youatt argued, that had produced pure lineages:

> Although in the seventh century the Arabs had no horses of value, yet the Cappadocian and other horses, which they had derived from their neighbours, were preserved with so much care, and propagated so uniformly and strictly from the finest of the breed, that in the thirteenth century the Arabian horse began to assume a just and unrivalled celebrity.[28]

The Arabs had primarily acquired their breeding stock from Cappadocia in Anatolia (modern Turkey), which was constantly being reinvigorated by horses from

Central Asia as successive generations of Turkic tribes, people of the horse and formidable mounted archers, migrated west. By the thirteenth century, after the defeat of the Seljuks of Rum, who had themselves defeated the Byzantines, Anatolia was controlled by various Mongol and Turcoman factions.[29] By the mid-fourteenth century, Anatolia had become home to a new generation of Muslim Turcoman emirates, including the Osmanlis or Ottomans,[30] many of whose names are the names of antique Anatolian breeds of horses: Teke (as in Akhal-Teke), Germiyan, Karaman. Nevertheless, when it came time for Youatt to characterize "Turkish" horses, he wrote: "The Turkish horses are descended principally from the Arab."[31]

How are we to account for this burying of the Turkic roots of the Eastern blood horse, and the elevation of Arabianness above all other forms of equine identity? Jeremy James speculates that anti-Turkish prejudice in Britain has a great deal to answer for. He himself, when he first embarked upon a long horseback expedition in Anatolia, assumed that the stallion he rode, Ahmed Pasha, was an Arabian: "He was big. Big for a Turkish horse: 15.2 hands. He was Arab. White. Stallion . . . The horse floated in front of me as only an Arab can."[32] Sixteen years later, James is now convinced that Ahmed Pasha, described by the local villagers as "Turkish," though "not pure," was in fact a descendant of the same Turkic bloodlines that produced the Byerley Turk. The legacy of the old Turkic breeds, those proto-Akhal-Tekes, appears to have produced a taller, larger-headed, leggier build and a fiercer, more hot-tempered character than was usually attributed to the Arabian:

> What coursed through his heart, red and hot, what made his sinews tremble, held his nostrils quivering, what pricked his ears, crested his neck and glittered in his big black eyes was blood and ancestry. Even years of apathy and chance breeding, diluted, sullied and muddied, could not alter that. His ancestry was there, ablaze, screaming and bursting with pride . . . I searched . . . for glimpses of the horses of the Turks. They are almost impossible to find. It's as though history has tried to eradicate them utterly. But they were there: they were there.[33]

After centuries of migration and mixing, which has complicated the genetic picture, finding either empirical or archival traces of old Anatolian breeds with Central Asian origins is likely to prove difficult, though in neighboring Iran some breakthroughs have been made. For many years Louise Firouz has promoted international awareness of Turkic and Iranian horses; she is perhaps best known for rescuing the miniature Caspian horse, a breed on the verge of extinction, and the most likely representative of the Turanian or "Scythian" horse of Sándor

Bökönyi's archaeozoological research.[34] Firouz's arguments in favor of the Caspian as the most ancient of the Eastern breeds—and indeed, as the ancestor of the Arabian—with the Caspian closely followed in genetic history by the Turkmen (including the strains of Akhal-Teke, Yamoud, Yabou, Jargalan, and Goklan) has recently received support from the equine geneticist Gus Cothran.[35] As Jason Elliot remarks, the idea of Caspian horses taking precedence over the Arabian in terms of equine ancestry, and of Turkmen horses carrying Parthian archers to victory against "the massed legionaries of Crassus and Mark Antony," and bearing in the sixteenth and seventeenth centuries the Ottoman sultans all the way to the gates of Vienna, "did not go down well in orthodox equestrian circles" because "Western equine history, hypnotized by the beauty of the Arab, tended to come to a halt at the Euphrates."[36]

We are left with the conclusion, therefore, that, in a number of cases his lordship's Arabian might very well have been his lordship's Turk. To have been bred from Turkic steppe bloodlines in Anatolia or the Balkans was as likely as a desert origin for a blood horse obtained from Ottoman territory. His lordship's Barb was also genetically crucial, as evidenced by Tregonwell's Natural Barb mare and other Barb mares whose mtDNA is still present in their female descendants.[37]

At this distance in time from the late seventeenth and early eighteenth centuries, we shall never know for certain precisely how the imported Eastern horses were bred, but their genetic impact and cultural influence are still measurable today. From the seventeenth century onward, utility and beauty were embodied, irresistibly combined, in the Eastern blood horse as these equine foreigners embarked upon their European sojourns. Inspired by their coming, abandoning the manège, and riding short, "after the Turkey fashion," horsemen and women in the British Isles would pursue the ideal of equestrian partnership not in dressage movements but in free forward movement over the green turf, where the love of galloping for its own sake, for the joy of liberty rather than collection and discipline, could be most keenly felt.

"They cannot represent themselves, they must be represented": Swift's Houyhnhmns were not exactly equine self-representations, or a supplement to history like the history of women by women for which Virginia Woolf called in *A Room of One's Own*. Swift's or Wootton's or Gilpin's or Stubbs's blood horses are hardly tokens of an equine identity politics. But Swift's Houyhnhnms do reveal that horses were both unfairly dismissed by many humans, especially philosophers, as brutes or machines, and that they figured a higher, nobler kind of self for the humans who became obsessed with them. The influence of these noble brutes on perception, representation, and social practice should not be underestimated. This kind of highly mediated exchange between horses and humans—might we dare to call it a trace of equine agency?—should surely figure in any history of animals in which their effects upon human society and culture are registered.

The best possible title for a book about horsemanship was *My Horses, My Teachers,* by Alois Podhajsky, director of the Spanish Riding School of Vienna—with the proviso that to say "my" about a horse is always both strange and estranging.* Some debts can never be adequately repaid by books alone.

This book was generously supported by the John Simon Guggenheim Foundation and by Wayne State University, Detroit. My thanks to the Guggenheim for a fellowship in 1995–96, to the Department of English at Wayne State for a Josephine Nevins Keal award in 1999, and to Walter Edwards and the Humanities Center for a fellowship in 2001–2. Research was very pleasantly carried out courtesy of the staff of the Manuscripts Room and Rare Books Room at the British Library, London; the Bodleian Library, Oxford; the Paul Mellon Centre for the Study of British Art, Bedford Square, London; the Manuscripts Room of the University of Nottingham Library; the Topkapı Palace, Istanbul; and Skaigh Stables, Belstone, near Okehampton, Devon.

For suggestions and encouragement along the way I should like to thank Malcolm Andrews, Ros Ballaster, John Barrell, Jennie Batchelor, Peter de Bolla, Jerry Brotton, Paddy Bullard, Niccolò Capponi, Rebecca Cassidy, Rod Edmond, Peter Edwards, Andrew and Caroline Finkel, David Fleming, Robert Folkenflik, Erica Fudge, Tim Fulford, Regenia Gagnier, John Goodridge, Andrew Graciano, Nick

---

*As the equine protagonist of Tolstoy's "Kholstomer," or "Strider: The Story of a Horse," puts it, "The words '*my* horse' applied to me, a live horse, seemed to me as strange as to say 'my land,' 'my air,' or 'my water' . . . I became convinced that not only as applied to us horses, but in regard to other things, the idea of *mine* has no other basis than a low, mercenary instinct in men, which they call the feeling or right of property . . . And men strive in life not to do what they think right, but to call as many things as possible *their own*." Leo Tolstoy, "Strider: The Story of a Horse," in *The Snow Storm and Other Stories,* trans. Louise and Aylmer Maude (London: Oxford University Press, 1974), 389–439; this passage 414–15.

Groom, Richard Grusin, Abdulrazak Gurnah, Elaine Hobby, Rachel Holmes, Rosemary Hooley, Sarah Hutton, Cora Kaplan, Peter Kitson, Jonathan Lamb, Nigel Leask, Briony Llewellyn, Kate Loveman, Paddy Lyons, Gerald MacLean, Philip Mansel, Garry Marvin, Nick Mills, Sarah Moss, Rhoads Murphey, Richard Nash, Felicity Nussbaum, Marion O'Connor, Bill Overton, Karen Raber, Dafydd Roberts, Michael Rogers, Caroline Rooney, Layla Saatchi, Cannon Schmitt, Dana Seitler, Ian and Christine Shalders, Scarlett Thomas, Treva J. Tucker, James Grantham Turner, Abigail Williams, and audiences at the Group for Early Modern Cultural Studies conferences at Rochester, New York, and Chicago, Illinois; the Humanities Center at Wayne State University in Detroit; Middlesex University; the Western Society for Eighteenth-Century Studies at the Huntington Library; the British Society for Eighteenth-Century Studies at St. Hugh's College, Oxford; the "Long Restoration: Leviathan to Licensing Act" conference at Loughborough University; the University of Glasgow; the Restoration to Reform Seminar at Oxford; the Eighteenth Century and Romanticism Seminar at Cambridge; the Humanities Faculty at Nottingham Trent University; and the School of English at the University of Kent.

Preliminary versions of parts of the book appeared in a special issue of *Criticism* 46, no. 1 (Winter 2004), edited by Cannon Schmitt; in Karen Raber and Treva J. Tucker's *Culture of the Horse* (Palgrave, 2005); in a special issue of *Prose Studies* 29, no. 1 (Spring 2007), edited by Elaine Hobby; and in *Remapping the Humanities: Identity, Community, Memory, (Post)modernity*, edited by Mary Garrett, Heidi Gottfried, and Sandra F. VanBurkleo, with the assistance of Walter Edwards (Wayne State University Press, 2007). I thank all the editors and publishers for permission to reuse the material here.

Without Harriet Ritvo's enthusiasm for the project, and her invaluable suggestions at an early stage, this book would not have assumed its current form. I am grateful to Robert J. Brugger and the staff at the Johns Hopkins University Press for their thoroughbred approach to academic book publishing, and to the anonymous reader for the press for a sharp-eyed and most encouraging reader's report. My special thanks to Duncan Barrett for his knowledge of the art world, and his industry in gathering illustrations and permissions.

For fellow-traveling across country, and inspired advice on both riding and writing, I am forever indebted to Gerald MacLean and Rosemary Hooley. As one of the last outposts of the advocacy of really free forward movement of the horse, Skaigh Stables has been a touchstone from the beginning. This is Rosemary's book in many ways, and it is dedicated to her, to the memory of David Moore, and to the horses, the many horses.

Introduction · What the Horses Said

1. Letter from Edward, Lord Harley, to Nathaniel Harley, 4 December 1716, quoted in C. M. Prior, *Early Records of the Thoroughbred Horse Containing Reproductions of Some Original Stud-Books, and Other Papers, of the Eighteenth Century* (London: Sportsman Office, 1924), 142.

2. Letter from Nathaniel Harley to his brother Edward "Auditor of the Imprest" Harley, 15 February 1715, Portland Papers, British Library Additional Manuscripts (hereafter cited as B. L. Add. Mss.) 70143 (Nathaniel Harley's letters 1682–1720), 225v.

3. B. L. Add. Mss. 70143, 225v.

4. B. L. Add. Mss. 70143, 225v.

5. B. L. Add. Mss. 70143, 225v–226r.

6. Nathaniel Harley, Letter to Edward "Auditor" Harley, 6 January 1720, B. L. Add. Mss. 70143, 303v–304r.

7. Nathaniel Harley died in Aleppo on 17 July 1720. *Historical Manuscripts Commission, Report on the Manuscripts of His Grace The Duke of Portland, K.G. Preserved at Welbeck Abbey,* vol. 5 (Norwich, UK: For Her Majesty's Stationery Office by the "Norfolk Chronicle" Co., 1899), 603.

8. Linda Colley, *Britons: Forging the Nation, 1701–1837* (New Haven and London: Yale University Press, 1992).

9. Alok Yadav, *Before the Empire of English: Literature, Provinciality, and Nationalism in Eighteenth-Century Britain* (New York and Houndmills, Basingstoke, UK: Palgrave Macmillan, 2004), 21–53.

10. P. J. Cain and A. G. Hopkins, *British Imperialism: Innovation and Expansion, 1688–1914* (London: Longman, 1993), 12.

11. G[ervase] M[arkham], *Countrey Contentments, In Two Books: The first, containing the whole art of riding great Horses in very short time, with the breeding, breaking, dyeting and ordring of them, and of running, hunting and ambling Horses, with the manner how to use them in their travell. Likewise in two newe Treatises the arts of hunting, hawking, coursing of Greyhounds with the lawes of the leash, Shooting, Bowling, Tennis, Baloone &c. The Second intituled, The English Huswife* . . . (London: Printed by J. B. for R. Jackson, 1615).

12. William Blackstone, *Commentaries on the Laws of England* (1765–69), 3:326, quoted in Paul Langford, *Polite and Commercial People: England, 1727–1783* (Oxford and New York: Oxford University Press, 1992), 1. See also Robert Brenner, *Merchants and Revolution: Commercial Change, Political Conflict, and London's Overseas Traders, 1550–1653* (Princeton: Princeton University Press, 1993), and Peter Earle, *The Making of the English Middle Class: Business, Society and Family Life in London, 1660–1730* (London: Methuen, 1989).

13. Between 1750 and 1850, what Robert C. Allen calls the second or landlords' agricultural revolution occurred, during which the last wave of enclosures transformed much of the landscape of the Midlands and Eastern England, where many fashionable packs of hounds were located. Allen, *Enclosure and the Yeoman* (Oxford: Clarendon, 1992), 21.

14. Lizzie Purbrick quoted in Adella Lithman, "Hell-Raiser with a Heart of Gold," *Horse and Hound*, 17 June 1993, 18.

15. [Leo Africanus], "Notes of principall things in John Leo his eight Booke of the Historie of Africa," in Samuel Purchas, *Hakluytus Posthumus or Purchas His Pilgrimes, Contayning a History of the World in Sea Voyages and Lande Travells by Englishmen and others*, 20 vols. (London: Printed by William Stansby for Henrie Fetherstone, 1625; rpt. New York: AMS, 1965), 6: 1–54; this passage 39–40.

16. [Thomas Pennant], *British Zoology. Illustrated by Plates and Brief Explanations* (London: Printed and Sold by B. White, 1770), 42–50, and Plate L.

17. G. L. Buffon, *The Natural History of the Horse, Translated from the French of the Celebrated M. de Buffon* (London: Printed for R. Griffiths, 1762), 65.

18. Ibid., 65–66.

19. [William Youatt], *The Horse; with a Treatise on Draught; and a Copious Index, Published under the Superintendence of the Society for the Diffusion of Useful Knowledge* (London: Baldwin and Cradock, 1831), 29.

20. Ibid., 29.

21. "The willingness of country gentlemen to 'indulge' their tenants and neighbours with sporting rights slackened noticeably after 1750. There were exceptions to this, of course, but it is clear that by the end of the century, 'indulgences' were being granted far less frequently than they had been fifty years earlier." P. B. Munsche, *Gentlemen and Poachers: The English Game Laws, 1671–1831* (Cambridge: Cambridge University Press, 1981), 32. Munsche attributes this shift in attitudes to a complex network of factors, in which a massive infusion of agricultural and colonial wealth, attendant changes in codes of politeness and sociability, changes in the legal system, and the redefining of game animals as property all played a part (133–34).

22. *Memoirs of the Late Thomas Holcroft, Written by Himself, and Continued to the Time of His Death, from His Diary, Notes, and Other Papers*, 3 vols. (London: Printed by J. McCreery for Longman, Hurst, Rees, Orme, and Brown, 1816), 71, 73.

23. Mike Huggins, *Flat Racing and British Society, 1790–1914: A Social and Economic History* (London and Portland, OR: Frank Cass, 2000), 20.

24. Ibid., 20.

25. Ibid., 233.

26. Ibid., 234.

27. Ross McKibbin, *The Ideologies of Class: Social Relations in Britain, 1880–1950* (Oxford: Oxford University Press, 1990), 131, cited in Huggins, *Flat Racing*, 94.

28. Sir William Foster, ed., *The Travels of John Sanderson in the Levant, 1584–1602, with His Autobiography and Selections from His Correspondence* (London: Hakluyt Society, 1931), 15.

29. Journals of Dr. J. Covel's Travels, 1670–1678, B. L. Add. Mss. 22912, 217v. J. Theodore Bent regrettably omitted this section from the well-known Hakluyt Society edition of Covel's diaries, *Early Voyages and Travels in the Levant. The Diary of Master Thomas Dallam, 1599–1600; Extracts from the Diaries of Dr. John Covel, 1670–1679. With Some Account of the Levant Company of Turkey Merchants* (rpt. New York: Burt Franklin, n.d.), 171–241.

30. Karl Marx, *The Eighteenth Brumaire of Louis Bonaparte*, (1852), in *The Marx-Engels Reader*, ed. Robert C. Tucker, 2nd ed. (New York and London: W. W. Norton, 1978), 608.

31. Erica Fudge, "A Left-Handed Blow: Writing the History of Animals," in *Representing Animals*, ed. Nigel Rothfels (Bloomington and Indianapolis: Indiana University Press, 2002), 3–18; this passage 5.

32. Ibid., 15.

33. See Steve Baker, "Guest Editor's Introduction: Animals, Representation, and Reality," *Society and Animals: Journal of Human-Animal Studies,* special issue on "The Representation of Animals," 9, no. 3 (2001): 189–200; this passage 193–94.

34. Donna Landry and Gerald MacLean, *Materialist Feminisms* (Oxford: Blackwell, 1993), 206–28.

35. Animal rights (Regan) and the critique of speciesism (Singer) both operate as social movements as well as philosophical arguments: Tom Regan, *The Case for Animal Rights* (Berkeley and Los Angeles: University of California Press, 1983); Peter Singer, *Animal Liberation,* 2nd ed. (1975; New York: New York Review Books, 1990). See also Marjorie Spiegel, *The Dreaded Comparison: Human and Animal Slavery* (1988; New York: Mirror Books/ IDEA, 1996).

36. See Keith Thomas, *Man and the Natural World: A History of the Modern Sensibility* (New York: Pantheon, 1983), and Harriet Ritvo, *The Animal Estate: The English and Other Creatures in the Victorian Age* (London and New York: Penguin, 1990).

37. Adrian Franklin, *Animals and Modern Cultures: A Sociology of Human-Animal Relations in Modernity* (London, Thousand Oaks, CA, and New Delhi: Sage, 1999), 175–99, and Keith Tester, *Animals and Society: The Humanity of Animal Rights* (London and New York: Routledge, 1991), 170–208.

38. See Tester, *Animals and Society,* 16, 176–200, and Ted Benton, *Natural Relations: Ecology, Animal Rights, and Social Justice* (London: Verso, 1993).

39. Donna Haraway, *The Companion Species Manifesto: Dogs, People, and Significant Otherness* (Chicago: Prickly Paradigm, 2003).

40. Vicki Hearne, *Adam's Task: Calling Animals by Name* (New York: Vintage/Random House, 1987), 21.

41. Ibid., 25.

42. Ibid., 106.

43. Ibid., 107.

44. Haraway, *Companion Species Manifesto,* 50.

45. Ibid., 53, 52, 54.

46. Ibid., 54, 52–54.

47. Paul Patton, "Language, Power, and the Training of Horses," in *Zoontologies: The Question of the Animal,* ed. Cary Wolfe (Minneapolis and London: University of Minnesota Press, 2003), 83–99; this passage 92.

48. Ibid., 95, 96.

49. Haraway, *Companion Species Manifesto,* 89–90.

50. Garry Marvin, "Wolves in Sheep's and Other Clothing," revised version of a paper originally delivered at the German Historical Institute conference on "Looking at Animals," 9 May 2005; "Wölfe in Schafs und anderen Pelzen," in *Tiere in der Geschichte,* ed. Dorothee Brantz and Christof Mauch (Paderborn: Schöningh, 2007). My thanks to Marvin for letting me read the English version in typescript.

51. Marvin, "Wolves," 10.

52. Ibid.

53. Karen Raber and Treva J. Tucker, "Introduction," *The Culture of the Horse: Status, Discipline, and Identity in the Early Modern World,* ed. Raber and Tucker (New York and Houndmills, Basingstoke, UK: Palgrave Macmillan, 2005), 1–41; this passage 2.

54. Elisabeth LeGuin, "Man and Horse in Harmony," in *Culture of the Horse,* 175–96; this passage 179.

55. Raber and Tucker, "Introduction," *Culture of the Horse,* 3.

Chapter 1 · *Horsemanship in the British Isles before the Eastern Invasion*

1. Joan Thirsk, *Horses in Early Modern England: For Service, for Pleasure, for Power,* the Stenton Lecture 1977 (Reading, UK: University of Reading, 1978), 6. For a general history of horses in early modern England, see Peter Edwards, *Horse and Man in Early Modern England* (London: Hambledon Continuum, 2007).

2. [Arthur Young], *The Farmer's Letters to the People of England: Containing the Sentiments of a Practical Husbandman, on Various Subjects of the Utmost Importance . . .* (London: Printed for W. Nicoll, 1767), 106, 103–7.

3. Diana Donald, "'Beastly Sights': The Treatment of Animals as a Moral Theme in Representations of London, 1820–1850," *Art History* 2, no. 4 (November 1999): 514–44, 515.

4. Ibid., 515.

5. Ibid., 521.

6. Ibid., 535, citing Carlyle's *Past and Present* (1843), ed. Donald Jerrold (London, 1960), 18, 213.

7. Donna Haraway, *The Companion Species Manifesto: Dogs, People, and Significant Otherness* (Chicago: Prickly Paradigm, 2003), 28.

8. Ibid., 28.

9. K. N. Chauduri, *Asia before Europe: Economy and Civilisation of the Indian Ocean from the Rise of Islam to 1750* (Cambridge and New York: Cambridge University Press, 1990).

10. Andre Gunder Frank, *ReOrient: Global Economy in the Asian Age* (Berkeley, Los An-

geles, and London: University of California Press, 1998), 4–5. As late as 1853, the Ottoman cavalry of previous centuries was being remembered as "the finest cavalry seen in Europe" by British observers. See Captain Lewis Edward Nolan, *Cavalry; Its History and Tactics* (London: Thomas Brown, 1853), 24.

11. K. N. Chauduri, *Trade and Civilisation in the Indian Ocean: An Economic History from the Rise of Islam to 1750* (Cambridge and New York: Cambridge University Press, 1985), 39. See also Kenneth Pomeranz and Steven Topik, *The World That Trade Created: Society, Culture, and the World Economy, 1400–the Present* (Armonk, NY, and London: M. E. Sharpe, 1999), 34.

12. Juliet Clutton-Brock, *A Natural History of Domesticated Mammals*, 2nd ed. (Cambridge and New York: Cambridge University Press and Natural History Museum, 1999), 105–6.

13. John F. Richards, "Outflows of Precious Metals from Early India," in *Precious Metals in the Late Medieval and Early Modern Worlds*, ed. J. F. Richards (Durham, NC: Carolina Academic Press, 1983).

14. Audrey Burton, Papers on Inner Asia #23, *Bukharan Trade, 1558–1718* (Bloomington: Indiana University Press, 1993).

15. Naimur Rahman Farooqi, *Mughal-Ottoman Relations: A Study of Political and Diplomatic Relations between Mughal India and the Ottoman Empire, 1556–1748* (Delhi: Idarah-i Adabiyat-i Delli, 1989), 224.

16. Ibid., 27–28.

17. Juliet Clutton-Brock, *Horse Power: A History of the Horse and the Donkey in Human Societies* (London: Natural History Museum Publications, 1992), 58, citing L. H. Van Wijngaarden-Bakker, "The Animal Remains from the Beaker Settlement at Newgrange, Co. Meath—First Report," *Proceedings of the Royal Irish Academy* 74 *(Section C)* (1974): 313–83.

18. Lynn White Jr., *Medieval Technology and Social Change* (London, Oxford, and New York: Oxford University Press, 1962), 138, n. 1 to p. 8, citing A. Heiermaier, "Westeuropäische Heimat und Namen des Pferdes," *Paideia* 6 (1951): 371–75.

19. A. A. Dent and Daphne Machin Goodall, *The Foals of Epona: A History of British Ponies from the Bronze Age to Yesterday* (London: Galley, 1962), 9.

20. White, *Medieval Technology and Social Change*, 138, note 1 to p. 8, citing A. Holder, *Alt-celtischer Sprachschatz* (Leipzig, 1904), 2:417.

21. Thirsk, *Horses in Early Modern England*, 5–6, quoting *Calendar of State Papers Venetian*, VI, iii (1557–58), 1672.

22. *Sidney's Apologie for Poetrie*, ed. J. Churton Collins (Oxford: Clarendon, 1907), 1.

23. Ibid., 2.

24. Ibid., 13.

25. For more on these early modern analogies as they operated in France, see the essays by Kate van Orden, "From *Gens d'armes* to *Gentilshommes:* Dressage, Civility, and the *Ballet à Cheval*," 197–222, and Treva J. Tucker, "Early Modern French Noble Identity and the Equestrian 'Airs above the Ground,'" 273–309, in *The Culture of the Horse: Status, Discipline, and Identity in the Early Modern World*, ed. Karen Raber and Treva J. Tucker (New York and Houndmills, Basingstoke, UK: Palgrave Macmillan, 2005).

26. J. P. Hore, *The History of Newmarket, and the Annals of the Turf: With Memoirs and*

Biographical Notices of the Habitués of Newmarket, and the Notable Turfites from the Earliest Times to the End of the Seventeenth Century, 3 vols. (London: A. H. Baily and Co., 1886), 1:21.

27. Like many other historians of racing, Hore acknowledges genetic hybridity in the Thoroughbred but makes nothing of it, asserting a stable native identity by means of English mares: "The superiority of the English thoroughbred horse is attributable, if not directly traceable, to the Eastern blood introduced and maintained by the Romans at the period above mentioned. Subsequently the best English mares were covered by Arabian stallions which continued to be imported during the early and middle ages, and in a more marked degree and more closely allied with the Turf, in the sixteenth, seventeenth, and eighteenth centuries." Ibid.

28. Quoted in Sidney, *An Apologie for Poetrie*, ed. Evelyn S. Shuckburgh (Cambridge: Cambridge University Press, 1905), 66.

29. Federico Grisone, *Gli Ordini di Cavalcare* (Naples: Guilio Terzo, 1550).

30. Claudio Corte, *Il Cavallenzzo . . . nel qual si tratta della natura de' Cavalli, delle Razze, del modo di governarli, domarli, & frenarli . . .* (Venice: Giordano Ziletti, 1573); Pasqual Caracciolo, *La Gloria Del Cavallo . . . Divisa In Dieci Libri: Ne' Quali Oltra Gli Ordini Pertinenti Alla Cavalleria, si descrivono tutti i particolari, che son necessari nell'allevare, custodire, maneggiare, & curar cavalli; accommodandovi estempi tratti da tutte l'historie antiche & moderne, con industria & giudicio dignisimo d'essere avertito da ogni Cavalliero* (Venice: Gabriel Giolito De' Ferrari, 1567). See also Cesare Fiaschi, "Gentil'huomo Ferrarese," *Trattato Del Modo Dell'Imbrigliare, Maneggiare, & ferrare cavalli, diviso in tre parti, Con alcuni discorsi sopra la natura di cavalli, con disegni di briglie, maneggi, & di Cavalieri à cavallo, & de'ferri d'esso* (Venice: Francesco de Leno, 1563).

31. Thirsk, *Horses in Early Modern England*, 19; C. M. Prior, *The Royal Studs of the Sixteenth and Seventeenth Centuries, Together with a Reproduction of the Second Earl of Godolphin's Stud-Book, and Sundry Other Papers Relating to the Thoroughbred Horse* (London: Horse and Hound, 1935), 1–2.

32. R. H. C. Davis, *The Medieval Warhorse: Origin, Development, and Redevelopment* (London: Thames and Hudson, 1989), 110.

33. Ibid., 110.

34. F. H. Huth, *Works on Horses and Equitation. A Bibliographical Record of Hippology* (London: Bernard Quaritch, 1887), 5.

35. As Thirsk notes, *Horses in Early Modern England*, 17, citing Huth, *Works on Horses and Equitation*.

36. John Astley, Master of the Queen's Jewell-House, and first in a long line of Astleys to profess horsemanship in England, *The Art of Riding, set foorth in a breefe treatise, with a due interpretation of certeine places alledged out of Xenophon, and Gryson, verie expert and excellent Horssemen* (London: Henrie Denham, 1584), 15.

37. Walter Liedtke, *The Royal Horse and Rider: Painting, Sculpture, and Horsemanship, 1500–1800* (New York: Abaris Books and the Metropolitan Museum of Art, 1989), 23.

38. [Thomas Blundeville], *A newe booke containing the arte of ryding, and breakinge greate Horses, together with the shapes and Figures, of many and divers kyndes of Byttes, mete to serve divers mouthes. Very necessary for all Gentlemen, Souldyours, Seruingmen, and for any man that delighteth in a horse* (London: Willyam Seres, n.d. [1560]).

39. In addition to Astley (n. 36 above), see Thomas Bedingfield's translation of Claudio Corte's *Il Cavallenzzo*, also published as *The Art of Riding* (London: Henrie Denham, 1584).

40. For general introductions to this reformulation, see Gerald MacLean, introduction to *Re-Orienting the Renaissance: Cultural Exchanges with the East* (Houndmills, Basingstoke, UK, and New York: Palgrave Macmillan, 2005); Jerry Brotton, *The Renaissance Bazaar: From the Silk Road to Michelangelo* (Oxford and New York: Oxford University Press, 2002); and Lisa Jardine, *Worldly Goods: A New History of the Renaissance* (London and Basingstoke, UK: Macmillan, 1996). Important specialized studies include Gülru Necipoğlu, "Süleyman the Magnificent and the Representation of Power in the Context of Ottoman-Hapsburg-Papal Rivalry," *Art Bulletin* 71 (1989): 401–27; Michael Rogers, "The Arts under Süleyman the Magnificent," in *Süleyman the Second and His Time*, ed. Halil İnalcık and Cemal Kafadar (Istanbul: Isis, 1993), 287–324; Deborah Howard, *Venice and the East* (New Haven: Yale University Press, 2000); and Julian Raby, *Venice, Dürer, and the Oriental Mode* (London: Islamic Art Publications, 1982). For the specific case of horsemanship, see Miklós Jankovich, *They Rode into Europe: The Fruitful Exchange in the Arts of Horsemanship between East and West*, trans. Anthony Dent (London: George G. Harrup, 1971), and Lisa Jardine and Jerry Brotton's chapter, "Managing the Infidel: Equestrian Art on Its Mettle," in *Global Interests: Renaissance Art between East and West* (London: Reaktion; Ithaca, NY: Cornell University Press, 2000), 132–85, which is indebted to Jankovich.

41. Liedtke, *Royal Horse*, 21. Naples was acknowledged as the leading center for riding schools in the sixteenth century, though Mantua is now credited with the earliest known still standing *cavallerizza*, built in 1538–39. Liedtke's source for Pignatelli's visit to Constantinople is a popular Italian history, Luigi Gianoli's *Horses and Horsemanship through the Ages*, trans. Iris Brooks (New York: Crown, 1969), 103, which makes no mention of available documentation. To complicate matters further, in an appendix to Liedtke's book, Alexander Mackay-Smith claims, on the basis of no named evidence, that the riding school at Naples was opened in 1532 by Grisone (90), and that Pignatelli, who had been a pupil of Cesare Fiaschi of Ferrara, merely joined Grisone's academy, becoming a celebrated instructor to Salomon de la Broue, Antoine de Pluvinel, and the Chevalier de St. Antoine, Charles I's riding master and equerry (89). Since I have been unable to do any primary research in Italian archives, I am suggesting that Gianoli's history offers at least grounds for speculation.

42. Giles Worsley, "A Courtly Art: The History of the 'Haute École' in England," *The Court Historian* 6 (May 2001): 29–47; this passage 31.

43. Charles Chenevix Trench, *A History of Horsemanship* (London: Longman, 1970), 151.

44. [Blundeville,] *The arte of ryding*, book 2, chap. 28, second page, fifth page.

45. Ibid., second page.

46. *A New Method and Extraordinary Invention, To Dress Horses, and Work Them according to Nature: as also, To Perfect Nature by the Subtilty of Art; Which was never found out, but by The Thrice Noble, High, and Puissant Prince William Cavendishe* (London: Printed by Thomas Milbourn, 1667), 20. Further references are to this edition. The influence of Arabic terms for horses and horsemanship in the New World through the mixing of Spanish and English vernaculars in Mexico and the southwestern United States has been noted by Gary Paul Nabhan, "Arabic in the Saddle," *Saudi Aramco World* 58 (March–April 2007): 39.

47. Cavendish, *New Method*, 70–71.

48. Ibid., 82.

49. Liedtke, *Royal Horse*, 21.

50. Nathaniel Harley, Letter to Mr. "Auditor" Edward Harley, Esq., Aleppo, 29 December 1705, B. L. Add. Mss. 70143, 179v–180r.

51. See Jankovich, *They Rode into Europe*, 80–87, for discussion of the interpenetration of Bactrian or Turanian horses and horse culture from the Central Asian steppe—the "Turkish" heritage—with Arab horse breeding and horse-keeping practices.

52. Shihab al-Sarraf, "Furusiyya Literature of the Mamluk Period," in *Furusiyya*, ed. David Alexander, 2 vols. (Riyadh: King Abdulaziz Public Library, 1996), 1:118–35; this passage 118.

53. "*Furusiyya*" (G. Douillet and D. Ayalon), in *Encyclopedia of Islam, New Edition*, ed. H. A. R. Gibb et al., 11 vols. (Leiden: E. J. Brill, 1960–2000), 2:952–55.

54. Rhoads Murphey, "Horsebreeding in Eurasia: Key Element in Material Life or Foundation of Imperial Culture?" *Central and Inner Asian Studies* 4 (1990): 1–13; these passages 1 and 10.

55. Robert Irwin, "Eating Horses and Drinking Mare's Milk," in *Furusiyya*, 1:148–51; this passage 151.

56. J. M. Rogers, "Ottoman Furusiyya," in *Furusiyya*, 1:176–83; this passage 176.

57. al-Sarraf, "Furusiyya Literature of the Mamluk Period," in *Furusiyya*, 1:118.

58. "*Maydan*" (F. Viré), in *Encyclopedia of Islam, New Edition*, 6:912–13.

59. Brotton, *Renaissance Bazaar*, 141–43. Costanzo di Moysis, also known as Costanzo da Ferrara, was active 1474–1524 and inscribed the reverse of this portrait medal of Mehmed II, circa 1478, as follows: HIC BELLI FULMEN POPULOS PRO STRAVIT ET URBES/ CONST/ANTIUS F. (This man, the thunderbolt of war, has laid low peoples and cities. Constantius made it.) See Caroline Campbell and Alan Chong, *Bellini and the East* (London: National Gallery Company; Boston: Isabella Stewart Gardner Museum, 2005), 71.

60. Caroline Finkel, *Osman's Dream: The Story of the Ottoman Empire, 1300–1923* (London: John Murray, 2005), 285–88.

61. Jeremy James, *The Byerley Turk* (Ludlow, UK: Merlin Unwin, 2005), 145.

62. John Ellis discusses the diminishing role of cavalry from the moment that infantry forces began to get its measure, but also early modern revivals of cavalry's tactical usefulness, e.g., as shock troops or for reconnaissance, harrassment, and outflanking, and the persistence of the cavalry's survival in warfare, partly as a consequence of the "continued aristocratic domination of the army, and their insistence upon the pre-eminence of the horse in war," despite the coming of new technology—"precision weapons in huge quantities"—and new rules of engagement. Ellis, *Cavalry: The History of Mounted Warfare* (New York: G. P. Putnam's Sons, 1978), 78–107; this passage 107.

63. Nolan, *Cavalry*, 24.

64. *The Training of Cavalry Remount Horses, by the Late Captain Nolan*, new ed. (London: Parker Son and Bourn, 1861), 1 n.

65. See Anthony Dent's "Translator's Preface" to Jankovich, *They Rode into Europe*, 6–8; this passage 7.

66. Ibid., 7–8.

67. Ibid., 8.

68. Edward W. Said, *Orientalism* (1978; London and New York: Penguin, 1995), 8.

69. Noël Denham-Young, "The Tournament in the Thirteenth Century," in *Studies in Medieval History Presented to Frederick Maurice Powicke,* ed. R. W. Hunt, W. A. Pantin, and R. W. Southern (Oxford: Clarendon, 1948), 240.

70. Quoted in Sidney, *Apologie,* ed. Shuckburgh, 65.

71. Quoted ibid., 66.

72. Quoted ibid.

73. For more on this relationship, see Elisabeth LeGuin, "Man and Horse in Harmony," in *Culture of the Horse,* 175–96.

74. Xenophon, *On the Art of Horsemanship,* in *Scripta Minora,* trans. E. C. Marchant (London: William Heinemann; New York: G. P. Putnam's Sons, 1925), 347.

75. Ibid.

76. Astley, *Art of Riding,* 4.

77. Cavendish, *New Method,* 42–43.

78. [Blundeville], *The arte of ryding,* book 3, chap. 12, first and second pages.

79. Ibid., second page.

80. Ibid., first page.

81. Thomas Bedingfield, *The Art of Riding, conteining diverse necessarie instructions, demonstrations, helps, and corrections apperteining to horssemanship, not heretofore expressed by anie other Author: Written at large in the Italian toong, by Maister Claudio Corte, a man most excellent in this Art* (London: Henrie Denham, 1584), 95.

82. Ibid., 112.

83. I quote from the English translation of Cavendish's French treatise of 1658, *Methode Et Invention Nouvelle de dresser Les Chevaux par le tres-noble, haut, et tres-puissant Prince Guillaume Marquis Et Comte De Newcastle . . .* (Antwerp: Jacques Van Meurs, 1658), which appeared in 1743 as *A General System of Horsemanship in all it's Branches: containing a Faithful Translation Of that most noble and useful Work of his Grace, William Cavendish, Duke of Newcastle, entitled The manner of Feeding, Dressing, and Training of Horses for the Great Saddle, and Fitting them for the Service of the Field in Time of War, or for the Exercise and Improvement of Gentlemen in the Academy at home: A Science peculiarly necessary throughout all Europe, and which has hitherto been so much neglected, or discouraged in England, that young Gentlemen have been obliged to have recourse to foreign Nations for this Part of their Education,* 2 vols. (London: Printed for J. Brindley, 1743), 1:11. Only the first volume is in fact Cavendish's work; the second is a translation of Gasper de Saunier.

84. Ibid., 13.

85. Ibid., 12.

86. Paul Patton, "Language, Power, and the Training of Horses," in *Zoontologies: The Question of the Animal,* ed. Cary Wolfe (Minneapolis and London: University of Minnesota Press, 2003), 83–99; this passage 93.

87. Margaret, Duchess of Newcastle, *The Life of the Thrice Noble, High and Puissant William Cavendishe, Duke, Marquess, and Earl of Newcastle* (London: Printed by A. Maxwell, 1667), book 2, 67.

88. Karen L. Raber is right to point to this tension in Cavendish's writing but perhaps exaggerates the contradiction that arises between his "ostensible purpose"—defending the authority of nobility—and his "emphasis on riding as a partnership, and on the rational, characterful nature of the horse" that "invests the horse with a nascent subjectivity, an individualized and self-motivated identity which mirrors cultural and political transformations of human subjectivity across class lines in seventeenth-century England." Raber, "'Reasonable Creatures': William Cavendish and the Art of Dressage," in *Renaissance Culture and the Everyday*, ed. Patricia Fumerton and Simon Hunt (Philadelphia: University of Pennsylvania Press, 1999), 42–66; this passage 61.

89. On the Restoration as an acknowledgment and product of the English Revolution, as well as a failure of political imagination, see Gerald MacLean, "Literature, Culture, and Society in Restoration England," in *Culture and Society in the Stuart Restoration*, ed. MacLean (Cambridge and New York: Cambridge University Press, 1995), 3–27.

90. This resonant phrase from David Underdown captures something of the self-identity of the English, and Britons, that also resonates with their ideas of horsemanship as distinguished from those of Continental Europe. Underdown, *Revel, Riot, and Rebellion: Popular Politics and Culture in England, 1603–1660* (Oxford: Clarendon, 1985).

91. Antoine de Pluvinel, *Maneige Royal Ou Lon Peut Remarquer Le Defaut Et La Perfection Du Chevalier* (Paris: Crispian de Pas, 1623).

92. *A New Method and Extraordinary Invention to Dress Horses, And work them according to Nature: as also, To Perfect Nature by the Subtilty of Art; Which was never found out, but by The Thrice Noble, High, and Puissant Prince William Cavendishe, Duke, Marquess, and Earl of Newcastle* . . . (Dublin: Printed for James Kelburn, 1740). See also n. 83 above.

93. Thirsk, *Horses in Early Modern England*, 22, n. 97.

94. Ibid., 22.

95. Cavendish, *New Method*, 5.

96. Ibid., 11.

97. Ibid., 46–47.

98. Harold B. Barclay, *The Role of the Horse in Man's Culture* (London and New York: J. A. Allen, 1980), 105.

99. Clutton-Brock, *Horse Power*, 72, 100. There is some evidence that donkeys at Tell Brak in Syria may have been harnessed with snaffle-type bits made of bone or hard rope as early as the third millennium B.C.E.. Clutton-Brock, "Were the Donkeys at Tell Brak (Syria) Harnessed with a Bit?" in *Prehistoric Steppe Adaptation and the Horse*, ed. Marsha Levine, Colin Renfrew, and Katie Boyle (Cambridge: McDonald Institute for Archaeological Research, n.d. [2003]), 126–27.

100. Barclay, *Role of the Horse*, 71 and 72–73. See also Sándor Bökönyi, *Data on Iron Age Horses of Central and Eastern Europe in the Mecklenberg Collection, Part I*, American School of Prehistoric Research Bulletin 25 (Cambridge: Peabody Museum, Harvard University Press, 1968), 1–71; this passage 46.

101. Barclay, *Role of the Horse*, 73–74, citing T. G. E. Powell, *The Celts* (London: Thames and Hudson, 1959), 106.

102. *An Hipponomie or The Vineyard of Horsemanship: Deuided into three Bookes, By*

Michaell Baret, Practitioner and Professor of the same Art (London: Printed by George Eld, 1618), 21.

103. On bits as forms of technology that in the later sixteenth and early seventeenth centuries appeared to hold the key to human mastery of the horse, see Pia Cuneo, "Just a Bit of Control: The Historical Significance of Sixteenth- and Seventeenth-Century German Bit Books," in *Culture of the Horse*, 141–73. After this time, technology such as bits ceases to be as important as rational negotiation between horse and rider (162–63).

104. Cavendish, *New Method*, 22.

105. John Lawrence, *The Horse in All His Varieties and Uses; His Breeding, Rearing, and Management, Whether in Labour or Rest; with Rules, Occasionally Interspersed, for His Preservation from Disease* (London: Printed for M. Arnold, Sold by Longman, Rees, Orme, et al., 1829), 40.

106. Richard Berenger, *The History and Art of Horsemanship*, 2 vols. (London: Printed for T. Davies and T. Cadell, 1771), 1:194–95.

107. Henry Herbert, tenth Earl of Pembroke, *Military Equitation: Or, a Method of Breaking Horses, and Teaching Soldiers to Ride. Designed for The Use of the Army* (Sarum: Printed and Sold by E. Easton; London: J. Dodsley and J. Wilkie, 1778), 20–21. In the Newberry Library copy, Henry Merrik Hoare has written, "3rd—first Quarto—and best edition [with additions] of the treatise on which was based the system of handling horses. Since adopted by the British Cavalry."

108. *The Compleat Horseman; or, the Art of Riding made easy: Illustrated by Rules drawn from Nature, and Confirmed by Experience; with Directions to the Ladies to sit gracefully, and ride with Safety, By Charles Hughes, Professor of Horsemanship, at his Riding-School, near Blackfriars Bridge* (London: Printed for F. Newbery, and Sold at Hughes's Riding-School, n.d. [1772]), 29–30.

109. Lawrence, *The Horse*, 168.

110. John Adams, *An Analysis of Horsemanship; Teaching the Whole Art of Riding, in the Manege, Military, Hunting, Racing, and Travelling System. Together with the Method of Breaking Horses, for Every Purpose to Which Those Noble Animals Are Adapted* 3 vols. (London: Printed by Albion Press, Published by James Cundee, and Sold by C. Chapple, 1805), 1:xviii.

111. Ibid., xviii–xix.

112. Lawrence, *The Horse*, 41.

113. See Landry, *The Invention of the Countryside: Hunting, Walking, and Ecology in English Literature, 1671–1831* (Houndmills, Basingstoke, UK, and New York: Palgrave, 2001), 21–22, and color plate 1.

114. *The Sportsman's Dictionary: Or, The Country Gentleman's Companion, In all Rural Recreations: with full and particular Instructions for Hawking, Hunting, Fowling, Setting, Fishing, Racing, Riding, Cocking*, 2 vols. (London: Printed for C. Hitch, C. Davis, S. Austen, 1735); *The Sportsman's Dictionary . . .* (London: Printed for Fielding and Walker, 1778); *The Sportsman's Dictionary . . .*, 3rd ed. (London: Printed for G. G. J. and J. Robinson, 1785); *The Sportsman's Dictionary . . .*, 4th ed. (London: Printed for G. G. J. and J. Robinson, 1792).

115. Lawrence, *A Philosophical And Practical Treatise On Horses, and on the Moral Duties Of Man towards The Brute Creation*, 2 vols. (London: Printed for T. Longman, 1796–98), 2:251.

116. Adams, *Analysis of Horsemanship*, 1:xvi–xvii.

117. V. S. Littauer, *More about the Forward Seat: Modern Methods of Schooling and Cross-Country Riding* (London: Hurst and Blackett, 1939), 30–32.

118. Quoted in Thirsk, *Horses in Early Modern England*, 28.

119. Jankovich, *They Rode into Europe*, 99.

120. Adams, *Analysis of Horsemanship*, 2:8.

121. Lawrence, *Philosophical And Practical Treatise*, 2:20.

122. *Sportsman's Dictionary*, 4th ed. (1800).

123. Baret, *Hipponomie*, 54.

124. *Memoirs of the Late Thomas Holcroft, Written by Himself, and Continued to the Time of His Death, from His Diary, Notes, and Other Papers*, 3 vols. (London: Printed by J. McCreery for Longman, Hurst, Rees, Orme, and Brown, 1816), 111.

125. T. Hornby Morland, *The Genealogy of the English Race Horse; with the natural history of his progenitors, from the earliest times down to the period when foreign blood was first introduced into this kingdom; collected from the best authorities: to which is added, the General Practice of the most judicious Breeders, whereby they have Improved & Perfected Our Breed Of Blood Horses So as to have acquired a decided Pre-eminence and Superiority in the essential Points of Size, Strength, Beauty, Speed, Bottom, &c. &c. Over Those Of other Countries: With Observations upon the Present Improved Method of Breeding for the Turf, on the selection of stallions, choice of brood mares, crossing the blood, or mixing races; treatment of brood mares and young colts intended for racing, &c. &c. The Result of Observation and Experience during an Acquaintance for many Years with the Turf . . .* (London: Printed by J. Barfield, 1810), 2.

126. Erica Fudge, *Animal* (London: Reaktion, 2002), 113–16.

Chapter 2 · The Making of the English Hunting Seat

1. Sir Walter Gilbey Bart., *Life of George Stubbs R.A.* (London: Vinton and Co., 1898), 143.

2. Martin Myrone, *George Stubbs* (London: Tate, 2002), 8, and fig. 2.

3. On hunting dress and frock coats in particular, see Philip Mansel, *Dressed to Rule: Royal and Court Costume from Louis XIV to Elizabeth II* (New Haven and London: Yale University Press, 2005), 57–58, 63–65.

4. *DNB*. See also Landry, *The Invention of the Countryside: Hunting, Walking, and Ecology in English Literature, 1671–1831* (Houndmills, Basingstoke, UK, and New York: Palgrave, 2001), 146–47, 277 n. 15.

5. Malcolm Warner, "Catalogue," in Malcolm Warner and Robin Blake, *Stubbs and the Horse* (New Haven and London: Yale University Press in Association with Kimbell Art Museum, Fort Worth, 2004), 161–213; catalogue entry 53, 189–90.

6. Kim F. Hall, *Things of Darkness: Economies of Race and Gender in Early Modern England* (Ithaca, NY, and London: Cornell University Press, 1995), 237.

7. Theodore Andrea Cook, *A History of the English Turf*, 3 vols. (London: H. Virtue and Co., 1901), 1:i–49.

8. William Cavendish, *A General System of Horsemanship in all it's Branches: containing*

a Faithful Translation Of that most noble and useful Work of his Grace, William Cavendish, Duke of Newcastle, entitled The manner of Feeding, Dressing, and Training of Horses for the Great Saddle, and Fitting them for the Service of the Field in Time of War, or for the Exercise and Improvement of Gentlemen in the Academy at home: A Science peculiarly necessary throughout all Europe, and which has hitherto been so much neglected, or discouraged in England, that young Gentlemen have been obliged to have recourse to foreign Nations for this Part of their Education, 2 vols. (London: Printed for J. Brindley, Bookseller to His Royal Highness the Prince of Wales, 1743), 1:21.

9. Walter Shaw Sparrow, *George Stubbs and Ben Marshall* (London: Cassell; New York: Charles Scribner's Sons, 1929), 14.

10. Henry Angelo, *Reminiscences of Henry Angelo, with Memoirs of His Late Father and Friends, Including Numerous Original Anecdotes and Curious Traits of the Most Celebrated Characters That Have Flourished during the Last Eighty Years* (London: Henry Colburn, 1828), 29.

11. Ibid., 1–2, and Angelo, *Reminiscences of Henry Angelo . . .* , vol. 2 (London: Henry Colburn and Richard Bentley, 1830), 54.

12. Antoine de Pluvinel, *Maneige Royal Ou Lon Peut Remarquer Le Defaut Et La Perfection Du Chevalier* (Paris: Crispian de Pas, 1623).

13. Alois Podhajsky, *The Complete Training of Horse and Rider,* trans. Eva Podhajsky and Col. V. D. S. Williams (London: Harrap, 1967), 17–19.

14. John Buchan, *Greenmantle* (1916; Harmondsworth, UK: Penguin, 1958), 248.

15. Ibid.

16. Ibid., 29.

17. Ibid., 248.

18. Lucinda Green, "Do We Really Need the Agonies of Dressage Judging and the Boredom of Average Show Jumping to Determine the Winners?" *Horse and Hound,* 25 August 1994, 8.

19. Robin Balfour quoted in Emmanuelle de Monléon, "Germans Retain Double Gold; Germany Proves Unbeatable While Britain Cannot Catch up after Falling Behind in the Dressage," *Horse and Hound,* 11 August 2005, 5.

20. Everyone agrees about 1897 as the year of Sloan's international impact, as that was the year in which he first came to Europe from America and raced at Saint-Cloud. See Charles Chenevix Trench, *A History of Horsemanship* (London: Longman, 1970), 186. Piero Santini, a pupil of Caprilli's, gives 1897 as the starting date for his master's work on his new system of horsemanship, to which he devoted the last ten years of his short life. Santini, *Riding Reflections* (1933; rev. ed. London: Country Life, 1950), 1.

21. Chenevix Trench, *History of Horsemanship,* 239.

22. Edward Hotaling, *The Great Black Jockeys: The Lives and Times of the Men Who Dominated America's First National Sport* (Rocklin, CA: Forum, 1999).

23. Ibid., 297–98.

24. Chenevix Trench, *History of Horsemanship,* 250.

25. See Captain F. C. Hitchcock, *To Horse!* (New York: Charles Scribner's Sons, 1938), 244.

26. Chenevix Trench, *History of Horsemanship,* 152–53.

27. Ibid., 153.

28. Elwyn Hartley Edwards, *Horses and Their Role in the History of Man* (London: Willow Books–Collins, 1987), 145.

29. Ibid., 145–46.

30. Lieutenant Colonel S. G. Goldschmidt, *Bridle Wise: A Key to Better Hunters—Better Ponies* (London: Country Life; New York: Charles Scribner's Sons, 1927), 9.

31. Edwards, *Horses and Their Role,* 146.

32. Hitchcock, *To Horse!* 245.

33. A cartoon, captioned "One of these Continental snaffle experts," portrays a Caprilli-like figure in Lieutenant Colonel M. F. McTaggart, D. S. O., *From Colonel to Subaltern: Some Keys for Horseowners* (London: Country Life, 1928), 143.

34. Santini writes of the "Weedon seat" in *Riding Reflections,* 3–4. In a later book, *The Forward Impulse* (London: Country Life, 1937), Santini notes that Capt. Bowden Smith, a graduate of the Italian Cavalry School at Pinerolo in 1920–21, was "at present [1937] and for some years past head of the British Cavalry School at Weedon" (113 n.).

35. These popular histories thus deserve consideration, since from the ethnographic point of view, what people in a field of endeavor regard as their history counts as valuable evidence. As it happens, I have found Charles Chenevix Trench's extensive use of primary sources to be judicious and fundamentally accurate, even in the case of quotations, despite the absence of footnotes in his book. Elwyn Hartley Edwards is often consulted and cited by art historians and archaeologists on matters equestrian.

36. *An Hipponomie or The Vineyard of Horsemanship: Devided into three Bookes, By Michaell Baret, Practitioner and Professor of the same Art* (London: Printed by George Eld, 1618), 54.

37. John Lawrence, *A Philosophical And Practical Treatise On Horses, and on the Moral Duties Of Man towards The Brute Creation,* 2 vols. (London: Printed for T. Longman, 1796–98), 2:20.

38. John Lawrence, *The Horse in All His Varieties and Uses; His Breeding, Rearing, and Management, Whether in Labour or Rest; with Rules, Occasionally Interspersed, for His Preservation from Disease* (London: Printed for M. Arnold, Sold by Longman, Rees, Orme, et al., 1829), 165.

39. Cavendish, *A New Method and Extraordinary Invention, To Dress Horses, and Work Them according to Nature: as also, To Perfect Nature by the Subtilty of Art; Which was never found out, but by The Thrice Noble, High, and Puissant Prince William Cavendishe* (London: Printed by Thomas Milbourn, 1667), 203–6.

40. Lawrence, *Philosophical And Practical Treatise,* 2:246–47.

41. Ibid., 250.

42. Ibid., 250–51.

43. *The Compleat Horseman: Discovering the Sweet Marks of the Beauty, Goodness, Faults and Imperfections of Horses: . . . By the Sieur de Solleysell, Querry to the present French King for his Great Horses, and one of the Royal Academy of Paris. To which is added, A most Excellent Supplement of Riding; Collected from the best Authors, By Sir William Hope, Kt. Deputy-Lieutenant of the Castle of Edinburgh* (London: Printed for M. Gillyflower, R. Bentley, et al., 1696), otherwise known as *The Parfait Mareschal, Or Compleat Farrier,* 96–97.

44. Thomas Lister, Lord Ribbesdale, Master of the Buckhounds from 1892 to 1895, *The Queen's Hounds and Stag-Hunting Recollections* (London: Longmans, Green, and Co., 1897), 301 n.

45. See Judy Egerton, *British Sporting and Animal Painting, 1655–1867* (London: Tate Gallery for the Yale Center for British Art, 1978), 42–43, catalogue entry 45.

46. Ibid.

47. Nathaniel Harley, Letter to Edward "Auditor" Harley, 4 November 1715, B. L. Add. Mss. 70143, 227r.

48. Miklós Jankovich, *They Rode into Europe: The Fruitful Exchange in the Arts of Horsemanship between East and West,* trans. Anthony Dent (London, Toronto, Wellington, and Sydney: George G. Harrup and Co., 1971), 83.

49. Lynn White Jr., *Medieval Technology and Social Change* (London, Oxford, and New York: Oxford University Press, 1962), 14–15. See also Hugh Kennedy, *The Armies of the Caliphs: Military and Society in the Early Islamic State* (London and New York: Routledge, 2001), 171–73.

50. White, *Medieval Technology,* 15.

51. Ibid., 18–19; Kennedy, *Armies of the Caliphs,* 172–73; Rachel Ward, "Stirrups from the Islamic World," in *Furusiyya,* ed. David Alexander, 2 vols. (Riyadh: King Abdulaziz Public Library, 1996), 1:84–91.

52. See, e.g., Bernard S. Bachrach, "*Caballus et Caballarius* in Medieval Warfare," in *The Study of Chivalry: Resources and Approaches,* ed. Howell Chickering and Thomas H. Seiler (Kalamazoo: Medieval Institute Publications, Western Michigan University, 1988), 194–97; Bernard S. Bachrach, "Animals and Warfare in Early Medieval Europe," in *L'uomo di fronte al mondo animale nell'alto Medioevo* (Spoleto: Centro italiano di studi sull'alto Medioevo, 1985), 733, 737–49; Matthew Bennett, "The Medieval Warhorse Reconsidered," in *Medieval Knighthood V: Papers from the Sixth Strawberry Hill Conference,* ed. Stephen Church and Ruth Harvey (Woodbridge, UK, and Rochester, NY: Boydell, 1995), 34; Carroll M. Gillmor, "Cavalry, European," in *Dictionary of the Middle Ages,* ed. Joseph R. Strayer, 13 vols. (New York: Scribner, 1982–89), 3:201–2. White, *Medieval Technology,* 27, dated the impact of the stirrup on Western military tactics to the time of Charles Martel, but more recent scholarship dates its role in military change to a much later period—the very late ninth or even early tenth century.

53. Richard Berenger, *The History and Art of Horsemanship,* 2 vols. (London: Printed for T. Davies and T. Cadell, 1771), 1:130.

54. Ibid., 113.

55. Ibid., 130.

56. See Jean Dumont [Baron de Carlscroon], *A New Voyage to the Levant: Containing An Account of the most Remarkable Curiosities in Germany, France, Italy, Malta, and Turkey; With Historical Observations relating to the Present and Ancient State of those Countries,* 2nd ed. (London: Printed by T. H. for M. Gillyflower et al., 1696), 263–65, and Frederick Hasselquist, M.D., *Voyages and Travels in the Levant; In the years 1749, 50, 51, 52. Containing Observations in Natural History, Physick, Agriculture, and Commerce: Particularly On the Holy Land, and the Natural History of the Scriptures,* trans. Charles Linnaeus (London: Printed for L. Davis and C. Reymers, 1766), 72.

57. Captain Lewis Edward Nolan, *Cavalry; Its History and Tactics* (London: Thomas Brown, 1853), 141; British Library shelfmark 8827.d.59.

58. Earl Leslie Griggs, ed., *Collected Letters of Samuel Taylor Coleridge*, 6 vols. (Oxford: Clarendon, 1956–71), 1:66, quoted in Richard Holmes, *Coleridge: Early Visions* (1989; London and New York: Penguin, 1990), 54.

59. Griggs, ed., *Letters*, 1:73; quoted in Holmes, *Early Visions*, 58.

60. Charles MacFarlane, Esq., *Constantinople in 1828. A Residence of Sixteen Months in the Turkish Capital and Provinces: With an Account of the Present State of the Naval and Military Power, and of the Resources of the Ottoman Empire*, 2nd ed., 2 vols. (London: Saunders and Otley, 1829), 2:179, 1:504, 2:174–80.

61. Ibid., 1:503.

62. Ibid., 2:179, 180, 1:504.

63. Ibid., 1:504; 2:179, 187.

64. Ibid., 2:188.

65. Ibid., 187.

66. [Frederick William Robert Stewart], Viscount Castlereagh, M. P. [later fourth Marquis of Londonderry], *A Journey to Damascus through Egypt, Nubia, Arabia Petraea, Palestine, and Syria*, 2 vols. (London: Henry Colburn, 1847), 1:73.

67. Nolan, *Cavalry*, 26.

68. Ibid., 25–26.

69. Ibid., 27.

70. Frontispiece, "The Military Seat As It Ought To Be," from ibid., British Library shelfmark 8827.d.59.

71. Frontispiece from Major-General Geoffrey Brooke, *Introduction to Riding and Stablecraft*, Beaufort Library vol. 2 (London: Seeley Service and Co., 1953), British Library shelfmark W.P.B. 352/2.

72. Piero Santini, *Forward Impulse*, 113–17.

73. Karen Raber and Treva J. Tucker, "Introduction," *The Culture of the Horse: Status, Discipline, and Identity in the Early Modern World* (New York and Houndmills, Basingstoke, UK: Palgrave Macmillan, 2005), 1–41; this passage 40 n. 47.

74. Ibid., 28, 40 n. 47.

75. Ibid., 40 n. 47.

76. Witness the character Stepan Kopenkin in Andrei Platonov's novel *Chevengur*, written in the 1920s. Kopenkin is a Bolshevik cavalryman who rides a horse called Proletarian Strength and, in memory of Rosa Luxemburg, for whose image he feels a tender devotion, devotes himself to socialist revolution, which means abolishing the love of property and substituting the love of one's comrades. Platonov, *Chevengur*, trans. Anthony Olcott (Ann Arbor, MI: Ardis, 1978), see esp. 84–104.

77. Horace Walpole, *Anecdotes of Painting in England; With some Account of the principal Artists; And incidental Notes on other Arts; Collected by the late Mr. George Vertue; And now digested and published from his original MSS. By Mr. Horace Walpole. To which is added The History of The Modern Taste in Gardening*, 4 vols. (Strawberry-Hill: Printed by Thomas Kirgate, 1771), 4:139, 147.

78. Lawrence, *Philosophical And Practical Treatise*, 2:251.

79. John Adams, *An Analysis of Horsemanship; Teaching the Whole Art of Riding, in the Manege, Military, Hunting, Racing, and Travelling System. Together with the Method of Breaking Horses, for Every Purpose to Which Those Noble Animals Are Adapted,* 3 vols. (London: Printed by Albion Press, Published by James Cundee, and Sold by C. Chapple, 1805), 2:36.

80. Ibid., 6.

81. Hannah More, *Strictures on the Modern System of Female Education. With a View of the Principles and Conduct Prevalent Among Women of Rank and Fortune,* 2 vols. (London: Cadell and Davies, 1799), 1:135.

82. The English horse that Swift brought over to Ireland with him was called Bolingbroke. Harold Williams, ed., *The Correspondence of Jonathan Swift,* 5 vols. (Oxford: Clarendon, 1963; rpt 1965), 1:364, 2:133, 153, 171, 193.

83. Lord Bolingbroke, *Contributions to the Craftsman,* ed. Simon Varey (Oxford: Clarendon, 1982), no. 430 (Saturday, 28 September 1734), 172–78; this passage 176.

84. Bolingbroke, *Craftsman,* 176.

85. Christine Gerrard, *The Patriot Opposition to Walpole: Politics, Poetry, and National Myth, 1725–1742* (Oxford: Clarendon, 1994), esp. 108–49.

86. Samuel Chifney, *Genius Genuine, . . . A Fine Part in Riding a Race, Known Only to the Author. Why There Are So Few Good Runners; or Why the Turf Horses Degenerate. A Guide to Recover Them to Their Strength and Speed; as Well as to Train Horses for Running, and Hunters and Hacks for Hard Riding. To Preserve Their Strength, and Their Sinews from Being So Often Destroyed; with Reasons for Horses Changing in Their Running. Likewise a Full Account of the Prince's Horse Escape Running at Newmarket on the 20th and 21st Days of October 1791. With Other Interesting Particulars* (London: Printed by Shury, Sold only for the Author, n.d. [1803]), 158.

87. Ibid.

88. See Christopher Lennox-Boyd, Rob Dixon, and Tim Clayton, *George Stubbs: The Complete Engraved Works* (Abingdon, UK: Stipple, 1989), catalogue 65b: *Baronet, with Sam Chifney Up,* State 3, stipple with etching printed in color by George Townly Stubbs, republished by Edward Orme (4 June 1817), based on oil on canvas by George Stubbs (1791) in the collection of Lord Halifax.

89. Chifney, *Genius Genuine,* 160.

90. Laura Thompson, *Newmarket From James I to the Present Day* (London: Virgin, 2000), 109.

91. Ibid.

92. Ozias Humphry, *Particulars of the life of Mr. Stubbs . . . given to the author of this Memoir by himself and committed from his own relation* [1797], manuscript in the Liverpool Central Library, Liverpool Libraries and Information Services (collection reference 920 May), reproduced as an appendix by Helen Macintyre in Nicholas H. J. Hall, *Fearful Symmetry: George Stubbs, Painter of the English Enlightenment,* exhibition catalogue (New York: Hall and Knight, 2000), 195–212; this passage 203. I have compared microfilm of the original manuscript memoir with Macintyre's transcript in Hall's book, and corrected her transcript in accordance with the original. I give page references to the latter for the reader's convenience.

93. Note by Mary Spencer in Humphry, *Memoir,* in Hall, *Fearful Symmetry,* 203. Next to

Richard Grosvenor is his brother Thomas Grosvenor, gesturing with a whip, and, moving to the right, Sir Roger Mostyn, Fifth Baronet of Mostyn, Flintshire, and Mr. Bell Lloyd; the Huntsman blows his horn on the far left; he and the other hunt servants wear green livery; Judy Egerton, *George Stubbs 1724–1806* (London: Tate Gallery, 1984), 66–67, catalogue entry 39; this passage 66.

94. Basil Taylor, *Animal Painting in England from Barlow to Landseer* (Harmondsworth, UK: Penguin, 1955), 24.

95. Stephen Deuchar, *Sporting Art in Eighteenth-Century England: A Social and Political History* (New Haven and London: Yale University Press, 1988), 108.

96. Robin Blake, *George Stubbs and the Wide Creatioon: Animals, People, and Places in the Life of George Stubbs, 1724–1806* (London: Chatto and Windus, 2005), 138–43.

97. Theodore Andrea Cook, *A History of the English Turf*, 3 vols. (London: H. Virtue and Co., 1901), 1:i:98.

98. Gerald MacLean, "Ottomanism before Orientalism? Bishop King Praises Henry Blount, Passenger in the Levant," in *Travel Knowledge: European "Discoveries" in the Early Modern Period*, ed. Ivo Kamps and Jyotsna G. Singh (New York and Houndmills, Basingstoke, UK: Palgrave, 2001), 85–96. See also MacLean, *Looking East: English Writing and the Ottoman Empire before 1800* (Houndmills, Basingstoke, UK, and New York: Palgrave Macmillan, 2007), and Edward W. Said, *Orientalism* (1978; London and New York: Penguin, 1995), who defines Orientalism as a systematic discourse in the service of European imperialism beginning in the late eighteenth century. For a later refinement of Said's position, see "East Isn't East," *Times Literary Supplement*, February 1995, 6.

99. Lisa Jardine and Jerry Brotton, *Global Interests: Renaissance Art between East and West* (London: Reaktion; Ithaca, NY: Cornell University Press, 2000), 119, 133.

100. Ibid., 133.

101. "Sandy, of course, had no European ulster, for it was months since he had worn proper clothes." Buchan, *Greenmantle*, 248.

102. Ibid., 271.

103. It would be inappropriate to read Sandy Arbuthnot as exemplary of early modern British imperial agency, since Buchan's is clearly a later formation. See Daniel Goffman's *Britons in the Ottoman Empire, 1642–1660* (Seattle and London: University of Washington Press, 1998), 3–6, on the need for historical particularity. Buchan's characters may not belong to the early modern period, but they are, like a twentieth-century English hunting seat, products of a process initiated then.

Chapter 3 · *Steal of a Turk*

Epigraph: James Buchan, *High Latitudes* (New York: Farrar, Straus, Giroux, 1996), 75–76.

1. The most recent work on Thoroughbred genetics, from the Smurfit Institute of Genetics at Trinity College, Dublin, has revealed errors in the *General Stud-Book* and suggests that the number of foundation mares for the English Thoroughbred is even smaller than had been thought. E. W. Hill et al., "History and Integrity of Thoroughbred Dam Lines Revealed in Equine mtDNA Variation," *Animal Genetics* 33 (August 2002): 287–94. In 2005

Patrick Cunningham delivered a paper at the British Association's Festival of Science in Dublin, in which he claimed that "a combination of modern molecular genetics and a trawl through 300 years of pedigree stud books" revealed that the Darley's "Y chromosome, which carries the male genes, is found in 95 per cent of modern thoroughbred stallions," while Tregonwell's Natural Barb "contributed the largest proportion—14 per cent—of the genes passed down the female line of racehorses." Steve Connor, "Modern Racehorses Can Be Traced to a Single Ancestor," *The Independent*, 6 September 2005, 16.

2. Franco Varola, *Typology of the Racehorse* (1974; London and New York: J. A. Allen, 1977), 2.

3. See, e.g., Caroline Bankes, "An Eye for a Horse," *The Field* 273, no. 7048 (November 1991): 52–57.

4. Juliet Clutton-Brock, personal communication to the author, January 2004.

5. Juliet Clutton-Brock, *Horse Power: A History of the Horse and the Donkey in Human Societies* (London: Natural History Museum, 1992), 61.

6. S. Bökönyi, *History of Domestic Mammals in Central and Eastern Europe*, trans. Lili Halápy with revisions by Ruth Tringham (Budapest: Akadémiai Kiadó, 1974), 252–54.

7. Ibid., 255.

8. S. Bökönyi, *Data on Iron Age Horses of Central and Eastern Europe in the Mecklenberg Collection, Part I*, American School of Prehistoric Research Bulletin 25 (Cambridge, MA: Peabody Museum, Harvard University Press, 1968), 52.

9. Bökönyi, *History of Domestic Mammals*, 255.

10. Recent champions of native British racing stock include Alexander Mackay-Smith, *Speed and the Thoroughbred: The Complete History* (Lanham, MD: Derrydale and Millwood House, 2000), 1–4, 19–82, and Richard Nash, "'Honest English Breed': The Thoroughbred as Cultural Metaphor," in *The Culture of the Horse: Status, Discipline, and Identity in the Early Modern World*, ed. Karen Raber and Treva J. Tucker (New York and Houndmills, Basingstoke, UK: Palgrave Macmillan, 2005), 245–72; this passage 265, 271–72 n. 36.

11. Mackay-Smith, *Speed and the Thoroughbred*, 138–50; Nash, "'Honest English Breed,'" 264–65. Jeremy James suggests that "the Ottoman Empire produced fabulous horses of great variety, of which Arabs formed one part, but the vast majority of military horses used by the Ottoman Turks were of Turkik origin"; *The Byerley Turk* (Ludlow, UK: Merlin Unwin, 2005), 339. James substantiates the claim for a majority of Turkic or Anatolian breeds demographically dominating the Arabian by measuring the "chanfrons," protective face plates used for horses, in collections of armor in the Askeri Museum in Istanbul and the Stibberts Museum in Florence, noting the disparity that emerges: "Chanfrons to fit spoon- or dished-faced horses may be found in the Stibberts Museum in Florence, which houses collections of Mameluke armour from Egypt. This would be consistent with the use of Arab horses. The chanfrons in Stibberts were made to fit faces considerably smaller than the Ottoman chanfrons in Istanbul, which measure from 58 cm to 71 cm, so they would fit horses ranging from 15.3 hh to 17.2 hh" with "straight" or "slightly convex faces" (344).

12. Gerald MacLean, *The Rise of Oriental Travel: English Visitors to the Ottoman Empire, 1580–1720* (Houndmills, Basingstoke, UK, and New York: Palgrave Macmillan, 2004), 162–63.

13. William Cavendish, *A New Method and Extraordinary Invention, To Dress Horses, and Work Them according to Nature: as also, To Perfect Nature by the Subtilty of Art . . .* (London: Printed by Thomas Milbourn, 1667), 72.

14. Laurence D'Arvieux, *The Chevalier D'Arvieux's Travels in Arabia the Desart; Written by Himself, and Publish'd by Mr. De la Roque: Giving a very accurate and entertaining Account of the Religion, Rights, Customs, Diversions, &c. of the Bedouins, or Arabian Scenites. Undertaken by Order of the late French King. To which is added, A General Description of Arabia, by Sultan Ishmael Abulfeda, translated from the best Manuscripts; with Notes, Done into English by an Eminent Hand* (London: Printed for B. Barker, C. King, and J. Brown, 1718), 169–70.

15. Richard Berenger, Esq., Gentleman of the Horse to His Majesty, *The History and Art of Horsemanship,* 2 vols. (London: Printed for T. Davies and T. Cadell, 1771), 1:116–18; Thomas Pennant, *British Zoology, Illustrated by Plates and Brief Explanations* (London: Printed and Sold by B. White, 1770), 46.

16. Also noted by Nash, "Honest English Breed," 266.

17. Elwyn Hartley Edwards, ed., *Encyclopedia of the Horse* (New York: Crescent Books, 1990), 41, citing Lady Wentworth.

18. Philip K. Hitti, *History of the Arabs from the Earliest Times to the Present,* rev. 10th ed. (1937; Houndmills, Basingstoke, UK, and New York: Palgrave, 2002), 21.

19. C. M. Prior, *Early Records of the Thoroughbred Horse Containing Reproductions of Some Original Stud-Books, and Other Papers, of the Eighteenth Century* (London: Sportsman Office, 1924), 15.

20. Major-General W. Tweedie, *The Arabian Horse, His Country and People* (1894; rpt. Alhambra, CA: Borden, 1961), title page and 246 n.

21. See the Museum of the Horse, "The Akhal-Teke," <http://www.imh.org/imh/bw/akhal.html>; Miklós Jankovich, *They Rode into Europe: The Fruitful Exchange in the Arts of Horsemanshiip between East and West,* trans. Anthony Dent (London: George G. Harrap, 1971), 29–35, 132–33; Ann Hyland, *The Medieval Warhorse from Byzantium to the Crusades* (Phoenix Mill, UK: Sutton, 1996), 19–20, 110.

22. Peter Edwards, *The Horse Trade of Tudor and Stuart England* (Cambridge: Cambridge University Press, 1988), 41, n. 46.

23. See Rebecca Cassidy, *The Sport of Kings: Kinship, Class, and Thoroughbred Breeding in Newmarket* (Cambridge: Cambridge University Press, 2002).

24. See Margaret E. Derry, *Bred for Perfection: Shorthorn Cattle, Collies, and Arabian Horses since 1800* (Baltimore and London: Johns Hopkins University Press, 2003), xii, 103–55.

25. William Osmer, *A Dissertation on Horses: Wherein it is Demonstrated, by Matters of Fact, as well as from the Principles of Philosophy, that Innate Qualities do not exist, and that the excellence of this Animal is altogether mechanical and not in the Blood* (London: T. Waller, 1756), 26.

26. Lady Wentworth [Judith Anne Dorothea Blunt Lytton, Baroness Wentworth], *Thoroughbred Racing Stock and Its Ancestors: The Authentic Origin of Pure Blood* (London: George Allen and Unwin, 1938).

27. Connor, "Modern Racehorses," 16.

28. Daniel Defoe, *A Tour through the Whole Island of Great Britain,* ed. Pat Rogers (1724–26; London and New York: Penguin, 1971), 512–13.

29. Mackay Smith, *Speed and the Thoroughbred,* 33–94, 163, 170–73; Nash, "'Honest English Breed,'" 271–72 n. 36.

30. Defoe, *Tour,* 512.

31. Prior, *Early Records,* 102.

32. Peter Willett, *An Introduction to the Thoroughbred* (London: Stanley Paul, 1966), 21.

33. J. B. Robertson, *The Principles of Heredity Applied to the Racehorse* (London: Winning Post, n.d. [1910?]), 35.

34. Willett, *Introduction to the Thoroughbred,* 19.

35. Ibid., 35–36.

36. Nicholas Russell, *Like Engend'ring Like: Heredity and Animal Breeding in Early Modern England* (Cambridge: Cambridge University Press, 1986), 219.

37. Ibid.

38. Ibid., 61, 99, 101.

39. Varola, *Typology of the Racehorse,* 2. Varola observes that the prepotency of the three progenitor stallions who continue "to monopolise virtually all tail-male ancestries of the present-day Thoroughbreds, is a strong indication that the Thoroughbred is destined to be characterised by the emergence of a relatively few influential individuals at every stage of its development" (5–6).

40. Felicity A. Nussbaum, *The Limits of the Human: Fictions of Anomaly, Race, and Gender in the Long Eighteenth Century* (Cambridge and New York: Cambridge University Press, 2003), 254, 255.

41. Ibid., 254. Although a bill was passed in 1833 emancipating British colonial slaves, slavery was not abolished until 1838.

42. Ibid., 256.

43. T. Hornby Morland, *The Genealogy of the English Race Horse; with the natural history of his progenitors, from the earliest times down to the period when foreign blood was first introduced into this kingdom; collected from the best authorities: to which is added, the General Practice of the most judicious Breeders, whereby they have Improved & Perfected Our Breed Of Blood Horses So as to have acquired a decided Pre-eminence and Superiority in the essential Points of Size, Strength, Beauty, Speed, Bottom, &c. &c. Over Those Of Other Countries: With Observations upon the Present Improved Method of Breeding for the Turf, on the selection of stallions, choice of brood mares, crossing the blood, or mixing races; treatment of brood mares and young colts intended for racing, &c. &c. The Result of Observation and Experience during an Acquaintance for many Years with the Turf* (London: Printed by J. Barfield, Printer to His Royal Highness the Prince of Wales, 1810), vii.

44. Heneage Finch, second Earl of Winchilsea, Letter to Count Lesley, Pera, 24 February–6 March 1666/7, Historical Manuscripts Commission, *Report on the Manuscripts of Allan George Finch, Esq., of Burley-on-the-Hill, Rutland,* 2 vols. (London: His Majesty's Stationery Office, 1913–22), 1:457–58; this passage 458.

45. See Nash, "'Honest English Breed,'" 249–50, who follows Mackay-Smith, *Speed and the Thoroughbred,* 122–27, who cites no sources for this claim.

46. Kate Fleet, *European and Islamic Trade in the Early Ottoman State: The Merchants of*

Genoa and Turkey (Cambridge and New York: Cambridge University Press, 1999), 29–30. After describing the importance of the horse trade for the Ottoman economy, Fleet carefully states, "The Turks were not always willing to export their horses" (29). Her example is the Hospitallers, who in 1365 were forced, "due to Turkish annoyance over the capture of Alexandria that year by King Peter of Cyprus," to buy horses in Apulia rather than Turchia (29–30). Elizabeth Tobey discusses how extensive Ottoman trade with Europe was in "The *Palio* Horse in Renaissance and Early Modern Italy," in *Culture of the Horse*, 63–90; see esp. 67–73.

47. Nathaniel Harley, Letter to Edward "Auditor" Harley, Aleppo, 29 December 1705, B. L. Add. Mss. 70143, 180r.

48. K. N. Chauduri, *Trade and Civilisation in the Indian Ocean: An Economic History from the Rise of Islam to 1750* (Cambridge and New York: Cambridge University Press, 1985), 39; Andre Gunder Frank, *ReOrient: Global Economy in the Asian Age* (Berkeley, Los Angeles, and London: University of California Press, 1998), 4–5; Kenneth Pomeranz and Steven Topik, *The World That Trade Created: Society, Culture, and the World Economy 1400–the Present* (Armonk, NY, and London: M. E. Sharpe, 1999), 34.

49. P. J. Cain and A. G. Hopkins, *British Imperialism: Innovation and Expansion, 1688–1914* (London: Longman, 1993), 12. For "fiscal-military state," see John Brewer, *The Sinews of Power: War, Money, and the English State, 1688–1783* (London: Unwin Hyman, 1989), xvii–xxi.

50. Frances Parthenope Verney and Margaret M. Verney, eds., *Memoirs of the Verney Family During the Seventeenth Century Compiled from the Papers and Illustrated by the Portraits at Claydon House*, 2 vols., 2nd ed. (London: Longmans, Green, and Co., 1907), 2:219.

51. Ibid., 218.

52. Alexander Pope, "The First Epistle of the Second Book of Horace Imitated; To Augustus," in *The Poems of Alexander Pope: A One-Volume Edition of the Twickenham Text with Selected Annotations*, ed. John Butt (London: Methuen, 1963), 640–41, lines 139–44.

53. [Thomas Warton], *New-Market, a Satire* (London: Printed for J. Newbery, 1751), 13–14.

54. Willett, *Introduction to the Thoroughbred*, 17.

55. *The Sportsman's Evening Brush, Consisting of the best and most Approved Songs, of the Chace; Ancient and modern (some entirely new) Calculated to give Sporting a Zest, and Enhance the Delights of Conviviality, most of them Written by the greatest Wits of the last and present Centuries. To which is added, The Sportsman's Toast Assistant, or President's Sentimental Guide. (Entirely New)* (London: Printed for J. Roach, and Sold by All the Booksellers in Great-Britain and Ireland, n.d. [Bodley catalogue gives 1792]), 15–16.

56. James Weatherby, *An Introduction to a General Stud-Book; containing (with few exceptions) The Pedigree of every Horse, Mare, &c. of note, That has appeared on the Turf for the last fifty Years, with many of an earlier date; together with a short account of the Most noted Arabians, Barbs, &c. connected therewith* (London: Printed by H. Reynell for J. Weatherby, 1791), part 4, "Arabians, Barbs, and Turks," 203.

57. C. M. Prior, *The Royal Studs of the Sixteenth and Seventeenth Centuries, Together with*

a Reproduction of the Second Earl of Godolphin's Stud-Book, and Sundry Other Papers Relating to the Thoroughbred Horse (London: Horse and Hound, 1935), ix.

58. Paul Rycaut, Letter to the Earl of Winchilsea, London, 26 November 1663, Historical Manuscripts Commission, *Finch Manuscripts,* 1:290–91; this passage 290.

59. Sonia Anderson remarks that the horse had encumbered Rycaut's journey from Adrianople to Smyrna, having to have an eye operation and copious bleeding, and that she has found no subsequent record of this horse: "Either it had a relapse, or it was not after all very fleet." Anderson, *An English Consul in Turkey: Paul Rycaut at Smyrna, 1667–1678* (Oxford: Clarendon, 1989), 33, 35 n. 48.

60. The Levant Company, London, 10 September 1657, Letter to Sir Thomas Bendish, Ambassador at Constantinople, in *Calendar of State Papers, Domestic Series, 1657–8,* ed. Mary Anne Everett Green (London: Longmans and Co., 1884), 95–96; this passage 96.

61. Levant Company, London, 10 September 1657, Letter to Henry Riley, Consul at Aleppo, ibid., 96–97; this passage 97.

62. Cavendish, *New Method,* 61.

63. Thomas Birch, ed., *A Collection of the State Papers of John Thurloe, Esq., Secretary, First, to the Council of State, And afterwards to The Two Protectors, Oliver and Richard Cromwell,* 7 vols. (London: Printed for the Executor of Fletcher Gyles, Thomas Woodward, and Charles Davis, 1742), 4:464, 3:526.

64. Ibid., 3:526.

65. *Calendar of State Papers, Domestic;* 453; cited in Roy Sherwood, *The Court of Oliver Cromwell* (London: Croom Helm, 1977), 57.

66. Prior, *Royal Studs,* 82; Mackay-Smith, *Speed and the Thoroughbred,* 124–27, 156–58, 164, 173.

67. Prior, *Royal Studs,* 82.

68. Mackay-Smith, *Speed and the Thoroughbred,* 12–13, 122–27, 131–50.

69. Jerry Brotton, *The Sale of the Late King's Goods: Charles I and His Art Collection* (London: Macmillan, 2006). Prior acknowledges that the dispersal of Tutbury horses may have had "a good and far reaching influence on the breed of thoroughbred stock in this country." Prior, *Royal Studs,* 54.

70. Monsieur de Bordeaux, Letter to Cardinal Mazarin, London, 4 February 1655, in Le Comte de Cosnac [Gabriel-Jules], *Les Richesses du Palais Mazarin* (Paris: Librarie Renouard, 1884), 233. My thanks to Dafydd Roberts and Jerry Brotton for this reference.

71. Monsieur de Bordeaux, Letter to Cardinal Mazarin, London, 12 February 1655, in de Cosnac, *Les Richesses du Palais Mazarin,* 233–34; this passage 234.

72. Prior, *Royal Studs,* 61, 62–63.

73. Ibid., 63; Landry, "'Delight Makes All of the One Mind': Irish Collectivity at the Races," paper delivered at "Romantic Ireland: From Tone to Gonne," University of Glasgow, 22–24 June 2007. For a history of Irish horse racing, see Tony and Annie Sweeney, in association with Francis Hyland, *The Sweeney Guide to the Irish Turf from 1501 to 2001* (Dublin: Éamonn de Búrca for Edmund Burke, 2002).

74. Jean Rougé, *Ships and Fleets of the Ancient Mediterranean,* trans. Susan Frazer (orig.

pub. in French as *La Marine dans l'antiquité* by Presses Universitaires de France, 1975; Middletown, CT: Wesleyan University Press, 1981), 180.

75. Ibid.

76. Lisa Jardine and Jerry Brotton, *Global Interests: Renaissance Art between East and West* (London: Reaktion; Ithaca, NY: Cornell University Press, 2000), 148, 208 n. 51.

77. Ibid., 208 n. 51.

78. Ralph Davis, *The Rise of the English Shipping Industry In the Seventeenth and Eighteenth Centuries*, National Maritime Museum Modern Maritime Classics Reprint no. 3 (1962; rpt. Newton Abbot, UK: David and Charles, [1978]), 251.

79. *Journal Kept during the Russian War: From the Departure of the Army from England in April, 1854, to the Fall of Sebastopol, by Mrs. Henry Duberly* (London: Longman, Brown, Green, and Longmans, 1855), 5.

80. Ibid., 8.

81. M. Horace Hayes, *Horses on Board Ship: A Guide to their Management* (London: Hurst and Blackett, 1902), 1.

82. Eight other horses besides the Dun, the small "Scrub" who accompanied him, and the Bloody-Shouldered Arabian are mentioned in Nathaniel Harley's letters, B. L. Add. Mss. 70143, 181r, 194r, 215v, and 227r, and in Prior, *Early Records*, 137, 138. The ninth we have no record of shipping for, but the Welbeck stud-book records that Lady Henrietta Cavendish Holles, who in 1713 married Edward, Lord Harley, received a "Barb Mare Creem Coller 5 years old" given her "by Cousen Harley" which may have been an import from Aleppo. "An Acct of What Horses belongs to the Stud July ye 24th 1711," Portland Collection, University of Nottingham Library, Manuscripts Department, P W 2/331: fol. 4. Also quoted in Prior, *Early Records*, 122.

83. Hayes, *Horses on Board Ship*, 4, 10.

84. Ibid., 2–4.

85. Thirsk, *Horses in Early Modern England*, 7.

86. Jeremy James notes the prevalence of *"saman"* in *Saddletramp: From Ottoman Hills to Offa's Dyke* (London and New York: Pelham Books/Stephen Greene and Penguin Group, 1989), 18.

87. These were reported by Lady Anne Blunt as fed to horses by Bedouins in *A Pilgrimage to Nejd: The Cradle of the Arab Race*, 2nd ed., 2 vols. (London: John Murray, 1881; rpt London: Frank Cass, 1968), 2:5, 58, 79.

88. This last was the usual diet of the Turkmen or Akhal-Teke. Because "the sandy Kara Kum desert occupies 90% of Turkmenistan," fresh grass was available only a few months of the year. "The Akhal-Teke," Museum of the Horse website: http://www.imh.org/imh/bw/akhal.html.

89. Prior, *Early Records*, 137–38.

90. K. N. Chaudhuri, "The English East India Company's Shipping (c. 1660–1760)," in *Ships, Sailors, and Spices: East India Companies and their Shipping in the 16th, 17th, and 18th Centuries*, ed. Jaap R. Bruijn and Femme S. Gaastra (Amsterdam: NEHA, 1993), 49–80; this passage 66.

91. Prior, *Early Records*, 137.

92. Ibid.

93. Ibid., 138.

94. Willett, *Introduction to the Thoroughbred*, 22.

95. Nash, "Honest English Breed," 257–62.

96. Eugéne Sue, *Histoire de Arabian Godolphin* (Paris: La Presse, 1838), trans. into English for the London *Sunday Times* and reproduced in book form as *The Godolphin Arabian; or, the History of a Thorough-Bred* (London: Chapman and Elcoate, 1845). Sue's romance inspired the Australian J. Brunton Stephens's narrative in verse, *The Godolphin Arabian: The Story of a Horse* (Brisbane: Watson and Co; London: Sampson Low, Son, and Marston, 1873), and the American Marguerite Henry's children's book, *King of the Wind* (Chicago: Rand McNally, 1948).

97. Linda Colley, *Britons: Forging the Nation, 1701–1837* (New Haven and London: Yale University Press, 1992).

98. Prior, *Royal Studs*, 83.

99. Mackay-Smith, *Speed and the Thoroughbred*, 128–29.

100. James, *Byerley Turk*, 348–49.

101. Prior, *Royal Studs*, 83.

102. Prior, *Early Records*, 144.

103. John Evelyn, *Kalendarium, 1673–1689: The Diary of John Evelyn*, ed. E. S. deBeer, 6 vols. (Oxford: Clarendon, 1955), 4:398.

104. Ibid., 398–99.

105. Ogier Ghiselin de Busbecq, *Travels into Turkey: Containing the most accurate Account of the Turks, and Neighbouring Nations, Their Manners, Customs, Religion, Superstition, Policy, Riches, Coins, &c. The whole being a series of remarkable observations and events, interspers'd with great variety of entertaining incidents, never before printed, Translated from the Original Latin of the Learned A. G. Busbequius, With Memoirs of the Life of the Illustrious Author* (London: Printed for J. Robinson; and W. Payne, 1744), 131. See also Edward Seymour Forster, ed., *The Turkish Letters of Ogier Ghiselin de Busbecq, Imperial Ambassador at Constantinople 1554–1562, Newly Translated from the Latin of the Elzevir Edition of 1633* (Oxford: Clarendon, 1927), 105–6.

106. On English merchants in Aleppo, see Susan E. Whyman, *Sociability and Power in Late-Stuart England: The Cultural Worlds of the Verneys, 1660–1729* (Oxford and New York: Oxford University Press, 1999), 48–54.

107. Letters quoted in Prior, *Early Records*, 124–25, 129.

108. Public Record Office Admiralty (PRO ADM) 52/254 [packet no. 3], Master's Log of the *Preston*, 4 Dec 1717 to 3 March 1718/19, 14r. They sailed on July 5.

109. Weatherby, *General Stud-Book*, 205.

110. Nathaniel Harley, Aleppo, Letter to Edward "Auditor" Harley, London, 29 December 1710, B. L. Add. Mss. 70143, 184r.

111. Nathaniel Harley, Letter to nephew Robert Harley, n.d. [ca. 1716], B. L. Add. Mss. 70143, 264r.

112. Thomas Darley, Aleppo, 21 December 1703, Letter to Henry Darley, Aldby Park, North Yorkshire County Archives, ZDA DAR CP1. My thanks to Richard Nash and Nick Mills for their transcriptions of this letter.

113. Lady Wentworth, *Thoroughbred Racing Stock*, 213.

114. [William Youatt], *The Horse; with a Treatise on Draught; and a Copious Index*, Published under the Superintendence of the Society for the Diffusion of Useful Knowledge (London: Baldwin and Cradock, 1831), 44.

115. Rebecca Cassidy, "Turf Wars: Arab Dimensions to British Racehorse Breeding," *Anthropology Today* 19 (June 2003): 13–18; this passage 15. Cassidy gives no sources for this story, though her article is otherwise well documented. The story also appears on the well-researched and sumptuously illustrated Thoroughbred Heritage website managed by Patricia Erigero: http://www.tbheritage.com.

116. Nathaniel Harley, Letter to Edward "Auditor" Harley, 29 December 1705, B. L. Add. Mss. 70143, 179v.

117. Ibid., 180v.

118. Quoted in Prior, *Early Records*, 126.

119. Quoted ibid., 126–27.

120. Letters and accounts quoted ibid., 137–38.

121. Nathaniel Harley, Letter to Edward "Auditor" Harley, Esq., in London, under cover to Mr. Kingston, Aleppo, 15 February 1714/15, B. L. Add. Mss. 70143, 225r–225v.

122. Edward, Lord Harley, Letter to Nathaniel Harley, 4 December 1716, quoted in Prior, *Early Records*, 142.

123. Bridget Tempest, *Turkmen at Wimpole: Artists from Turkmenistan* (Ashgabat: Visiting Artists, n.d. [2001]), 20.

124. Prior, *Early Records*, 141

125. C. M. Prior, *The History of the Racing Calendar and Stud-Book From Their Inception in the Eighteenth Century, with Observations on Some of the Occurrences Noted Therein* (London: Sporting Life, 1926), 123.

126. Ibid., 131.

127. Ibid., 123.

Chapter 4 · About a Horse

1. Nathaniel Harley, Letter to Edward "Auditor" Harley, 21 February 1717, B. L. Add. Mss. 70143, 275r.

2. Edward, Lord Harley, Letter to Nathaniel Harley, 4 December 1716, quoted in C. M. Prior, *Early Records of the Thoroughbred Horse Containing Reproductions of Some Original Stud-Books, and Other Papers, of the Eighteenth Century* (London: Sportsman Office, 1924), 142.

3. As translated by Lady Wentworth in *Thoroughbred Racing Stock and Its Ancestors: The Authentic Origin of Pure Blood* (London: George Allen and Unwin, 1938), 217.

4. N. Harley to "Auditor" Harley, 21 February 1717, B. L. Add. Mss. 70143, 275r.

5. N. Harley to "Auditor" Harley, 15 May 1717, B. L. Add. Mss. 70143, 285r.

6. "The Great Northern War did not end until 1721; Charles was killed in Norway fighting the Danes in 1718; and Peter died in 1725; neither was succeeded by a sovereign as able as themselves." Caroline Finkel, *Osman's Dream: The Story of the Ottoman Empire, 1300–1923* (London: John Murray, 2005), 336.

7. N. Harley to "Auditor" Harley, 18 May 1717, B. L. Add. Mss. 70143, 289r.

8. N. Harley to "Auditor" Harley, 6 January 1720, B. L. Add. Mss. 70143, 303v–304v.

9. N. Harley to "Auditor" Harley, 29 December 1705, B. L. Add. Mss. 70143, 179v.

10. Michael Levey, *Painting at Court* (London: Weidenfeld and Nicolson, 1971), 277, plate 104; Walter Liedtke, *The Royal Horse and Rider: Painting, Sculpture, and Horsemanship, 1500–1800* (New York: Abaris Books and Metropolitan Museum of Art, 1989), 131, plate 126.

11. See the version of the Bloody Shouldered Arabian's portrait, labeled *Oxford or Basset Bloody-Shouldered Arabian,* reproduced in Lady Wentworth, *Thoroughbred Racing Stock* (1938 ed.), plate 128, near p. 212.

12. Arline Meyer, *John Wootton, 1682–1764: Landscapes and Sporting Art in Early Georgian England* (London: Greater London Council, 1984), 34.

13. Arjun Appadurai, "Introduction: Commodities and the Politics of Value," in *The Social Life of Things: Commodities in Cultural Perspective,* ed. Appadurai (Cambridge: Cambridge University Press, 1986), 3–63; this passage 38.

14. Lisa Jardine and Jerry Brotton, *Global Interests: Renaissance Art between East and West* (London: Reaktion; Ithaca, NY: Cornell University Press, 2000), 172, 212 n. 88.

15. Ibid., 133.

16. Ibid.

17. John Monk's "An exact account of all ye horses Mares Geldings & Ffouls in ye Lordpp of Welbeck And of other Quick Stock, March 8th 1716," Portland Collection, University of Nottingham Library, Manuscripts Department, Pl C 1/284.

18. John Cossen, Wimpole, 11 July 1727, Letter to Lord Oxford, Dover Street, University of Nottingham Library, Pl C 1/579.

19. Isaac Hobart, Letters to Edward, Lord Harley, later Lord Oxford, Portland Papers, B. L. Add. Mss. 70385 and 70386 [unfoliated].

20. Hobart, B. L. Add. Mss. 70385.

21. John Cossen, Wimpole, 1 August 1727, to Lord Oxford in Dover Street: "The head and neck of ye Arabian is very much broke out wth a Scab by some extraordinary usage or other." University of Nottingham Library, Pl C 1/581. Five days later, 6 August 1727, the mystery appeared to have been solved, according to the farrier, and Cossen wrote to Oxford, "The Knots about ye Head and Neck of ye Arabian seem to be somewht faln: he is in good health and ye Farrier thinks he is kept too much in Cloaths." Pl C 1/582, fol. 2v.

22. John Cossen wrote on 14 February 1724/25, to Lord Oxford in Dover Street, "Have discoursed John Elsom who says that the Arabian is very well altho his Codd be somewhat larger thro the ailment he had." University of Nottingham Library, Pl C 1/484; Isaac Hobart, Letters to Lord Oxford, 21 August 1725, reported "The Arabian's being taken ill last Tuesday in the same manner as he was the last Winter at Wimpole, but is not so much swelled as then. John Bowron has rowel'd him and will proceed wth him in the same method, if wee find no relief from what he has done, I resolve to send on Monday for Mr Marriot & will not fail every post to let Yr. Ldp. know how it is with him"; on 23 August 1725, Hobart advised, "The Arabian is in a fair way to recover once more, I design'd to have sent for Mr Marriot, but John Bowron thinks he will do well without any other advice"; on 28 August 1725, Hobart assured his lordship, "John Bowron tells me I may assure Yr. Ldp. that The Arabian is now out of Danger—-I wish he may never have another return"; B. L. Add. Mss. 70385.

23. Hobart to Lord Oxford, 21 May 1726: "The Arabian also is fallen off very much, I don't hear that any of The Mares wch were Sent to him the last year proved to be in foal." B. L. Add. Mss. 70385.

24. Cavendish, *A General System of Horsemanship in all it's Branches: containing a Faithful Translation Of that most noble and useful Work of his Grace, William Cavendish, Duke of Newcastle . . .* , 2 vols. (London: John Brindley, 1743), 1:21–22.

25. William Osmer, *A Dissertation on Horses: Wherein it is Demonstrated, by Matters of Fact, as well as from the Principles of Philosophy, that Innate Qualities do not exist, and that the excellence of this Animal is altogether mechanical and not in the Blood* (London: T. Waller, 1756), 14–15.

26. As translated by Lady Wentworth in *Thoroughbred Racing Stock*, 217.

27. Regarding Tillemans's *George I at Newmarket* (1722), Walter Shaw Sparrow observes, "The nearest string of horses belongs to the Duke of Devonshire; its leader is Flying Childers. The other horses on Warren Hill are portraits also, but I cannot find out their names. One of the greys is the Bloody-shouldered Arabian, probably." Walter Shaw Sparrow, *British Sporting Artists from Barlow to Herring* (London: John Lane, the Bodley Head Limited; New York: Charles Scribner's Sons, 1922), 67.

28. Hobart to Lord Harley, 1 December 1722, B. L. Add. Mss. 70385.

29. N. Harley to "Auditor" Harley, 15 May 1717 and 6 January 1720, B. L. Add. Mss. 70143, 285r and 304r.

30. Alexander Mackay-Smith asserts, without providing any evidence, that Nathaniel Harley had tried the Bloody Shouldered Arabian for speed during the four years he owned him, "presumably over 4-mile distances," and found that he had "spirit, quality, and stamina," but not the middle-distance speed that Mackay-Smith attributes to "Turcoman" (Akhal-Teke), rather than Arabian, horses; this was the most desired Thoroughbred characteristic that had been lacking in native Irish racing hobbies and Yorkshire running-horses. Mackay-Smith, *Speed and the Thoroughbred: The Complete History* (Lanham, MD: Derrydale and Millwood House, 2000), 103–4.

31. Hobart to Lord Harley, 27 April 1723, B. L. Add. Mss. 70385.

32. For Berkshire, see Prior, *Early Records*, 139; for Sir Gervas Clifton, Letters to Lord Oxford, 9 April 1726 and 7 May 1726, B. L. Add. Mss. 70374, 87r and 89r.

33. Cossen, Wimpole, 8 April 1729, to Lord Oxford, Dover Street: "At the beginning of last Week came the Duke of Bridgwaters mair and Saturday last the Duke of Ancasters Mair have bin both coverd by the Arabian, and are kept at the Tigar Inne." University of Nottingham Library, Pl C 1/646.

34. Hobart to Lord Oxford, 15 April 1728, B. L. Add. Mss. 70386.

35. Hobart to Lord Harley, 18 November 1723, B. L. Add. Mss. 70385.

36. Lord Oxford wrote to Isaac Hobart from Dover Street on 28 February 1727, "I shall not cover any more mares with the Arabian I would have you dispose of all the brood mares except the young Arabian mare and the old Dunn Pad Mare"; the dun mare may have been Lady Henrietta's favorite, who had been painted several times by Wootton twelve years before. B. L. Add. Mss. 70385.

37. Cossen, Wimpole, 30 March 1729, to Lord Oxford: "The Grey Mair was coverd by ye Arabian ye 26th past." University of Nottingham Library, Pl C 1/641. A week later, 8

April 1729, Cossen reported further aristocratic couplings: "At the beginning of last Week came the Duke of Bridgwaters mair and Saturday last the Duke of Ancasters Mair have bin both coverd by the Arabian, and are kept at the Tigar Inne." Pl C 1/646.

38. Cossen, Wimpole, 8 April 1729, to the Earl of Oxford, in Dover Street, University of Nottingham Library, Pl C 1/646.

39. Letter from the sixth Duke of Somerset to the second Earl of Oxford, dated Newmarket, 29 April 1729, quoted in Prior, *Early Records*, 143.

40. Cossen, Wimpole, 4 May 1729, to Lord Oxford, in Dover Street, University of Nottingham Library, Pl C 1/652.

41. [George Coleman and Bonnell Thornton], *The Connoisseur*, no. 63 (Thursday, 10 April 1755) (London: Printed for J. Walker, 1798), 144–46; this passage 144.

42. Other Portland Papers are housed at University of Nottingham Library.

43. Humfrey Wanley, *The Diary of Humfrey Wanley, 1715–1726*, ed. C. E. Wright and Ruth C. Wright, 2 vols. (London: Bibliographical Society, 1966).

44. See *DNB* and Landry, *The Invention of the Countryside: Hunting, Walking, and Ecology in English Literature, 1671–1831* (Houndmills, Basingstoke, UK, and New York: Palgrave, 2001), 146–47, 157–59, 277 n. 15.

45. As his friend Jonathan Swift observed. See Harold Williams, ed., *The Correspondence of Jonathan Swift*, 5 vols. (Oxford: Clarendon, 1963–65), 2:383 and n.; 5:205–6.

46. Linda Colley, *In Defiance of Oligarchy: The Tory Party, 1714–60* (Cambridge: Cambridge University Press, 1982), 162.

47. Arline Meyer, "Wootton at Wimpole," *Apollo*, September 1985, 212–19; this passage 213.

48. Wootton received twenty-six pounds five shillings for Lord Harley's *Dun Arabian*, painted sometime before 1720; at 84×68 inches, a larger picture than the *The Bloody Shouldered Arabian* at $40\frac{3}{4} \times 50$ inches; ten pounds fifteen shillings for what would become known as *The Countess of Oxford's Dun Mare*, painted in 1715, $50 \times 40\frac{1}{2}$ inches, so roughly the same size as *The Bloody Shouldered Arabian* but referred to as a "sketch"; and as much as forty guineas for *The Countess of Oxford's Dun Mare, with Thomas Thornton the Groom*, also from 1715, at 106×132 inches, a picture "as big as ye Life." Richard C. Goulding and C. K. Adams, *Catalogue of the Pictures Belonging to His Grace the Duke of Portland, K.G. at Welbeck Abbey, 17 Hill Street, London, and Langwell House* (Cambridge: Cambridge University Press, 1936), 113, 167, 112.

49. Captain Frank Siltzer, *Newmarket: Its Sport and Personalities* (London, New York, Toronto, and Melbourne: Cassell, 1923), 194–214.

50. Ibid., 200.

51. See Jardine and Brotton, *Global Interests*, 149–50, for images and commentary, and for further details, Elizabeth Tobey, "The *Palio* Horse in Renaissance and Early Modern Italy," in *Culture of the Horse: Status, Discipline, and Identity in the Early Modern World*, ed. Karen Raber and Treva J. Tucker (New York and Houndmills, Basingstoke, UK: Palgrave Macmillan, 2005), 63–90.

52. Sheila Canby, "Persian Horse Portraits and Their Cousins," in *Furusiyya*, ed. David Alexander, 2 vols. (Riyadh: King Abdulaziz Public Library, 1996), 1:190–95.

53. Sparrow, *British Sporting Artists from Barlow to Herring*, 12.

54. Ibid.

55. *"The Bloody Shouldered Arabian* (see Goulding and Adams, No. 957), was purchased by the Duke of Portland at Christie's, 24 July, 1914, Lot 114 and is almost an exact replica of No. 293 which was painted for Harley." Meyer, "Wootton at Wimpole," 213, 219 n. 12.

56. See Landry, *Invention of the Countryside*, colour plate 4, for the 1723 portrait, misdated there as 1724.

57. Guy Paget, "John Wootton, Father of English (Sporting) Painting, 1685–1765," *Apollo* 39 (February 1944): 136–45; this passage 145; Meyer, "Wootton at Wimpole," 214–16.

58. Paget, "John Wootton," 139, citing Captain Frank Siltzer, *The Story of British Sporting Prints* (London: Hutchinson and Co., n.d. [1925]), 316–17, 375.

59. Meyer, *John Wootton*, 34.

60. "I send also a little Greyhound Bitch of this Countrey that has been used to the Hawkes, and designed as a Curiosity rather then pretending to vie with those you have in England which run so much better," wrote Nathaniel Harley to his brother Edward, "Auditor" Harley, from Aleppo, 15 February 1715, B. L. Add. Mss. 70143, 225r.

61. Linda Colley, *Captives: The Story of Britain's Pursuit of Empire and How Its Soldiers and Civilians Were Held Captive by the Dream of Global Supremacy* (New York: Pantheon, 2003).

62. Joan Thirsk, ed., *The Agrarian History of England and Wales, Volume V.ii., 1640–1750: Agrarian Change* (Cambridge: Cambridge University Press, 1985), 578.

63. Harriet Ritvo, "Possessing Mother Nature: Genetic Capital in Eighteenth-Century Britain," in *Early Modern Conceptions of Property,* ed. John Brewer and Susan Staves (London and New York: Routledge, 1995), 413–26; this passage 414.

64. Ibid., 415.

65. Daniel Defoe, *The Life and Adventures of Robinson Crusoe,* ed. Angus Ross (1719; Harmondsworth, UK: Penguin, 1974), 27.

66. Thirsk, *Agrarian History,* 578.

67. Harriet Ritvo, *The Animal Estate: The English and Other Creatures in the Victorian Age* (London and New York: Penguin, 1990), 1–3.

68. Osmer, *Dissertation*, 50–51.

69. Ibid., 9–10, 25–26.

70. Rebecca Cassidy, *The Sport of Kings: Kinship, Class, and Thoroughbred Breeding in Newmarket* (Cambridge: Cambridge University Press, 2002), 140–60.

71. [Gervase Markham], *How to chuse, ride, traine, and diet, both Hunting-horses and running Horses. With all the secrets thereto belonging discouered: an Arte neuer heere-to-fore written by any Authour. Also a discourse of horsmanship, wherein the breeding, and ryding of Horses for seruice, in a briefe manner, is more methodically sette downe, then hath beene heeretofore: vvith a more easie and direct course for the ignorant, to attaine to the sayd Arte or knowledge. Together with a newe addition for the cure of horses diseases, of what kinde or nature soeuer* (1593; London: James Roberts, 1599), A3v.

72. Noël Denham-Young, "The Tournament in the Thirteenth Century," in *Studies in Medieval History Presented to Frederick Maurice Powicke,* ed. R. W. Hunt, W. A. Pantin, and R. W. Southern (Oxford: Clarendon, 1948), 240–68; this passage 240.

73. My thanks to Layla Saatchi for first pointing out the connection to Shi'a iconography.

74. *"Ta'ziya"* (P. Chelkowski), in *The Encyclopedia of Islam, New Edition*, ed. H. A. R. Gibb et al., 11 vols. (Leiden: E. J. Brill, 1960–2000), 10:406–8.

75. David Pinault, *Horse of Karbala: Muslim Devotional Life in India* (New York and Houndmills, Basingstoke, UK: Palgrave, 2001), 109–32.

76. [William Youatt], *The Horse; with a Treatise on Draught; and a Copious Index, Published under the Superintendence of the Society for the Diffusion of Useful Knowledge* (London: Baldwin and Cradock, 1831), 12.

77. *Narrative of a Journey through the Upper Provinces of India, from Calcutta to Bombay, 1824–1825, (with notes upon Ceylon,) an Account of a Journey to Madras and the Southern Provinces, 1826, and Letters Written in India, by the Late Right Reverend Reginald Heber, D.D., Lord Bishop Of Calcutta*, 2 vols. (London: John Murray, 1828), 2:319.

78. Ibid.

79. Youatt, *The Horse*, 15.

80. Prior, *Early Records*, 142.

81. John Cheny, *An Historical List, of all Horse-Matches Run, And of All Plates and Prizes Run for in England and Wales (of the Value of Ten Pounds or upwards) in 1729. Containing the Names of the Owners of the Horses, that have Run, as above, and the Names and Colours of the said Horses also. With The Winner distinguished of every Match, Plate, Prize or Stakes: The Conditions of Running, as to Weight, Age, Size, &c. and the Places in which the losing Horses have come in. With a List also of all the Principal Cock-Matches, of the Year above, and who were the Winners and Losers of them, &c.* (London: Printed in the Year 1729), 20.

82. Cheny, *An Historical List . . . Run for in 1730*, 18; *An Authentic Historical Racing Calendar of all the Plates, Sweepstakes, Matches, &c. Run for at York, from the First Commencement of the Races There in the Year 1709, to the Year 1785 inclusive; . . . , by W. Pick of York* (York: Printed by W. Blanchard and Co., n.d. [1785?]), 25.

83. Cheny, *An Historical List . . . Run for in 1729*, 172; Cheny, *An Historical List . . . Run for in 1730*, 14.

84. Cheny, *An Historical List . . . Run for in 1728*, 13.

85. Ibid., 21.

86. Ibid., 23.

87. Ibid., 9.

88. Cheny, *An Historical List . . . Run for in 1731*, 26, 30, 7.

89. Cheny, *An Historical List . . . Run for in 1740*, 47, 49, 58, 64.

90. James Bramston, Letter to Lord Oxford, 8 October 1729, Portland Papers, B. L. Add. Mss. 70373, 150v–151r; this passage 150v.

91. Swift, *Correspondence*, 2:415; 3:5 and n.

92. Ibid., 1:173, 223–25, 226–27; 3:39–41.

93. See Albert J. Rivero, ed., *Gulliver's Travels: A Norton Critical Edition* (1726; New York and London: W. W. Norton, 2002), 273–74, and *Correspondence*, 3:258 and n.

94. Swift, *Correspondence*, 2:338–39.

95. Ibid., 127, 171, 348, 418.

96. Ibid., 311, 133, 171, 390.

97. Ibid., 29, 40.

98. Gulliver steers hopefully eastward from the island of Houyhnhnmland toward "New-Holland," a Dutch skipper is reported to have found Houyhnhnmland by sailing south from New-Holland, and the map for Part 4 of *Gulliver's Travels* depicts a mainland north and east of Houyhnhnmland labelled "Edel's land, Lewins land, and Nuyts Land." Swift, *Gulliver's Travels*, ed. Rivero, 239, 242, 186.

99. Note Linda Colley's comment on Sir William Yonge's wondering "how men who cherished the prerogative could support a motion whereby the King 'would not have so much Power left him as the Stadtholder of the Republick of Holland',—an invidious parallel selected for a tory audience." Colley, *In Defiance of Oligarchy*, 103.

100. [Reverend James Bramston], *The Art of Politicks, In Imitation of Horace's Art of Poetry* (London: Printed for Lawton Gillver, 1729). "I have made some little alterations in the Art of Politicks, which I will communicate to your Lordship, & when I come to London will publish it without a name, unless your Lordship enters a protest against my So doing. If it will be big enough to sell for two Shillings (& I can sell two thousand in a twelve months time,) I shall get money enough to buy me a large parcel of good books." Bramston, Letter to Lord Oxford, B. L. Add. Mss. 70373, 151r.

101. There are always exceptions to the rule, such as the series of fifty-five gouaches painted for the tenth Earl of Pembroke at Wilton House by the riding master and artist Baron Reis d'Eisenberg around 1747. Baron Reis d'Eisenberg and Dorian Williams, *The Classical Riding School: The Wilton House Collection* (New York: Vendome, 1979). Giles Worsley, in "A Courtly Art: The History of 'Haute École' in England," *The Court Historian* 6, no. 1 (May 2001): 29–47, remarks upon several other noblemen and gentlemen who revived the *haute école* in the later eighteenth century (45–46).

Chapter 5 · The Noble Brute

1. Although the satire exceeds the targeting of Britain's maritime-mercantile and imperial ambitions, Swift's critique of imperialism and settler-colonialism has often been noted. As Howard Erskine-Hill observes, the final chapter of Part 4 is "a trenchant critique of colonization and empire," and as an "account of the origin of the European sea-borne empires could hardly be improved on as a piece of devastating, reductive, humanist satire." *Gulliver's Travels*, Landmarks of World Literature series, J. P. Stern, gen. ed. (Cambridge and New York: Cambridge University Press, 1993), 91.

2. Felicity A. Nussbaum, *The Limits of the Human: Fictions of Anomaly, Race, and Gender in the Long Eighteenth Century* (Cambridge and New York: Cambridge University Press, 2003), 254.

3. Ibid., 254.

4. Howard Erskine-Hill has suggested, "The replacement of the horse by the internal combustion engine as a source of energy has probably facilitated the reaction against the Houyhnhnms in our time." *Gulliver's Travels*, 104, Endnote.

5. Jonathan Swift, *Gulliver's Travels*, ed. Claude Rawson and Ian Higgins (1726, 1735; Oxford and New York: Oxford University Press, 2005), 224. All further references are to this edition unless otherwise noted.

6. Ibid., 271.

7. Ibid., 224.

8. Ibid.

9. Ibid.

10. Erskine-Hill, *Gulliver's Travels*, 64.

11. Swift, *Gulliver's Travels*, 224.

12. Erskine-Hill, *Gulliver's Travels*, 65.

13. [John Hawkesworth], *The Adventurer* no. 37, Tuesday, 13 March 1753, [217]-222; this passage 220. Hawkesworth specifically dismisses what radical vegetarians had insisted: that to be against cruelty meant giving up killing animals for food. Hawkesworth envisaged domestic livestock and game animals as competitors with humans for vegetable resources, observing, "[B]y him that kills merely to eat, life is sacrificed only to life; and if man had lived upon fruits and herbs, the greater part of those animals which die to furnish his table, would never have lived; instead of increasing the breed as a pledge of plenty, he would have been compelled to destroy them to prevent a famine" (218).

14. Ibid., 221.

15. Ibid.

16. Ibid.

17. Malcolm Warner, "Ecce Equus: Stubbs and the Horse of Feeling," in Malcolm Warner and Robin Blake, *Stubbs and the Horse* (New Haven and London: Yale University Press in Association with Kimbell Art Museum, Fort Worth, 2004), 1–17; see 5–7, 17 n. 18.

18. Swift, *Gulliver's Travels*, 276.

19. Swift emerges from Irvin Ehrenpreis's biography as a "sharp-eyed, if appreciative (and generous) master" to his servants, particularly his grooms; Ehrenpreis comments that "the delight in horses and the acute observation of them which appear in Houyhnhnmland are derived from an immense firsthand knowledge," and that "the contrast with humans was drawn in part from Swift's trials with grooms and footmen." *Swift: The Man, His Works, and the Age, Volume Three: Dean Swift* (Cambridge, MA: Harvard University Press, 1983), 432.

20. Swift, *Gulliver's Travels*, 210–14.

21. Ogier Ghiselin de Busbecq, *Travels into Turkey: Containing the most accurate Account of the Turks, and Neighbouring Nations, Their Manners, Customs, Religion, Superstition, Policy, Riches, Coins, &c. The whole being a series of remarkable observations and events, interspers'd with great variety of entertaining incidents, never before printed. Translated from the Original Latin of the Learned A. G. Busbequius. With Memoirs of the Life of the Illustrious Author* (London: Printed for J. Robinson; and W. Payne, 1744), 131–32.

22. *A New Method and Extraordinary Invention, To Dress Horses, and Work Them according to Nature: as also, To Perfect Nature by the Subtilty of Art; Which was never found out, but by The Thrice Noble, High, and Puissant Prince William Cavendishe* (London: Printed by Thomas Milbourn, 1667), 82.

23. Busbecq, *Travels into Turkey*, 132.

24. English visitors, in particular, found much to admire in the Ottoman empire between 1580 and 1720; fear gave way to fascination, and imperial envy was often the order of the day, as Gerald MacLean recounts in *The Rise of Oriental Travel: English Visitors to the*

Ottoman Empire, 1580–1720 (Houndmills, Basingstoke, UK, and New York: Palgrave Macmillan, 2004).

25. Busbecq, *Travels into Turkey*, 132.

26. For Bankes's Marocco, see John Dando the wier-drawer of Hadley and Harrie Runt, head Ostler of Bosomes Inn, *Maroccus Extaticus. Or, Bankes Bay Horse in a Trance. A Discourse set downe in a merry Dialogue, between Bankes and his beast: Anatomizing some abuses and bad trickes of this age* (London: Printed for Cuthbert Burby, 1595). My thanks to Mat Dimmock for the last reference. See also Matthew Dimmock, ed., *William Percy's Mahomet and His Heaven: A Critical Edition* (Aldershot, UK: Ashgate, 2006); *Chrestoleros. Seuen bookes of Epigrammes written by T. B.* (London: Imprinted by Richard Bradocke for I. B., 1598), 62; and *A Strappado for the Diuell. Epigrams And Satyres alluding to the time, with diuers measures of no lesse Delight* (London: Printed by I. B. for Richard Redmer, 1615), 159–60.

27. See Erica Fudge, *Animal* (London: Reaktion, 2002), 113–16.

28. Gervase Markham, *Cavelarice, Or The English Horseman: Contayning all the Arte of Horse-manship, as much as is necessary for any man to understand, whether he be horse-breeder, horse-ryder, horse-hunter, horse-runner, horse-ambler, horse-farrier, horse-keeper, Coachman, Smith, or Sadler. Together, with the discouery of the subtill trade or mistery of horse-coursers, & an explanatio[n] of the excellency of a horses vndersta[n]ding, or how to teach them to doe trickes like Bankes his Curtall: And that horses may be made to drawe drie-foot like a Hound. Secrets before vnpublished, & now carefully set down for the profit of this whole nation,* 8 books (London: Printed for Edward White, 1607), 8: mispaginated as 28.

29. Ibid., mispaginated as 34.

30. S. R., *The Art Of Jugling Or Legerdemaine. Wherein Is Deciphered, all the conveyances of Legerdemaine and Jugling , how they are effected, and wherein they chiefly consist. Cautions to beware of cheating at Cardes and Dice. The detection of the beggerly Art of Alcumistry. And, The foppery of foolish cousoning Charmes. All tending to mirth and recreation, especially for those that desire to have the insight and priuate practise thereof* (London: Printed by George Eld, 1614), [Sig. Gv].

31. Heath W. Lowry's revisionist view of the early Ottoman state attributes its success as a "predatory confederacy" in the fourteenth and fifteenth centuries to a policy of accommodation with local populations, rather than forced conversion to Islam or force of arms. *The Nature of the Early Ottoman State* (Albany: State University of New York Press, 2003), 95, 99, 101, 139.

32. James Weatherby, *The Supplement to the General Stud-Book, Being the Produce of Mares, Continued to 1799, Inclusive: By the Same Author. To Which Is Added, a Short Dissertation on Horses, by Colonel Gilbert Ironside* (London: Printed by H. Reynell for J. Weatherby, 1800), 22.

33. Ibid.

34. *The Chevalier's Travels in Arabia the Desart; Written by Himself, and Publish'd by Mr. De la Roque: Giving a very accurate and entertaining Account of the Religion, Rights, Customs, Diversions, &c. of the Bedouins, or Arabian Scenites, Undertaken by Order of the late French King, Done into English by an Eminent Hand* (London: Printed for B. Barker and C. King and J. Brown, 1718).

35. Ibid., 170–74.

36. [Gervase Markham], *How to chuse, ride, traine, and diet, both Hunting-horses and running Horses. With all the secrets thereto belonging discovered: an Arte never heere-to-fore written by any Authour. Also a discourse of horsmanship, wherein the breeding, and ryding of Horses for service, in a briefe manner, is more methodically sette downe, then hath beene heeretofore: with a more easie and direct course for the ignorant, to attaine to the sayd Arte or knowledge. Together with a newe addition for the cure of horses diseases, of what kinde or nature soever* (1593; London: James Roberts, 1599), A3v.

37. James Sharpe, *Dick Turpin: The Myth of the English Highwayman* (London: Profile Books, 2004), 156–57, citing William Harrison Ainsworth, *Rookwood*, 5th ed. (1834; London: Richard Bentley, 1837).

38. Sharpe, *Dick Turpin*, 157.

39. William Cowper, Book 6, "The Winter Walk at Noon," *The Task* (1785), in *The Poetical Works of William Cowper*, ed. H. S. Milford, 3rd. ed. (London: Oxford University Press and Humphrey Milford, 1926), 230–31, lines 516–20.

40. *Memoirs of the Late Thomas Holcroft, Written by Himself, and Continued to the Time of His Death, from His Diary, Notes, and Other Papers*, 3 vols. (London: Printed by J. McCreery for Longman, Hurst, Rees, Orme, and Brown, 1816), 75.

41. Ibid., 111.

42. Ibid., 172.

43. Having been lent the *Spectator* and *Gulliver's Travels*, Holcroft was asked by the shoemaker which he liked best, and when he answered that he preferred Swift ten times over, the shoemaker replied as follows: "'Aye,' said he, 'I would have laid my life on it, boys and young people always prefer the marvellous to the true.' I acquiesced in his judgment, which, however, only proved that neither he nor I understood Gulliver, though it afforded me infinite delight." Ibid., 137–38.

44. T. Hornby Morland, *The Genealogy of the English Race Horse; with the natural history of his progenitors, from the earliest times down to the period when foreign blood was first introduced into this kingdom; collected from the best authorities: to which is added, the General Practice of the most judicious Breeders, whereby they have Improved & Perfected Our Breed Of Blood Horses So as to have acquired a decided Pre-eminence and Superiority in the essential Points of Size, Strength, Beauty, Speed, Bottom, &c. &c. Over Those Of other Countries: With Observations upon the Present Improved Method of Breeding for the Turf, on the selection of stallions, choice of brood mares, crossing the blood, or mixing races; treatment of brood mares and young colts intended for racing, &c. &c. The Result of Observation and Experience during an Acquaintance for many Years with the Turf* . . . (London: Printed by J. Barfield, 1810), 1–2.

45. Ibid., 2.

46. See Landry, *The Invention of the Countryside: Hunting, Walking, and Ecology in English Literature, 1671–1831* (Houndmills, Basingstoke, UK, and New York: Palgrave, 2001), 12–15, 168–201.

47. John Adams, *An Analysis of Horsemanship; Teaching the Whole Art of Riding, in the Manege, Military, Hunting, Racing, and Travelling System. Together with the Method of Breaking Horses, for Every Purpose to Which Those Noble Animals Are Adapted*, 3 vols. (London: Printed by Albion Press, Published by James Cundee, and Sold by C. Chapple, 1805), 2:36.

48. *DNB.* See also Landry, *Invention of the Countryside,* 67–68.

49. See Gerald MacLean, Donna Landry, and Joseph P. Ward, eds., *The Country and the City Revisited: England and the Politics of Culture, 1550–1850* (Cambridge and New York: Cambridge University Press, 1999), 1–23.

50. E. K. Waterhouse, "Lord Fitzwilliam's Sporting Pictures by Stubbs," *Burlington Magazine* 88 (August 1946): 199.

51. Ibid.

52. A. C. Sewter, "Four English Illustrative Pictures," *Burlington Magazine* 74 (March 1939): 122–27; this passage 122.

53. The Reverend Dr. Franklin, "The Triumph of the Arts," in William Sandby, *The History of The Royal Academy of Arts from Its Foundation in 1768 to the Present Time,* 2 vols. (London: Longman, Green, Longman, Roberts, and Green, 1862), 1:130.

54. "Song," composed by Mr. Hull, and sung by Mr. Vernon, ibid., 130.

55. [Robert Strange], "A Dialogue between Pallet, an Academician; Easel, a Fellow of the Society of Artists; and Plain Truth, a Lover of the Arts," for the *Public Advertiser,* cutting inserted into British Library copy containing MS notes by Sir Joshua Reynolds, of *The Conduct of the Royal Academicians, while Members of the Incorporated Society of Artists of Great Britain, viz. From the Year 1760, to their Expulsion in the Year 1769. With some Part of their Transactions since* (London: Printed by J. Dixwell, 1771) and *An Inquiry into the Rise and Establishment of the Royal Academy of Arts. To which is prefixed, A Letter to the Earl of Bute, by Robert Strange, Member of the Royal Academy of Painting at Paris, of the Academies of Rome, Florence, Bologna; Professor of the Royal Academy of Parma, &c.* (London: Printed for E. and C. Dilly, J. Robson, and J. Walter, 1775), B. L. Shelfmark 741.a.13.(2.).

56. Swift, *Gulliver's Travels,* 265.

57. Michael DePorte, "Avenging Naboth: Swift and Monarchy," *Philological Quarterly* 69, no. 1 (Winter 1990): 419–33; this passage 429.

58. Ian Higgins, ed., *Gulliver's Travels,* 350, citing Richard Nash, "Of Sorrels, Bays, and Dapple Greys," *Swift Studies* 15 (2000): 110–15.

59. Harold Williams, ed., *The Correspondence of Jonathan Swift,* 5 vols. (Oxford: Clarendon, 1963–65), 2:133.

60. Ian Higgins notices both these possible equi-political allusions, "Sorrel" and "Bolingbroke," in his notes to *Gulliver's Travels,* 351–52.

61. Williams, ed., *Correspondence,* 2:171.

62. Swift, *Gulliver's Travels,* 239. Many thanks to Paddy Bullard for his comments on the suppression of this passage from the first edition.

63. *Stubbs and the Horse* was a combined effort by the Kimbell Art Museum of Fort Worth, Texas, the Walters Art Museum, Baltimore, Maryland, and the National Gallery in London. I saw the exhibition in London in June 2005.

64. Judy Egerton, "George Stubbs and the Landscape of Creswell Crags," *Burlington Magazine* 126 (December 1984): 738–43; this passage 738.

65. Warner, "Catalogue," *Stubbs and the Horse,* entry number 57, 193–94; this passage 193.

66. Egerton, "Stubbs and Creswell Crags," 738; Warner, "Catalogue," *Stubbs and the Horse,* 193–94.

67. Warner, "Catalogue," *Stubbs and the Horse,* 193.

68. Ibid.

69. Judy Egerton was the first to broach the likely significance of Creswell Crags for Stubbs, with its cave containing prehistoric animal bones, including horses and big cats, in "Stubbs and Creswell Crags," 738–43. Malcolm Warner makes the bold move of suggesting that Creswell Crags, with its prehistoric remains, came to represent for Stubbs a Barbary landscape and hence an allusion to the origins of the Thoroughbred, in "Stubbs and the Origin of the Thoroughbred," in *Stubbs and the Horse,* 101–21; this passage 110–11.

70. T. N., Obituary for George Stubbs, *The Sporting Magazine,* May 1808; see Barnaby Rogerson, "Did Stubbs Go to Morocco?" *Country Life,* 2 March 2000, 60–61.

71. Rebecca Cassidy, "Turf Wars: Arab Dimensions to British Racehorse Breeding," *Anthropology Today* 19, no. 3 (June 2003): 13–18, see esp. 16–18; Chris McGrath, "Abscess Explains Discreet Cat's Defeat as Maktoum's Grand Plans Gather Pace," *The Independent,* Monday, 2 April 2007, 48.

72. Martin Myrone, *George Stubbs* (London: Tate, 2002), 38.

73. Myrone reproduces a photograph of the painting projected onto the exterior wall of the National Gallery during the campaign for its acquisition. Ibid., 37, fig. 25. Robin Blake felicitously calls the background "honey-coloured" in *George Stubbs and the Wide Creation: Animals, People, and Places in the Life of George Stubbs, 1724–1806* (London: Chatto and Windus, 2005), 148.

74. Whistlejacket's sire was Mogul, a son of the Godolphin Arabian, out of Sachrissa, or "the Large Hartley Mare." C. M. Prior, *The Royal Studs of the Sixteenth and Seventeenth Centuries, Together with a Reproduction of the Second Earl of Godolphin's Stud-Book, and Sundry Other Papers Relating to the Thoroughbred Horse* (London: Horse and Hound, 1935), 171. His dam was by Sweepstakes, who was by the Bloody Shouldered Arabian, as we have seen. His maternal grand-dam was by the Hampton-Court Chestnut Arabian; Place's White Turk and the Layton Barb Mare also appear in his pedigree. W. Pick, of York, *An Authentic Historical Racing Calendar of all the Plates, Sweepstakes, Matches, &c. Run for at York, from the First Commencement of the Races There in the Year 1709, to the Year 1785 inclusive . . . , including "Pedigrees and Performances of the most celebrated Race-Horses, that have appeared upon The English Turf, since the time of Basto, Flying Childers, &c. with An Historical Account of the most favourite Arabians, Turks, Barbs, English Stallions, and Brood-Mares; alphabetically digested"* (Printed by W. Blanchard and Co., York, n.d. [1786?]): "Whistlejacket, the property of *Sir William Middleton,* Bart. was got by Mogul, (own brother to Babram); his dam by Sweepstakes, (son of the Oxford Bloody-shouldered Arabian); his grandam by the Hampton-Court Chestnut Arabian, a daughter of Makeless—Brimmer—Place's White Turk—Dodsworth, and out of a Layton Barb Mare" (117).

75. Whistlejacket was bred by Sir William Middleton of Belsay Castle, Northumberland, and foaled in 1749. Warner, "Catalogue," *Stubbs and the Horse,* entry 39, 178–79; this passage 178. He may have been named for a Yorkshire toddy of gin and treacle, more or less the same color as his coat. National Gallery, *Stubbs and the Horse, Exhibition Guide: 29 June–25 September 2005* (London: National Gallery, 2005), entry for exhibit 29, catalogue 39: "Whistlejacket, evidently named after a medicinal drink of gin and treacle." Martin Hesp,

"Don't Let Wild Horses Keep You," *Western Morning News*, Saturday, 9 July 2005, 26–27, writes, "What the gallery staff have discovered is that Whistlejacket was the name of a Yorkshire hot-toddy made of gin and treacle, which may or may not have shared the same colour as the reddish brown of the horse's coat" (27).

76. Warner, "Catalogue," *Stubbs and the Horse*, 178.

77. William Pick (1786) quoted in C. M. Prior, *The History of the Racing Calendar and Stud-Book from Their Inception in the Eighteenth Century, with Observations on Some of the Occurrences Noted Therein* (London: Sporting Life, 1926), 268.

78. Holcroft, *Memoirs*, 131–32.

79. Ibid., 132–34.

80. Humphry, *Memoir*, in Nicholas H. J. Hall, *Fearful Symmetry: George Stubbs, Painter of the English Enlightenment*, exhibition catalogue (New York: Hall and Knight, 2000), 205.

81. Sir Joshua Reynolds, *Discourses on Art*, ed. Robert R. Wark, Paul Mellon Centre for Studies in British Art (London) (New Haven and London: Yale University Press, 1975), 41.

82. Ibid.

83. Ibid., 43.

84. Ibid., 57.

85. Ibid., 50.

86. John Barrell, *The Political Theory of Painting from Reynolds to Hazlitt* (New Haven and London: Yale University Press, 1986), 85.

87. Humphry, *Memoir*, in Hall, *Fearful Symmetry*, 209.

88. On the white horse of Hanover, see Robin Blake, "A Different Form of Art: Stubbs and Rockingham's Young Whigs in the 1760s," in Warner and Blake, *Stubbs and the Horse*, 42–63; this passage 57–58; and Blake, *Stubbs*, 150–52. On anti-Bute and anti-Hanoverian allegory in the Rockingham commissions *Lion Attacking a Stag* and *Lion Attacking a Horse* (1762), Blake cites Douglas Fordham, "The Class Menagerie, 1762–1765," in Fordham's "Raising Standards: Art and Imperial Politics in London, 1745–1776," Yale Ph.D. diss., 2003. "Seen everywhere he went emblazoned on the sides of his carriage," the stag and horse were Bute's heraldic supporters, Blake comments, and thus the paintings "show the Lion of England, symbolic custodian of liberty and history, gralloching the supporters of the presumptuous Scottish Earl." *Stubbs*, 151–52.

89. "His Lordship accordingly ordered Mr Stubbs to begin a fresh picture and fixed upon Scrubb, a dark bay Horse with a Black Mane and Tail, which was immediately executed.T T [*Note attached in Upcott in the hand of Mary Spencer:*] Upon some dispute with Lord Rockingham Mr. Stubbs brought it away afterwards and sold it to Mr. Ryland, who sent it to India with other pictures which were neer landed but returned to England, and it was so much Injured by the voyage that Mr. Stubbs took it back, in part of payment, new lined and repaired it, and it was finally disposed of at his sale, to Miss Saltonstall, and is now at her House, at Hatchford near Cobham, Surrey." Humphry, *Memoir*, in Hall, *Fearful Symmetry*, 205.

90. Keith Tester, *Animals and Society: The Humanity of Animal Rights* (London and New York: Routledge, 1991), 192–93.

91. Virginia Woolf, "Jack Mytton," in *The Common Reader: Second Series*, ed. Andrew McNeillie (1932; London: Hogarth, 1986), 127.

92. Balfour quoted in Emanuelle de Monléon, "Germans Retain Double Gold. Germany Proves Unbeatable, While Britain Cannot Catch up after Falling behind in the Dressage," *Horse and Hound*, 11 August 2005, 26.

93. Humphry, *Memoir*, in Hall, *Fearful Symmetry*, 211.

94. Petrus Camper implicitly distinguished between his own and Stubbs's relation to horses in a letter of 27 July 1772, in which he observed, "I dissect, but I do not love horses, though I keep them for proper use & for my family." In Hall, *Fearful Symmetry*, 210.

95. Matthew Reynolds, "Barbarous marks of Breeding: George Stubbs' Unflinching Reflections on Horse and Society," *Times Literary Supplement*, 29 July 2005, 16–17; this passage 17.

96. George Stubbs, *Self-Portrait on a Grey Hunter* (1782). Enamel on Wedgwood biscuit earthenware. Merseyside County Council, The Lady Lever Art Gallery, Port Sunlight. See Judy Egerton, *George Stubbs, 1724–1806* (1984; London: Tate Gallery, 1996), fig. 4, p. 18.

97. Holcroft, *Memoirs*, 111.

98. Isaac Hobart, Letter to Edward, Lord Harley, 18 November 1723, B. L. Add. Mss. 70385, 1–2.

Epilogue · Her Ladyship's Arabian

1. Lady Mary Wortley Montagu, Letter to [Anne] Thistlethwayte, Adrianople, 1 April 1717, in *The Complete Letters of Lady Mary Wortley Montagu*, ed. Robert Halsband, 3 vols. (Oxford: Clarendon, 1965–67), 1:341. For elaboration, see Landry, "Horsy and Persistently Queer: Imperialism, Feminism, and Bestiality," *Textual Practice* 15 (November 2001): 467–85, and "Love Me, Love My Turkey Book: Letters and Turkish Travelogues in Early Modern England," in *Epistolary Histories: Letters, Fiction, Culture*, ed. Amanda Gilroy and W. M. Verhoeven (Charlottesville and London: University Press of Virginia, 2000), 51–73.

2. Isaac Hobart to Lord Harley, 18 November 1723, B. L. Add. Mss. 70385.

3. Lord Oxford to Isaac Hobart, Dover Street, 28 February 1727, B. L. Add. Mss. 70385.

4. Isaac Hobart to Lord Oxford, 4 March 1727, B. L. Add. Mss. 70385.

5. *An Apology for the Life of George Anne Bellamy, Late of Covent-Garden Theatre, Written By Herself*, 2nd ed., 5 vols. (London: Printed for the Author and Sold by J. Bell, 1785), 3:52.

6. Lord Ribbesdale, Master of the Buckhounds from 1892 to 1895, *The Queen's Hounds and Stag-Hunting Recollections* (London: Longmans, Green, and Co., 1897), 79.

7. Records from the Duke of Newcastle's stud at Welbeck include "An Acct of What Horses belongs to the Stud July ye 24th 1711," which lists on the last page under "Hunters": "Lady Hen: Barb mare Creem Coller 5 years old 1712 given her by Cousen Harley"; Portland Welbeck Papers 2, 331: 4, University of Nottingham Library, Manuscripts Department. Also quoted in C. M. Prior, *Early Records of the Thoroughbred Horse Containing Reproductions of Some Original Stud-Books, and Other Papers, of the Eighteenth Century* (London: Sportsman Office, 1924), 122. Lady Henrietta's mare, painted several times by Wootton, is a cream or silver dun since she has a silver mane and tail, rather than a dun's black mane and tail and black stockings. If this mare was a present from Nathaniel Harley in Aleppo, it is curious that she was called a Barb rather than an Arabian or a Turk.

8. John Wootton, *Lady Henrietta Harley, out Hunting with Harriers* (ca. 1720s), collection of Lady Thompson. On the basis of architectural evidence of alterations to Wimpole, Arline Meyer dates this picture to somewhere between 1721 and 1730. Meyer, *John Wootton, 1682–1764: Landscapes and Sporting Art in Early Georgian England* (London: Iveagh Bequest, Kenwood, and Greater London Council, 1984), 37–38.

9. Gina M. Dorré argues for a partial cross-gendering of the horse as a literary trope in Victorian culture, from "an emblem of masculine prerogative" to "a feminine ideal of duty, docility, and acquiescence." Dorré, *Victorian Fiction and the Cult of the Horse* (Aldershot, UK, and Burlington, VT: Ashgate, 2006), 10.

10. R. S. Surtees, *Mr. Sponge's Sporting Tour* (1853; Gloucester, UK: Alan Sutton, 1984), 533, 579, 498, 533.

11. John Lawrence, *The Horse in All His Varieties and Uses; His Breeding, Rearing, and Management, Whether in Labour or Rest; with Rules, Occasionally Interspersed, for His Preservation from Disease* (London: Printed for M. Arnold, Sold by Longman, Rees, Orme, et al., 1829), 144–45.

12. Mrs. J. Stirling Clarke, *The Habit & the Horse; A Treatise on Female Equitation* (London: Day and Son, 1860), 101–3. Amanda Gilroy argues convincingly for nineteenth-century parallels between the suburbanization of gardening, and of riding, for women. Both became fashionable pastimes thought to inculcate the good taste and moral discipline necessary for successful domestic management. Gilroy, "The Habit and the Horse, or, the Suburbanisation of Female Equitation," in *Green and Pleasant Land: English Culture and the Romantic Countryside,* ed. Amanda Gilroy, Groningen Studies in Cultural Change 8, M. Gosman, gen. ed. (Leuven, Paris, and Dudley, MA: Peeters, 2004), 45–55.

13. Jane Austen, *Mansfield Park,* ed. Tony Tanner (1814; Harmondsworth, UK: Penguin, 1966), 98.

14. See Landry, "Learning to Ride at Mansfield Park," in *The Postcolonial Jane Austen,* ed. You-me Park and Rajeswari Sunder Rajan (London and New York: Routledge, 2000), 56–73.

15. R. S. Surtees, *Mr. Facey Romford's Hounds* (London: Bradley and Evans, 1865; rpt. Methuen, 1939), 409.

16. *"To Whom the Goddess . . ."* Hunting and Riding for Women, by Lady Diana Shedden and Lady Apsley (London: Hutchinson and Co., 1932), 75.

17. Ibid.

18. Ibid., 76.

19. Ibid.

20. Lady Anne Blunt, Friday, 29 November 1907, B. L. Add. Mss. 54020, 5. Like Lady Anne, Lady Mary Wortley Montagu abandoned her side-saddle in later life when she discovered that her Italian aristocratic friends rode astride. *Letters,* 2:444.

21. A. Blunt, Monday, 23 December 1907, B. L. Add. Mss. 54020, 22–23.

22. A. Blunt, Journal entry for 25 May 1917, quoted in *Lady Anne Blunt: Journals and Correspondence, 1878–1917,* ed. Rosemary Archer and James Fleming (Northleach, Cheltenham, UK: Alexander Heriot and Co., 1986), 384.

23. See the report on Cunningham's research in Steve Connor, "Modern Racehorses Can Be Traced to a Single Ancestor," *The Independent,* Tuesday, 6 September 2005, 16.

24. Roger D. Upton, *Newmarket and Arabia: An Examination of the Descent of Racers and Coursers* (1873; Reading, UK: Garnet/Folios Archive Library, 2001).

25. [William Youatt], *The Horse; with a Treatise on Draught; and a Copious Index, Published under the Superintendence of the Society for the Diffusion of Useful Knowledge* (London: Baldwin and Cradock, 1831), 12.

26. *Narrative of a Journey through the Upper Provinces of India, from Calcutta to Bombay, 1824–1825, (with Notes upon Ceylon,) an Account of a Journey to Madras and the Southern Provinces, 1826, and Letters Written in India, by the late Right Reverend Reginald Heber, D.D., Lord Bishop Of Calcutta,* 2 vols. (London: John Murray, 1828), 2:319.

27. Youatt, *The Horse,* 4.

28. Ibid., 11.

29. Caroline Finkel, *Osman's Dream: The Story of the Ottoman Empire, 1300–1923* (London: John Murray, 2005), 4.

30. Ibid.

31. Youatt, *The Horse,* 19.

32. Jeremy James, *Saddletramp* (Lexington, MA: Pelham Books/Stephen Greene; Harmondsworth, UK: Penguin, 1989), 16.

33. Jeremy James, *The Byerley Turk* (Ludlow, UK: Merlin Unwin, 2005), 16, 17.

34. Sándor Bökönyi, *Data on Iron Age Horses of Central and Eastern Europe in the Mecklenberg Collection, Part I,* American School of Prehistoric Research Bulletin 25 (Cambridge, MA: Peabody Museum, Harvard University Press, 1968), 1–71; S. Bökönyi, *History of Domestic Mammals in Central and Eastern Europe,* trans. Lili Halápy with revisions by Ruth Tringham (Budapest: Akadémiai Kiadó, 1974).

35. Louise Firouz, personal communication to the author, March 2007.

36. Jason Elliot, *Mirrors of the Unseen: Journeys in Iran* (London, Basingstoke, and Oxford: Picador/Pan Macmillan, 2006), 114–16.

37. E. W. Hill et al., "History and Integrity of Thoroughbred Dam Lines Revealed in Equine mtDNA Variation," *Animal Genetics* 33 (August 2002): 287–94. According to Patrick Cunningham, it was Tregonwell's Natural Barb who "contributed the largest proportion—14 per cent—of the genes passed down the female line of racehorses." Connor, "Modern Racehorses Can Be Traced to a Single Ancestor," 16.

This book contributes to cultural history and animal studies. I hope that my arguments will reveal new facets of East-West relations in the long eighteenth century and provoke further thinking regarding agency and human-animal relations.

The manuscript sources upon which this study is based are the Portland Papers held in the Manuscripts Room of the British Library, London, but also held in part by the Manuscripts Department of the University of Nottingham Library. Nathaniel Harley's letters from Aleppo (1682–1720), British Library Additional Manuscripts 70143, provide unusual enlightenment concerning the horse-trade of the Levant, as does Thomas Darley's letter from Aleppo, North Yorkshire County Archives, ZDA DAR CP1. Isaac Hobart's correspondence with Edward, Lord Harley, afterward the second Earl of Oxford—British Library Additional Manuscripts 70385 (1720–26) and 70386 (1727–38)—reveals much of the infrastructure of horse-keeping in the eighteenth century, as does the Wimpole steward John Cossen's correspondence with Lord Oxford, held by the University of Nottingham's Manuscripts and Special Collections Department, Portland Papers Pl C 1. The Journals of Dr. J. Covel's Travels, 1670–1678, British Library Additional Manuscripts 22912, offers a rare eyewitness account of Ottoman racing and horsemanship. Public Record Office Admiralty (PRO ADM) 52/254 [packet no. 3], Master's Log of the *Preston*, 4 December 1717 to 3 March 1718/19, documents Lady Mary Wortley Montagu and her husband's return to England after Edward Wortley Montagu's embassy to the Porte was terminated, much to their mutual chagrin. Ozias Humphry, *Particulars of the life of Mr. Stubbs . . . given to the author of this Memoir by himself and commited from his own relation* [1797], Manuscript in the Liverpool Central Library, Liverpool Libraries and Information Services (collection reference 920 May), reproduced as an "Appendix" by Helen Macintyre in Nicholas H. J. Hall, *Fearful Symmetry: George Stubbs, Painter of the English Enlightenment*, exhibition catalogue (New York: Hall and Knight, 2000), 195–212, is a crucial resource for George Stubbs. The manuscript diaries of Lady Anne Blunt in the British Library, including the one quoted from here, B. L. Add. Mss. 54020, and the one cited in Rosemary Archer and James Fleming, eds., *Lady Anne Blunt: Journals and Correspondence, 1878–1917* (Northleach, UK: Alexander Heriot and Co., 1986), deserve a study in themselves.

Valuable sources for early modern Ottoman and Bedouin horse culture are Ogier Ghiselin de Busbecq, *Travels into Turkey: Containing the most accurate Account of the Turks . . .*

Translated from the Original Latin of the Learned A. G. Busbequius, With Memoirs of the Life of the Illustrious Author (London: Printed for J. Robinson; and W. Payne, 1744); Edward Seymour Forster, ed., *The Turkish Letters of Ogier Ghiselin de Busbecq, Imperial Ambassador at Constantinople 1554–1562, Newly Translated from the Latin of the Elzevir Edition of 1633* (Oxford: Clarendon, 1927); and Laurence D'Arvieux, *The Chevalier D'Arvieux's Travels in Arabia the Desert; Written by Himself, and Publish'd by Mr. De la Roque: Giving a very accurate and entertaining Account of the Religion, Rights, Customs, Diversions, &c. of the Bedouins, or Arabian Scenites. Undertaken by Order of the late French King . . . Done into English by an Eminent Hand* (London: Printed for B. Barker, C. King, and J. Brown, 1718). Fascinating material is to be found in Sir William Foster, ed., *The Travels of John Sanderson in the Levant, 1584–1602, with His Autobiography and Selections from His Correspondence* (London: Hakluyt Society, 1931); John Evelyn, *Kalendarium, 1673–1689: The Diary of John Evelyn*, ed. E. S. de-Beer, 6 vols. (Oxford: Clarendon, 1955); Robert Halsband, ed., *The Complete Letters of Lady Mary Wortley Montagu*, 3 vols. (Oxford: Clarendon, 1965–67); Charles MacFarlane, Esq., *Constantinople in 1828. A Residence of Sixteen Months in the Turkish Capital and Provinces: With an Account of the Present State of the Naval and Military Power, and of the Resources of the Ottoman Empire*, 2nd ed., 2 vols. (London: Saunders and Otley, 1829); and *Narrative of a Journey through the Upper Provinces of India, from Calcutta to Bombay, 1824–1825, (with Notes upon Ceylon,) an Account of a Journey to Madras and the Southern Provinces, 1826, and Letters Written in India, by the Late Right Reverend Reginald Heber, D.D., Lord Bishop of Calcutta*, 2 vols. (London: John Murray, 1828).

Levant Company business during the Interregnum was tracked through Thomas Birch, ed., *A Collection of the State Papers of John Thurloe, Esq., Secretary, First, to the Council of State, And afterwards to The Two Protectors, Oliver and Richard Cromwell*, 7 vols. (London: Printed for the Executor of Fletcher Gyles, Thomas Woodward, and Charles Davis, 1742), and Mary Anne Everett Green, ed., *Calendar of State Papers, Domestic Series, 1657–8* (London: Longmans and Co., 1884). For the Restoration, see Historical Manuscripts Commission, *Report on the Manuscripts of Allan George Finch, Esq., of Burley-on-the-Hill, Rutland*, 2 vols. (London: His Majesty's Stationery Office, 1913–22); Sonia P. Anderson, *An English Consul in Turkey: Paul Rycaut at Smyrna, 1667–1678* (Oxford: Clarendon, 1989); and Susan E. Whyman, *Sociability and Power in Late-Stuart England: The Cultural Worlds of the Verneys, 1660–1729* (Oxford and New York: Oxford University Press, 1999).

Early modern discourse on horses and horsemanship is rich and varied. See Xenophon's *On the Art of Horsemanship*, in *Scripta Minora*, trans. E. C. Marchant (London: William Heinemann; New York: G. P. Putnam's Sons, 1925), for a modern edition of the work that inspired a renaissance in European horsemanship. The key English texts for the sixteenth century are Thomas Blundeville, *A newe booke containing the arte of ryding, and breakinge greate Horses* (London: Willyam Seres, n.d. [1560?]); John Astley, Master of the Queen's Jewell-House, *The Art of Riding, set foorth in a breefe treatise, with a due interpretation of certeine places alledged out of Xenophon, and Gryson, verie expert and excellent Horssemen* (London: Henrie Denham, 1584); Thomas Bedingfield's translation of Claudio Corte's *Il Cavallenzzo*, published as *The Art of Riding, conteining diverse necessarie instructions, demonstrations, helps, and corrections apperteining to horssemanship, not heretofore expressed by anie other Author* (London: Henrie Denham, 1584); Sir Philip Sidney, *An Apologie for Poet-*

rie, ed. Evelyn S. Shuckburgh (Cambridge: Cambridge University Press, 1905) and *Sidney's Apologie for Poetrie,* ed. J. Churton Collins (Oxford: Clarendon, 1907); and Gervase Markham, *How to chuse, ride, traine, and diet, both Hunting-horses and running Horses* (1593; London: James Roberts, 1599).

See for the seventeenth century, see Gervase Markham's *Cavelarice, Or The English Horseman: Contayning all the Arte of Horse-manship, as much as is necessary for any man to understand,* 8 books (London: Printed for Edward White, 1607) and *Countrey Contentments, In Two Books: The first, containing the whole art of riding great Horses in very short time, with the breeding, breaking, dyeting and ordring of them, and of running, hunting and ambling Horses, with the manner how to use them in their travell* . . . (London: Printed by J. B. for R. Jackson, 1615); *An Hipponomie or The Vineyard of Horsemanship: Deuided into three Bookes, By Michaell Baret, Practitioner and Professor of the same Art* (London: Printed by George Eld, 1618); *The Compleat Horseman: Discovering the Sweet Marks of the Beauty, Goodness, Faults and Imperfections of Horses:* . . . *By the Sieur de Solleysell, Querry to the present French King for his Great Horses, and one of the Royal Academy of Paris. To which is added, A most Excellent Supplement of Riding; Collected from the best Authors, By Sir William Hope, Kt. Deputy-Lieutenant of the Castle of Edinburgh* (London: Printed for M. Gillyflower, R. Bentley, et al., 1696).

The works of William Cavendish, Duke of Newcastle, were the most influential written by an Englishman: *Methode Et Invention Nouvelle de dresser Les Chevaux par le tres-noble, haut, et tres-puissant Prince Guillaume Marquis Et Comte De Newcastle* . . . (Antwerp: Jacques Van Meurs, 1658), which appeared in English in 1743 as *A General System of Horsemanship in all it's Branches,* 2 vols. (London: Printed for J. Brindley, 1743); and Cavendish's earlier English treatise, *A New Method and Extraordinary Invention, To Dress Horses, and Work Them according to Nature: as also, To Perfect Nature by the Subtilty of Art* (London: Printed by Thomas Milbourn, 1667).

Continental European works crucial for understanding the development of manège riding and the *haute école* are Federico Grisone, *Gli Ordini di Cavalcare* (Naples: Guilio Terzo, 1550); Claudio Corte, *Il Cavallenzzo . . . nel qual si tratta della natura de' Cavalli, delle Razze, del modo di governarli, domarli, & frenarli* (Venice: Giordano Ziletti, 1573); Pasqual Caracciolo, *La Gloria Del Cavallo* (Venice: Gabriel Giolito De' Ferrari, 1567); Cesare Fiaschi, "Gentil'huomo Ferrarese," *Trattato Del Modo Dell'Imbrigliare, Maneggiare, & ferrare cavalli, diviso in tre parti* (Venice: Francesco de Leno, 1563); and Antoine de Pluvinel, *Maneige Royal Ou Lon Peut Remarquer Le Defaut Et La Perfection Du Chevalier* (Paris: Crispian de Pas, 1623). The best modern study is Giles Worsley, in "A Courtly Art: The History of 'Haute École' in England," *The Court Historian* 6, no. 1 (May 2001): 29–47. Long eighteenth-century works of note include Thomas Pennant, *British Zoology. Illustrated by Plates and Brief Explanations* (London: Printed and Sold by B. White, 1770); G. L. Buffon, *The Natural History of the Horse* (London: Printed for R. Griffiths, 1762); William Youatt, *The Horse; with a Treatise on Draught; and a Copious Index* (London: Baldwin and Cradock, 1831); Richard Berenger, *The History and Art of Horsemanship,* 2 vols. (London: Printed for T. Davies and T. Cadell, 1771); Charles Hughes, *The Compleat Horseman; or, the Art of Riding made easy: Illustrated by Rules drawn from Nature, and Confirmed by Experience; with Directions to the Ladies to sit gracefully, and ride with Safety* (London: Printed for F. Newbery and Sold at Hughes's Riding-School, n.d. [1772]); John Adams, *An Analysis of Horsemanship; Teaching the Whole Art of Riding, in the Manege, Military, Hunting, Racing, and Travelling System. Together with the Method of Breaking Horses, for Every Purpose to Which Those Noble Animals Are Adapted*, 3 vols. (London: Printed by Albion Press, Published by James Cundee, and Sold by C. Chapple, 1805); and John Lawrence's *A Philosophical And Practical Treatise On Horses, and on the Moral Duties Of Man towards The Brute Creation*, 2 vols. (London: Printed for T. Longman, 1796–98) and *The Horse in All His Varieties and Uses; His Breeding, Rearing, and Management, Whether in Labour or Rest; with Rules, Occasionally Interspersed, for His Preservation from Disease* (London: Printed for M. Arnold, Sold by Longman, Rees, Orme, et al., 1829).

I have argued throughout that the European context in which English horsemanship has usually been understood needs to be supplemented by attention to Near Eastern and Central Asian influences. Important work in cultural history and Ottoman studies that prepares the ground for these arguments includes Gerald MacLean, ed., *Re-Orienting the Renaissance: Cultural Exchanges with the East* (Houndmills, Basingstoke, UK, and New York: Palgrave Macmillan, 2005), and MacLean's monographs *Looking East: English Writing and the Ottoman Empire before 1800* (Houndmills, Basingstoke, UK, and New York: Palgrave Macmillan, 2007) and *The Rise of Oriental Travel: English Visitors to the Ottoman Empire, 1580–1720* (Houndmills, Basingstoke, UK, and New York: Palgrave Macmillan, 2004); Jerry Brotton, *The Renaissance Bazaar: From the Silk Road to Michelangelo* (Oxford and New York: Oxford University Press, 2002); Ros Ballaster, *Fabulous Orients: Fictions of the East in England, 1662–1785* (Oxford and New York: Oxford University Press, 2005); and Lisa Jardine, *Worldly Goods: A New History of the Renaissance* (London and Basingstoke, UK: Macmillan, 1996). For an introduction to revisionist Ottoman history that debunks popular myths, see Caroline Finkel's breathtakingly comprehensive *Osman's Dream: The Story of the Ottoman Empire, 1300–1923* (London: John Murray, 2005), and Heath W. Lowry's more focused *The Nature of the Early Ottoman State* (Albany: State University of New York Press, 2003). For a brilliant theoretical and archival study of Ottoman historiography, see Gabriel Piterberg, *An Ottoman Tragedy: History and Historiography at Play* (Berkeley and Los Angeles: University of California Press, 2003). *The Encyclopedia of Islam, New Edition*, ed. H. A. R. Gibb et al., 11 vols. (Leiden: E. J. Brill, 1960–2000), remains indispensable. Important specialized studies include Gülru Necipoğlu, "Süleyman the Magnificent and the Representation of Power in the Context of Ottoman-Hapsburg-Papal Rivalry," *Art Bulletin* 71 (1989): 401–27; Michael Rogers, "The Arts under Süleyman the Magnificent," in *Süleyman the Second and His Time*, ed. Halil İnalcık and Cemal Kafadar (Istanbul: Isis, 1993), 287–324; Deborah Howard, *Venice and the East* (New Haven, CT: Yale University Press, 2000); Julian Raby, *Venice, Dürer, and the Oriental Mode* (London: Islamic Art Publications, 1982); Naimur Rahman Farooqi, *Mughal-Ottoman Relations: A Study of Political and Diplomatic Relations between Mughal India and the Ottoman Empire, 1556–1748* (Delhi: Idarah-i Adabiyat-i Delli, 1989); Kate Fleet, *European and Islamic Trade in the Early Ottoman State: The Merchants of Genoa and Turkey* (Cambridge and New York: Cambridge University Press, 1999); Daniel Goffman, *Britons in the Ottoman Empire, 1642–1660* (Seattle and London: University of Washington Press, 1998); Philip K. Hitti, *History of the Arabs from the Earliest Times to the Present*, rev. 10th ed. (1937; Houndmills, Basingstoke, UK, and New York: Palgrave, 2002); and David Pinault, *Horse of Karbala: Muslim Devotional Life in India* (New York and Houndmills, Basingstoke, UK: Palgrave, 2001).

The new global economic history that foregrounds the power of the Eastern empires before the rise of European economic and imperial dominance may be grasped by reading K. N. Chauduri's *Asia before Europe: Economy and Civilisation of the Indian Ocean from the Rise of Islam to 1750* (Cambridge and New York: Cambridge University Press, 1990) and *Trade and Civilisation in the Indian Ocean: An Economic History from the Rise of Islam to 1750* (Cambridge and New York: Cambridge University Press, 1985); Andre Gunder Frank, *Re-Orient: Global Economy in the Asian Age* (Berkeley, Los Angeles, and London: University of California Press, 1998); and Kenneth Pomeranz and Steven Topik, *The World That Trade Created: Society, Culture, and the World Economy, 1400–the Present* (Armonk, NY, and London: M. E. Sharpe, 1999).

On writing cultural biographies of commodities, see Arjun Appadurai, "Introduction: Commodities and the Politics of Value," in *The Social Life of Things: Commodities in Cultural Perspective,* ed. Appadurai (Cambridge: Cambridge University Press, 1986), 3–63.

Edward W. Said's *Orientalism* (1978; London and New York: Penguin, 1995) remains the *locus classicus* of postcolonial studies with regard to the Islamic Middle East. For a spirited defense of Orientalists, see Robert Irwin, *For Lust of Knowing: The Orientalists and Their Enemies* (London: Allen Lane, 2006). Although highly critical of Said's history of the various strands of scholarly Orientalism, Irwin agrees with Said about the deleterious effect of "Orientalist" prejudices on Anglo-U.S. foreign policy since 1948. The work of Nabil Matar broke new ground in restoring something of a shared history; of his many books, see especially *Islam in Britain, 1558–1685* (Cambridge and New York: Cambridge University Press, 1998). More recent work in this vein includes Matthew Dimmock, *New Turkes: Dramatizing Islam and the Ottomans in Early Modern England* (Aldershot, UK, and Burlington, VT: Ashgate, 2005), and Dimmock, ed., *William Percy's Mahomet and His Heaven: A Critical Edition* (Aldershot, UK: Ashgate, 2006); Matthew Birchwood and Matthew Dimmock, eds., *Cultural Encounters between East and West, 1453–1699* (Newcastle-upon-Tyne, UK: Cambridge Scholars, 2005); and Daniel Vitkus, *Turning Turk: English Theater and the Multicultural Mediterranean, 1570–1630* (New York and Houndmills, Basingstoke, UK: Palgrave Macmillan, 2003).

For the specific case of Eastern influences on global horsemanship, see Miklós Jankovich, *They Rode into Europe: The Fruitful Exchange in the Arts of Horsemanship between East and West,* trans. Anthony Dent (London: George G. Harrup, 1971), and Lisa Jardine and Jerry Brotton, *Global Interests: Renaissance Art between East and West* (London: Reaktion; Ithaca, NY: Cornell University Press, 2000), which is indebted to Jankovich. The best single source on Asian and Islamic horsemanship is the magnificent *Furusiyya,* ed. David Alexander, 2 vols. (Riyadh: King Abdulaziz Public Library, 1996). See also Rhoads Murphey, "Horsebreeding in Eurasia: Key Element in Material Life or Foundation of Imperial Culture?" *Central and Inner Asian Studies* 4 (1990): 1–13, and, more fancifully presented but thought-provoking nevertheless, Jeremy James's *The Byerley Turk* (Ludlow, UK: Merlin Unwin, 2005).

For understanding horse culture from a zoological and archaeological point of view, the work of Sándor Bökönyi and Juliet Clutton-Brock is invaluable. See Peter Anreiter et al., eds., *Man and the Animal World: Studies in Archaeozoology, Archaeology, Anthropology, and Palaeolinguistics in Memoriam Sándor Bökönyi* (Budapest: Archaeolingua Alapítvány, 1998);

Sándor Bökönyi, *Data on Iron Age Horses of Central and Eastern Europe in the Mecklenberg Collection, Part I*, American School of Prehistoric Research Bulletin 25 (Cambridge, MA: Peabody Museum, Harvard University Press, 1968), 1–71; S. Bökönyi, *History of Domestic Mammals in Central and Eastern Europe*, trans. Lili Halápy with revisions by Ruth Tringham (Budapest: Akadémiai Kiadó, 1974); Juliet Clutton-Brock, *Horse Power: A History of the Horse and the Donkey in Human Societies* (London: Natural History Museum Publications, 1992); Juliet Clutton-Brock, *A Natural History of Domesticated Mammals*, 2nd ed. (Cambridge and New York: Cambridge University Press and Natural History Museum, 1999); and Juliet Clutton-Brock, "Were the Donkeys at Tell Brak (Syria) Harnessed with a Bit?" in *Prehistoric Steppe Adaptation and the Horse*, ed. Marsha Levine, Colin Renfrew, and Katie Boyle (Cambridge: McDonald Institute for Archaeological Research, n.d. [2003]), 126–27. See also Harold B. Barclay, *The Role of the Horse in Man's Culture* (London and New York: J. A. Allen, 1980), and L. H. Van Wijngaarden-Bakker, "The Animal Remains from the Beaker Settlement at Newgrange, Co. Meath—First Report," *Proceedings of the Royal Irish Academy* 74 *(Section C)* (1974): 313–83.

All historians of the Thoroughbred have been indebted to James Weatherby, *An Introduction to a General Stud-Book* (London: Printed by H. Reynell for J. Weatherby, 1791), and *The Supplement to the General Stud-Book, Being the Produce of Mares, Continued to 1799, Inclusive: By the Same Author. To Which Is Added, a Short Dissertation On Horses, by Colonel Gilbert Ironside* (London: Printed by H. Reynell for J. Weatherby, 1800), as well as to C. M. Prior, whose archival labors in *Early Records of the Thoroughbred Horse Containing Reproductions of Some Original Stud-Books, and Other Papers, of the Eighteenth Century* (London: Sportsman Office, 1924), *The History of the Racing Calendar and Stud-Book from Their Inception in the Eighteenth Century, with Observations on Some of the Occurrences Noted Therein* (London: Sporting Life, 1926), and *The Royal Studs of the Sixteenth and Seventeenth Centuries, Together with a Reproduction of the Second Earl of Godolphin's Stud-Book, and Sundry Other Papers Relating to the Thoroughbred Horse* (London: Horse and Hound, 1935) brought to light important primary sources.

Useful approaches to Thoroughbred genetics and pedigrees include E. W. Hill et al., "History and Integrity of Thoroughbred Dam Lines Revealed in Equine mtDNA Variation," *Animal Genetics* 33 (August 2002): 287–94; see the report on a 2005 paper by Patrick Cunningham in Steve Connor, "Modern Racehorses Can Be Traced to a Single Ancestor," *The Independent*, Tuesday, 6 September 2005, 16; Nicholas Russell, *Like Engend'ring Like: Heredity and Animal Breeding in Early Modern England* (Cambridge: Cambridge University Press, 1986); William Osmer, *A Dissertation on Horses: Wherein it is Demonstrated, by Matters of Fact, as well as from the Principles of Philosophy, that Innate Qualities do not exist, and that the excellence of this Animal is altogether mechanical and not in the Blood* (London: T. Waller, 1756), T. Hornby Morland, *The Genealogy of the English Race Horse* (London: Printed by J. Barfield, 1810); J. B. Robertson, *The Principles of Heredity Applied to the Racehorse* (London: Winning Post, n.d. [ca. 1910?]); Lady Wentworth [Judith Anne Dorothea Blunt Lytton, Baroness Wentworth], *Thoroughbred Racing Stock and Its Ancestors: The Authentic Origin of Pure Blood* (London: George Allen and Unwin, 1938); Peter Willett, *An Introduction to the Thoroughbred* (London: Stanley Paul, 1966); Franco Varola, *Typology of the Racehorse* (1974; London and New York: J. A. Allen, 1977); Donald Lesh, *A Treatise on Thoroughbred Selection* (London and New York: J. A. Allen, 1978); and Alexander Mackay-Smith, *Speed and the Thoroughbred: The Complete History* (Lanham, MD: Derrydale and Millwood House, 2000).

Debates within animal studies can best be approached by beginning with Erica Fudge's ground-breaking essay, "A Left-Handed Blow: Writing the History of Animals," in *Representing Animals*, ed. Nigel Rothfels (Bloomington and Indianapolis: Indiana University Press, 2002), and Garry Marvin, "Wölfe in Schafs und anderen Pelzen," in *Tiere in der Geschichte*, ed. Dorothee Brantz and Christof Mauch (Paderborn: Schöningh, 2007). Tom Regan, *The Case for Animal Rights* (Berkeley and Los Angeles: University of California Press, 1983), and Peter Singer, *Animal Liberation*, 2nd ed. (1975; New York: New York Review Books, 1990), are canonical texts within the discourse. Countering animal rights approaches to human-animal relations with the model of training are Donna Haraway, *The Companion Species Manifesto: Dogs, People, and Significant Otherness* (Chicago: Prickly Paradigm, 2003), Vicki Hearne, *Adam's Task: Calling Animals by Name* (New York: Vintage / Random House, 1987), and Paul Patton, "Language, Power, and the Training of Horses," in *Zootologies: The Question of the Animal*, ed. Cary Wolfe (Minneapolis and London: University of Minnesota Press, 2003), 83–99. Donna Haraway's important follow-up to *The Companion Species Manifesto* appeared too late for me to incorporate it here: Donna J. Haraway, *When Species Meet* (Minneapolis and London: University of Minnesota Press, 2008).

The classic historical studies are Keith Thomas, *Man and the Natural World: A History of the Modern Sensibility* (New York: Pantheon, 1983), and Harriet Ritvo, *The Animal Estate: The English and Other Creatures in the Victorian Age* (London and New York: Penguin, 1990). See also Ritvo, "Possessing Mother Nature: Genetic Capital in Eighteenth-Century Britain," in *Early Modern Conceptions of Property*, ed. John Brewer and Susan Staves (London and New York: Routledge, 1995), 413–26. For excellent new work on animals and humans from an anthropological perspective, see Rebecca Cassidy, *The Sport of Kings: Kinship, Class, and Thoroughbred Breeding in Newmarket* (Cambridge: Cambridge University Press, 2002), and from an historical perspective, Margaret E. Derry, *Bred for Perfection: Shorthorn Cattle, Collies, and Arabian Horses since 1800* (Baltimore and London: Johns Hopkins University Press, 2003), and Erica Fudge, *Perceiving Animals: Humans and Beasts in Early Modern English Culture* (Houndmills, Basingstoke, UK, and London: Macmillan; New York: St. Martin's, 2000).

Useful recent studies of why animals have appeared on social and academic agendas are Adrian Franklin, *Animals and Modern Cultures: A Sociology of Human-Animal Relations in Modernity* (London, Thousand Oaks, CA, and New Delhi: Sage, 1999); Keith Tester, *Animals and Society: The Humanity of Animal Rights* (London and New York: Routledge, 1991); Ted Benton, *Natural Relations: Ecology, Animal Rights, and Social Justice* (London: Verso, 1993); Steve Baker, "Guest Editor's Introduction: Animals, Representation, and Reality," *Society and Animals: Journal of Human-Animal Studies*, special issue on "The Representation of Animals," 9, no. 3 (2001): 189–200; and Erica Fudge, *Animal* (London: Reaktion, 2002).

Karen Raber and Treva J. Tucker's edited collection *The Culture of the Horse: Status, Discipline, and Identity in the Early Modern World* (New York and Houndmills, Basingstoke, UK: Palgrave Macmillan, 2005), puts horses and horsemanship into a revisionist historical context. Older valuable studies are Joan Thirsk, *Horses in Early Modern England: For Service, for*

Pleasure, for Power, the Stenton Lecture 1977 (Reading, UK: University of Reading, 1978), and Peter Edwards, *The Horse Trade of Tudor and Stuart England* (Cambridge: Cambridge University Press, 1988). For a general history of horses in early modern England, see Peter Edwards, *Horse and Man in Early Modern England* (London: Hambledon Continuum, 2007).

Notable recent work on horses as literary and artistic representations includes Diana Donald, "'Beastly Sights': The Treatment of Animals as a Moral Theme in Representations of London, 1820–1850," *Art History* 22, no. 4 (November, 1999): 514–44; Amanda Gilroy, "The Habit and the Horse, or, the Suburbanisation of Female Equitation," in *Green and Pleasant Land: English Culture and the Romantic Countryside,* ed. Gilroy, Groningen Studies in Cultural Change 8, M. Gosman, gen. ed. (Leuven, Paris, and Dudley, MA: Peeters, 2004), 45–55; and Gina M. Dorré, *Victorian Fiction and the Cult of the Horse* (Aldershot, UK, and Burlington, VT: Ashgate, 2006).

Indispensable works in the field of art history are Sir Joshua Reynolds, *Discourses on Art,* ed. Robert R. Wark Paul Mellon Centre for Studies in British Art (London) (New Haven and London: Yale University Press, 1975); John Barrell, *The Political Theory of Painting from Reynolds to Hazlitt* (New Haven and London: Yale University Press, 1986); Judy Egerton, *British Sporting and Animal Painting, 1655–1867* (London: Tate Gallery for the Yale Center for British Art, 1978), *George Stubbs, 1724–1806* (1984; London: Tate Gallery, 1996), and "George Stubbs and the Landscape of Creswell Crags," *Burlington Magazine* 126 (December 1984): 738–43; Stephen Deuchar, *Sporting Art in Eighteenth-Century England: A Social and Political History* (New Haven and London: Yale University Press, 1988); Walter Liedtke, *The Royal Horse and Rider: Painting, Sculpture, and Horsemanship, 1500–1800* (New York: Abaris Books and Metropolitan Museum of Art, 1989); Arline Meyer, *John Wootton, 1682–1764: Landscapes and Sporting Art in Early Georgian England* (London: Greater London Council, 1984); Malcolm Warner and Robin Blake, *Stubbs and the Horse* (New Haven and London: Yale University Press in Association with Kimbell Art Museum, Fort Worth, 2004); Richard C. Goulding and C. K. Adams, *Catalogue of the Pictures Belonging to His Grace the Duke of Portland, K.G. at Welbeck Abbey, 17 Hill Street, London, and Langwell House* (Cambridge: Cambridge University Press, 1936); Robin Blake, *George Stubbs and the Wide Creation: Animals, People, and Places in the Life of George Stubbs, 1724–1806* (London: Chatto and Windus, 2005); E. K. Waterhouse, "Lord Fitzwilliam's Sporting Pictures by Stubbs," *Burlington Magazine* 88 (August 1946): 199; T. N., Obituary for George Stubbs, *The Sporting Magazine* (May 1808)—see Barnaby Rogerson, "Did Stubbs Go to Morocco?" *Country Life,* 2 March 2000, 60–61; Martin Myrone, *George Stubbs* (London: Tate, 2002); Guy Paget, "John Wootton, Father of English (Sporting) Painting, 1685–1765," *Apollo* 39 (February 1944): 136–45; Walter Shaw Sparrow, *British Sporting Artists from Barlow to Herring* (London: John Lane, the Bodley Head Limited; New York: Charles Scribner's Sons, 1922); Captain Frank Siltzer, *The Story of British Sporting Prints* (London: Hutchinson and Co., n.d. [1925]); Basil Taylor, *Animal Painting in England from Barlow to Landseer* (Harmondsworth: Penguin, 1955); Michael Levey, *Painting at Court* (London: Weidenfeld and Nicolson, 1971); and Bridget Tempest, *Turkmen at Wimpole: Artists from Turkmenistan* (Ashgabat, Turkmenistan: Visiting Artists, n.d. [2001]).

Works shedding light on the history of racing include John Cheny's series, beginning with *An Historical List, of all Horse-Matches Run, And of All Plates and Prizes Run for in England and Wales (of the Value of Ten Pounds or upwards) in 1729* . . . (London: Printed in the Year 1729); W. Pick, of York, *An Authentic Historical Racing Calendar of all the Plates, Sweepstakes, Matches, &c. Run for at York, from the First Commencement of the Races There in the Year 1709, to the Year 1785 inclusive* . . . (Printed by W. Blanchard and Co., York, n.d. [1786?]); Samuel Chifney, *Genius Genuine, . . . A Fine Part in Riding a Race, Known Only to the Author. Why There Are So Few Good Runners; or Why the Turf Horses Degenerate* (London: Printed by Shury, Sold only for the Author, n.d. [1803]); *Memoirs of the Late Thomas Holcroft, Written by Himself, and Continued to the Time of His Death, from His Diary, Notes, and Other Papers,* 3 vols. (London: Printed by J. McCreery for Longman, Hurst, Rees, Orme, and Brown, 1816); Roger D. Upton, *Newmarket and Arabia: An Examination of the Descent of Racers and Coursers* (1873; Reading, UK: Garnet/Folios Archive Library, 2001); J. P. Hore, *The History of Newmarket, and the Annals of the Turf: With Memoirs and Biographical Notices of the Habitués of Newmarket, and the Notable Turfites from the Earliest Times to the End of the Seventeenth Century,* 3 vols. (London: A. H. Baily and Co., 1886); Theodore Andrea Cook, *A History of the English Turf,* 3 vols. (London: H. Virtue and Co., 1901); Captain Frank Siltzer, *Newmarket: Its Sport and Personalities* (London, New York, Toronto, and Melbourne: Cassell, 1923); Mike Huggins, *Flat Racing and British Society, 1790–1914: A Social and Economic History* (London and Portland, OR: Frank Cass, 2000); and Edward Hotaling, *The Great Black Jockeys: The Lives and Times of the Men Who Dominated America's First National Sport* (Rocklin, CA: Forum, 1999).

For the history of cavalry, see Henry Herbert, tenth Earl of Pembroke, *Military Equitation: Or, a Method of Breaking Horses, and Teaching Soldiers to Ride. Designed for The Use of the Army* (Sarum: Printed and Sold by E. Easton; London: J. Dodsley and J. Wilkie, 1778); Captain Lewis Edward Nolan, *Cavalry; Its History and Tactics* (London: Thomas Brown, 1853), and *The Training of Cavalry Remount Horses, by the Late Captain Nolan,* new ed. (London: Parker Son and Bourn, 1861); John Ellis, *Cavalry: The History of Mounted Warfare* (New York: G. P. Putnam's Sons, 1978); Lynn White Jr., *Medieval Technology and Social Change* (London, Oxford, and New York: Oxford University Press, 1962); Hugh Kennedy, *The Armies of the Caliphs: Military and Society in the Early Islamic State* (London and New York: Routledge, 2001); Bernard S. Bachrach, *"Caballus et Caballarius* in Medieval Warfare," in *The Study of Chivalry: Resources and Approaches,* ed. Howell Chickering and Thomas H. Seiler (Kalamazoo: Medieval Institute Publications, Western Michigan University, 1988), 194–97; Carroll M. Gillmor, "Cavalry, European," in *Dictionary of the Middle Ages,* ed. Joseph R. Strayer, 13 vols. (New York: Scribner, 1982–89); Ann Hyland, *The Medieval Warhorse from Byzantium to the Crusades* (Phoenix Mill, UK: Sutton, 1996); and R. H. C. Davis, *The Medieval Warhorse: Origin, Development and Redevelopment* (London: Thames and Hudson, 1989).

Works particularly relevant from British historical studies include Harold Williams, ed., *The Correspondence of Jonathan Swift,* 5 vols. (Oxford: Clarendon, 1963; rpt 1965); Daniel Defoe, *A Tour through the Whole Island of Great Britain,* ed. Pat Rogers (1724–26; London and New York: Penguin, 1971); Linda Colley's *Britons: Forging the Nation, 1701–1837* (New Haven and London: Yale University Press, 1992), *In Defiance of Oligarchy: The Tory Party, 1714–60* (Cambridge: Cambridge University Press, 1982), and *Captives: The Story of Britain's*

Pursuit of Empire and How its Soldiers and Civilians Were Held Captive by the Dream of Global Supremacy (New York: Pantheon, 2003); Felicity A. Nussbaum, *The Limits of the Human: Fictions of Anomaly, Race, and Gender in the Long Eighteenth Century* (Cambridge and New York: Cambridge University Press, 2003); Irvin Ehrenpreis, *Swift: The Man, His Works, and the Age, Volume Three: Dean Swift* (Cambridge, MA: Harvard University Press, 1983); John Brewer, *The Sinews of Power: War, Money, and the English State, 1688–1783* (London: Unwin Hyman, 1989; Alok Yadav, *Before the Empire of English: Literature, Provinciality, and Nationalism in Eighteenth-Century Britain* (New York and Houndmills, Båsingstoke, UK: Palgrave Macmillan, 2004); P. J. Cain and A. G. Hopkins, *British Imperialism: Innovation and Expansion, 1688–1914* (London: Longman, 1993); Robert C. Allen, *Enclosure and the Yeoman* (Oxford: Clarendon, 1992); P. B. Munsche, *Gentlemen and Poachers: The English Game Laws, 1671–1831* (Cambridge: Cambridge University Press, 1981); Paul Langford, *Polite and Commercial People: England, 1727–1783* (Oxford and New York: Oxford University Press, 1992); Robert Brenner, *Merchants and Revolution: Commercial Change, Political Conflict, and London's Overseas Traders, 1550–1653* (Princeton: Princeton University Press, 1993); and Peter Earle, *The Making of the English Middle Class: Business, Society, and Family Life in London, 1660–1730* (London: Methuen, 1989).

Popular books about riding remain valuable sources of the riding fraternity's self-understanding. Particularly good ones are Lady Diana Shedden and Lady Apsley, *"To Whom the Goddess . . ." Hunting and Riding for Women* (London: Hutchinson and Co., 1932); Charles Chenevix Trench, *A History of Horsemanship* (London: Longman, 1970); Elwyn Hartley Edwards, *Horses and Their Role in the History of Man* (London: Willow Books–Collins, 1987); Piero Santini, *Riding Reflections* (1933; rev. ed. London: Country Life, 1950) and *The Forward Impulse* (London: Country Life, 1937); Alois Podhajsky, *The Complete Training of Horse and Rider*, trans. Eva Podhajsky and Col. V. D. S. Williams (London: Harrap, 1967); V. S. Littauer, *More about the Forward Seat: Modern Methods of Schooling and Cross-Country Riding* (London: Hurst and Blackett, 1939); and Luigi Gianoli, *Horses and Horsemanship through the Ages*, trans. Iris Brooks (New York: Crown, 1969).

I have quoted from the Oxford World's Classics edition of Jonathan Swift's *Gulliver's Travels*, ed. Claude Rawson and Ian Higgins (1726, 1735; Oxford and New York: Oxford University Press, 2005), except in chap. 4, where Albert J. Rivero's *Gulliver's Travels: A Norton Critical Edition* (1726; New York and London: W. W. Norton, 2002) contained pertinent information.